CW00676613

Lucid Dreams
The Films of Krzysztof Kieślowski

cinema voices

Series editor: Matthew Stevens, FLICKS BOOKS

This series provides critical assessments of film directors whose work is motivated by social, political or historical concerns, or reveals an opposition to conventional filmmaking systems and structures. The following titles are published• or in preparation:

•Auteur/provocateur: the films of Denys Arcand
Edited by André Loiselle and Brian McIlroy

•Dark alchemy: the films of Jan Švankmajer
Edited by Peter Hames

•Queen of the 'B's: Ida Lupino behind the camera
Edited by Annette Kuhn

•By angels driven: the films of Derek Jarman
Edited by Chris Lippard

•Poet of civic courage: the films of Francesco Rosi
Edited by Carlo Testa

•A call to action: the films of Ousmane Sembene
Edited by Sheila Petty

•Agent of challenge and defiance: the films of Ken Loach
Edited by George McKnight

•The last modernist: the films of Theo Angelopoulos
Edited by Andrew Horton

•Lucid dreams: the films of Krzysztof Kieślowski
Edited by Paul Coates

•The illusion of freedom : the films of Peter Watkins
James M Welsh

The enemy within: the films of Mrinal Sen
Edited by Sumita S Chakravarty

Identity and memory: the films of Chantal Akerman
Edited by Gwendolyn Audrey Foster

Lucid Dreams

The Films of Krzysztof Kieślowski

Edited by
Paul Coates

cinema voices series

FLICKS
BOOKS

A CIP catalogue record for this book is available from the British Library.

ISBN 0-948911-58-1 (Hb)
ISBN 0-948911-63-8 (Pb)

First published in 1999 by

Flicks Books
29 Bradford Road
Trowbridge
Wiltshire BA14 9AN
England
tel   +44 1225 767728
fax   +44 1225 760418
e-mail flicks.books@dial.pipex.com

© individual contributors, 1999

All rights reserved. No part of this publication may be reproduced, stored in a retrieval system or transmitted in any form or by any means: electronic, electrostatic, magnetic tape, mechanical, photocopying, recording or otherwise, without prior permission in writing from the publishers.

Printed and bound in Great Britain by Bookcraft (Bath) Ltd.

Contents

Acknowledgments

Many people have aided the completion of this book. I would like to thank the staff of Film Polski, particularly Helena Damętka, and of the Wytwórnia Filmów Dokumentalnych i Fabularnych (WFDiF; Documentary and Feature Production Studios) in Warsaw, for granting access to video copies of many of Kieślowski's films and screening others for me; the Carnegie Trust of the Universities of Scotland, for the travel and maintenance grant that funded much of my bibliographical reseach; the staff of the Warsaw Filmoteka Narodowa, who were unfailingly helpful; the University of Aberdeen English Department, for the six-week period of study leave which laid the groundwork for the research; and the British Academy, for the travel grant that enabled me to join the Kieślowski panel at the 1996 SCS Conference. Particularly warm thanks are due to Carmen Hendershott and Steven Main, as well as to *Dialog*, for selfless provision of bibliographical information, and to Tadeusz Lubelski, Serafino Murri, Mirosław Przylipiak and Jan Rek for other information and materials. No acknowledgments would be complete without mention of Irena Strzałkowska of TOR, and, of course, Krzysztof Kieślowski himself, whom I had the privilege of meeting twice, and who was unstintingly generous with his time and intellectual energy, even when his health was no longer of the best.

Introduction

Paul Coates

I.

Tragically cut down in his mid-fifties, by the last years of his life Krzysztof Kieślowski had established himself in the eyes of many as Europe's leading filmmaker. The agnostic spirituality of *Dekalog* (*The Decalogue*, 1988), the lyrical enigmas of *La Double Vie de Véronique* (*The Double Life of Véronique*, 1991), and the lucid pairings of colours and concepts in the *Trois couleurs* (*Three Colours*, 1993-94) trilogy had earned him fame well beyond his native Poland. His path had always been bravely personal, with the unflinchingness of the great documentarist. In the 1970s, such documentaries as *Z punktu widzenia nocnego portiera* (*From the Point of View of the Night Porter*, 1977), *Pierwsza miłość* (*First Love*, 1974) and *Dworzec* (*Station*, 1980) had recorded modern officialdom's pervasive and deep-seated will to control; others invoked the distress of the sick and disabled – *Byłem żołnierzem* (*I Was a Soldier*, 1970), *Prześwietlenie* (*X-Ray*, 1974) – while yet others reflected on transience and social aspiration – *Siedem kobiet w różnym wieku* (*Seven Women of Different Ages*, 1978), *Gadające głowy* (*Talking Heads*, 1980), *Robotnicy '71: nic o nas bez nas* (*Workers '71: Nothing About Us Without Us*, 1972) and *Murarz* (*Bricklayer*, 1973). Kieślowski's stringent scrupulosity bred a growing worry about the possible intrusiveness of all documentary work, prompting a shift to feature films and a leading position in the cinematic critique of power that helped precipitate Solidarność (Solidarity). Later, in *The Decalogue*, he would generalise his sense of the difficulties of daily Polish life into an empathetic quest for the grounds of moral action in modern society. This searching diagnosis of the state of Western culture's basic notions would conclude in *Three Colours*' meditation on the fate of the French Revolution's watchwords – liberté, égalité and fraternité – in the mid-1990s.

Kieślowski's last films were co-productions, all shot abroad, in part or *in toto*. His many interviews of the late-1980s suggest that work outside Poland grew out of disillusionment with the Polish response to his films. Yet, work in a foreign country may have been merely the logical conclusion of an œuvre whose characters so often inhabit bell-jars of silence and exile. Kieślowski motivated working in the West by an unwillingness to absorb domestic funds desperately needed by directors without his access to co-producers, but another reason may have been the way in which the deepening Western gulf between (official) religion and (unofficial) spirituality permitted pursuit of the mystical, while suspending the question of its relationship to any Church, a possibility not available within strongly Roman Catholic Poland.[1] In Iris Murdoch's *The Time of the Angels*, a Nietzschean priest remarks that where God is dead, then the angels are abroad.[2] If this is true, Kieślowski's spirituality may be less agnostic than atheistic; after all, his existentialism owes more to Camus than to Kierkegaard.

Where the early Kieślowski suffered at the hands of political censors, with film after film being shelved, the later one saw the native *critic* as his main adversary. Just why this should have been so is not entirely clear: People's Poland was never fully "totalitarian", and possessed some good and resourceful critics. And although Kieślowski's final turn to co-production is often attributed to domestic criticism, strictly speaking only *Bez końca* (*No End*, 1984) had encountered a predominantly negative reception, with even fair-minded critics having reservations – Tadeusz Szyma, for instance, found its intimate strand less convincing than its social one, disliked its "pseudo-metaphysics",[3] and was one of several critics whose mixed feelings led them to see it twice before making up their minds.[4] At the same time, Party hacks predictably decried its politics, Catholics its vision of suicide as existential choice, and Solidarity activists its pessimistic political prognosis. Beginning with *The Decalogue*, his next work, which was co-funded by Sender Freies Berlin, and deliberately universalised and abstracted by whiting out many of the realia of burdensome everyday Polish life, domestic objections allege artificial construction and psychological implausibility, but never become as overwhelming as Kieślowski's friends often maintain. The staff critics of *Polityka*, mostly liberal Communists doubly beleaguered by the aftermath of martial law, may perhaps have used aesthetic categories to mask their political animosity, but not all objectors can be suspected – however justly or unjustly – of having hidden agendas. Quite a few of the charges of implausibility, for instance, stem from female critics, a matter that deserves investigation; and, although it will not receive it here, Alicja Helman's remarks later in this volume, on the male-centered character of the majority of Kieślowski's works, suggest a partial explanation. The perceived "artificiality" of the films' construction could also be linked to their relentlessly hypothetical philosophico-legal quality, although for most viewers this dissolved into concretion before the sheer power and credibility of the performances Kieślowski elicited; the films offer "imaginary gardens with real toads in them", to use Marianne Moore's formula.[5] Mirosław Przylipiak's tabulation of 524 press reviews throughout Kieślowski's career shows 304 unequivocally positive, and another 72 generally positive; of 63 reviews of *The Decalogue* – or its parts – 48 are completely favourable. For Przylipiak, Polish critics contrasting a Kieślowski accepted abroad with one rejected at home partly reflect a domestic inferiority complex *vis-à-vis* the West – a hypothesis surely corroborated by the widespread negative Polish reaction to the one Kieślowski film to thematise that complex, *Trois couleurs: blanc* (*Three Colours: White*, 1994) (although even here the rejection level was only 38%).[6] Nevertheless, some Poles (mostly males?) did see the later Kieślowski as in breach of the long-standing unwritten contract between them and artists unofficially commissioned to speak of public affairs, *res publica*, not their own personal ones. In one of his very last interviews, he wondered whether his good friend Marcel Łoziński may not have been right to describe him as "betraying" the ordinary viewer by making increasingly esoteric films.[7]

Kieślowski's struggle with Polish critics in particular was one to peel off the main critical label glued to him – "socially committed" or "political" director. Although partly explicable as his reaction to the unexpected *débâcle* of *No End*, it reflects an existential pursuit of a free self-creation combating both the old self and anyone seeking to tie him to it, and the adjustment problems of a Polish culture whose "return to normality" after 1989 included a mourned loss of its old, "prophetic" role. (In reaction to this transition, the hagiographic atmosphere around some of the writing on Kieślowski preserved the "prophetic" status of art and artist by other means – a development not restricted to Poland,[8] although rendered most urgent there by the shocks of the post-1989 upheaval.) In the end, Kieślowski seems to have decided that co-production alone afforded insufficient liberty from the haunting afterlife of his old, "political" persona: he was ready to move from universalising things Polish to making films abroad.

If the West in its turn came to embrace Kieślowski, however, it was not simply because the last few films' greater gloss and "French" glamour rendered them more palatable than the "gritty" early ones (although Georgia Brown, writing in *The Village Voice*, was one of the few Westerners to prefer the "Polish frump" – as I did too).[9] After all, *The Decalogue* – the first co-production – had been sufficiently "gritty". Rather, Kieślowski's quizzical, sometimes pained and always thoughtful probings of coincidence and mystery resonated with West Europeans disenchanted both with institutional religion and the contrasting capitalist and Marxist economic gospels. But, if Kieślowski *is*, in a sense, "a mystic", his religion is unchurched. When one recalls the fraught age-old embrace of mystic and institution, his films' many cold authorities become hardly surprising. Think, for instance, of his sympathy with the girl expelled from school in *First Love*, or the dismissed Party member of *Życiorys* (*Curriculum Vitae*, 1975). The latter shows Kieślowski's rejection of politics as also a refusal of the widespread pre- and post-Solidarity Polish demonisation of Party members. In two of his alternative lives, the protagonist of *Przypadek* (*Blind Chance*, 1981) is a Party member and a Solidarity activist, and yet remains throughout the same – fundamentally decent – person, but the Renoir-like idea that the opponent could be *mon semblable, mon frère* was not one which many Solidarity sympathisers (which, given the union's ten million membership, meant few Poles) could comfortably entertain. Yet, no one could reasonably have accused Kieślowski of time-serving. Throughout the depressed early 1980s, he alone of the major Polish filmmakers continued working exclusively in Poland. As Wajda and Zanussi pursued co-productions' respite from fetid post-martial law "normalisation", and Agnieszka Holland sank ever-deeper roots in the France where she had been stranded, Kieślowski alone remained, stoically wed to a land he would later liken to the other partner in a bored couple. With *No End*, Kieślowski was alone in evoking the desolate aftermath of martial law, and only the contradictoriness of the Jaruzelski regime's situation, suspended between incompatible domestic and Soviet demands, and the film's pairing with the appallingly mediocre, pro-Party *Godność* (*Dignity*, 1985) permitted its screening abroad. (Local screenings were heavily restricted.)

An extremely peripatetic childhood had prepared Kieślowski for his mid-1980s solitude. The reception of *No End* must merely have confirmed his deepest fears. That isolation intensified his ability to speak from and for the loneliness that besets more and more of us, and dogs almost all his characters. Even the nervous, flicking camera movements of his early features not only are the typical *cinéma-vérité* scanning of groups for significant action, but also match the main characters' isolation, their unfocused, unattached glancing, as moments and milieux fail to hold them. One may recall his statement that "[a]ll my films, from the first to the most recent ones, are about individuals who can't quite find their bearings".[10] If the cigarette was an inseparable prop of his self-presentation, it was partly because nicotine is an anti-depressant. Indeed, it seems to me that Kieślowski's work essentially inhabits an experience of exile, derived perhaps from childhood rootlessness, but augmented by the widespread Polish alienation within "People's Poland". Raymond Williams suggestively attributes a similar experience to George Orwell, describing him as "an exile" for whom "society as such is totalitarian; he cannot commit himself, he is bound to stay out". Williams adds:

Yet Orwell was at the same time deeply moved by what he saw of avoidable or remediable suffering and poverty, and he was convinced that the means of remedy are social, involving commitment, involving association, and, to the degree that he was serious, involving himself. In his essay *Writers and Leviathan*...Orwell recognized this kind of deadlock, and his solution was that in such circumstances the writer must divide: one part of himself uncommitted, the other part involved. This indeed is the bankruptcy of exile, yet it was, perhaps, inevitable. He could not believe (it is not a matter of intellectual persuasion; it is a question of one's deepest experience and response) that *any* settled way of living exists in which a man's individuality can be socially confirmed.[11]

This passage is suggestive and can be used to pinpoint the intersection of Kieślowski's concern with suffering (most patent in the documentaries), non-commitment (the apoliticism and alternative scenarios) and thematisation of division (most apparent in the obsessive reflections of the late work), although "bankruptcy of exile" breathes a somewhat tired, dogmatic nativism. Williams argues that the tension of such a division may be mediated "[a]t the easy levels...in the depiction of society as a racket", while "[a]t the more difficult levels, with men of Orwell's seriousness" – and, one might add, of Kieślowski's – "the tension cannot be discharged":[12] the "consequent strain" has the desperation "of a man who, while rejecting the consequences of an atomistic society, yet retains deeply, in himself, its characteristic mode of consciousness".[13] The (internal) exile's intransigent honesty nurtures both isolation and the Kieślowskian dream of brotherhood.

Since *No End*, the names of Krzysztof Piesiewicz, Kieślowski's co-scriptwriter, and Zbigniew Preisner, the composer of his scores, become constants in his work. Their friendship and the fame he himself brought them echo Jean Renoir's view that "[t]he more you help your partners to express themselves, the more you express yourself".[14] The respect for co-workers (Kieślowski's definition of the director as someone who helps others), attested to in numerous anecdotes, yields the works' richness. In *The Decalogue*, the respect for co-workers dictates the privileging of actors by both screenplay and camera: by the screenplay's shaping of almost every scene as a one-on-one encounter; by the camera's bestowal of primacy on the face. His two meditations on the founding statements of Western culture – the ancient ones of the Ten Commandments, the modern ones of the French Revolution – both place the final accent on brotherhood, a leitmotif of his work beginning with *Szpital* (*Hospital*,

1976). The theme's attraction surely lay in the hope of an antidote to an isolation both reflected in and partly generated by some of the films' strategies. Sylvia Swift, situating *The Decalogue* in the context of reception theory, argues that it confounds Umberto Eco's distinction between "smart" and "naive" readers, the former being connoisseurs of the author's feints, the latter their victims:[15] "Kieślowski's variations are often so obvious that no one can be naïve (as in the repetitions in the segments of *Blind Chance* and *The Double Life of Véronique*), or so subtle that one wonders if one gets it".[16] No single mode of reading is privileged, no one excluded. Kieślowski's desire not to reject anybody, like Antek Gralak's in *Spokój* (*The Calm*, 1976), may also be one not to be rejected. (Witek in *Blind Chance* is described at the outset as universally popular.) Perhaps this is why the critical *débâcle* of *No End* hit him so hard – like a blow to an unprepared stomach, as he told Urszula Biełous.[17] Consequently, *The Decalogue* offers itself for appropriation on different levels – both as soap opera or time-travelling Balzac omnibus with randomly intersecting characters, and as modernist mystery.

The broad, tantalising appeal of "late Kieślowski" may also flow from the increasing centrality of female characters. As Alicja Helman points out later in this book, this had not been a feature of the earlier, male-dominated works. The consequences are as two-edged as the ambiguous combination of "smart" and "naïve" traits in the implicit viewer. The move to predominantly female protagonists may imprint a world whose negativity increasingly "feminises" – disempowers – us all (whence the male impotence of *Decalogue 9* or *Three Colours: White*; Tomek's inadequacy in *Krótki film o miłości* [*A Short Film About Love*, 1988]; the hero's phantomisation in *No End*; the helpless watching of the "angel" in all but one of the episodes of *The Decalogue*). Yet, it may also be deemed positive, with virtues culturally coded as "feminine", the right nostrum for many modern ills, as appears to occur in *Trois couleurs: rouge* (*Three Colours: Red*, 1994).

Potential universal appeal may nevertheless preclude precise address of anyone in particular. The sense of mystery so dear to late Kieślowski, a leitmotif of his interviews, can also feed misunderstandings. One may recall Rilke's description of fame as the cloud of misconceptions surrounding a name.[18] In 1994, Tony Rayns asked perspicaciously: "how much of the current critical backlash against the director is founded on a mishearing of his tone of voice?".[19] In the case of *Three Colours*, for instance, the intervals between each film's opening reduced the likelihood of viewers perceiving significant repetitions and variations, or the possibility of the parts constituting a single film. Most flags' colours are closely stitched together; the trilogy is, as it were, torn apart. Is it an accident that the one Kieślowski chooses has an interval, a blankness, at its centre? He could even deem the order of viewing a matter of indifference. The origin of *The Decalogue* in a television series, its suspension between "televisual" and "cinematic" aesthetics, caused further problems of distribution and comprehension. If the art film by definition requires close scrutiny and multiple viewings, can the television viewer, with a small screen and multiple distractions, even begin to do justice to it? Perhaps overmodestly, Kieślowski himself told Danusia Stok that his work had failed to match the television aesthetic. But how should one distribute a ten-hour film? Delivery in ten parts may indeed facilitate matters, but will a cinema viewer accept a single, 50-minute part – a *really* "short" film – as really "a film"? If not, how many parts should be seen together? (It was usually two – two hours' viewing time constituting a "movie-length" experience – although New York offered a continuous screening which Kieślowski himself felt would be a nightmare.) If Kieślowski hospitably offers his work for various appropriations, the lack of a single obvious "right" one may be frustrating, however nice the concord with his passion for alternative, equally valid scenarios.

The Decalogue was to be the turning-point of Kieślowski's career. The late fame dawns in 1988, with the award of the Félix for *Krótki film o zabijaniu* (*A Short Film About Killing*, 1988), and rises vertiginously thereafter. If Kieślowski had filmed the anecdote on which this work was based a decade earlier, as first intended, would the fame have come earlier too? (The 1970s release by Grzegorz Królikiewicz of *Na wylot* [*Through and Through*], a film with a similar plot-line, had caused the postponement.) But the extra time in which to hone his art may have made all the difference. Moreover, it was not until the late-1980s that Polish cinema began to shed the "political" label that had always limited its foreign distribution. The films of Wajda and the "Cinema of Moral Anxiety" enjoyed Western critical favour, but seemed too specialised for general appeal. In the dark days of late-1980s Poland, when the Polish regime and the opposition were locked in an increasingly bleak and ritualistic stalemate, Kieślowski and Piesiewicz decided to seek – and, if possible, touch – their culture's ethical bedrock. What better starting-point than the Ten Commandments, the core of Western ethics and legislation?

Both *The Decalogue* and the *Three Colours* trilogy would acquire the status of "cultural events". Kieślowski's serial aesthetic played intriguingly with familiarity and defamiliarisation, enticing viewers to return for the next variation. The interest is less in tracking recurring characters than in seeing how abstract maxims will be linked with specific situations. While concrete events blunt the maxims' abstraction, the maxims universalise the stories. Each becomes a talking-point, an extension of the open-ended ethics seminar which represents Kieślowski's own work *en abîme* in *Decalogue 8*. At the same time, the addition of the enigmatic witness figure resonated with the late-1980s discourse on angels, one arguably interested less in the possible presence of a distant God than in personalising the increasingly ubiquitous surveillance camera, imparting tenderness to its inclination above us. Meanwhile, the privileging of colours over concepts in the titles of the trilogy could appeal to a self-consciously "post-ideological era". "Liberty", "equality" and "brotherhood" may have pervaded Kieślowski's extra-filmic discourse and interviewers' questions, but only two of these words figure within the films themselves – as part of the Parisian Palais de Justice façade – and then only momentarily. As Julie trots up the Palais de Justice steps, "liberté" becomes visible on its façade. In *White*, a wider view reveals modernity's second fetish word, while, in *Red*, Kieślowski wisely eschews repetition of the device and leaves the third word unrepresented. Does this absence render it the most truly utopian of the three? It remains to be debated whether or not Kieślowski's apparent foregrounding of colour marks a partial withdrawal from the overtly ethical concerns of *The Decalogue*. Certainly, the colours carry no ideology: no red flag flies anywhere – not even parodically – in *Three Colours: Red*. Their significance is both more fundamental and more arbitrary, although the arbitrariness may be reduced by the uncanny correlation between the main elements of the narratives and some of Goethe's remarks on colour in his *Zur Farbenlehre* (*On the Theory of Colour*, 1810).[20] The "meanings" of blue, white or red are cloudy connotations, "outrunning" any cloth they might decorate. Kieślowski invites the viewer to a dialogue that may well lack a clear ending.[21]

II.

Earlier in this introduction, I quoted Rilke's definition of fame as the sum of the misunderstandings connected with a name. The following essays are, of course, expressions of Kieślowski's late fame and additions to it, written in the hope that Rilke's "bad" fame may have a "good" counterpart. My decision to ask several Polish critics to contribute acknowledges Kieślowski's own attachment to the Poland he could never leave for long, and where he wished to die, as he did, so terribly prematurely. Polish critics have the deepest – somatic – knowledge of where Kieślowski "was coming from". Their contextualisations of the late work are further justified by the Eliotic maxim that deems ends implicit in beginnings, as Bogusław Zmudziński in particular has argued Kieślowski's were.[22]

In the book's opening essay, Tadeusz Sobolewski – as Tadeusz

Lubelski later notes, Kieślowski's most faithful commentator over the years – gives an overview of his work, stressing in particular its denial of political dualisms and its position *vis-à-vis* the existentialist tradition, both agnostic (Camus) and religious (Paul Tillich). For Sobolewski, a metaphysical revolt underlies the work's philosophical questions, and culminates in what he describes as "the solidarity of sinners"[23] in *The Decalogue* – a community which renders untenable the position of judge (and so, one could add, anticipates *Three Colours: Red*), excluding no one.

My own essay on Kieślowski's documentaries proposes their cryptic colouration of autobiography – not only through subject-matter, as noted by several critics, but also through the way in which the voices we hear echo Kieślowski's own interview voice. Tracing his documentary practice's evolution from the simple registration of his film school days to the complexly punctuated later works, I note his growing fear of documentary's potential endangerment of its subjects and his response, firstly, by deindividualising them into "models" and, finally, by moving into fiction. The relationship between that step and the famous ending of *Amator* (*Camera Buff*, 1979) becomes part of the evolution of an aesthetic of transparency into one whereby the world's surfaces occlude any depths.

Tadeusz Lubelski analyses the "political" features Kieślowski made between 1975 and 1985, showing how they extend the documentary project of "describing reality", which was also that of the group known as "Młoda kultura" ("Young Culture") – the generation of 1968, the year of Kieślowski's own graduation from the Państwowa Wyższa Szkoła Filmowa i Teatralna (PWSFiT; Łódź Film School). Lubelski demonstrates that the various heroes of Kieślowski's political features not only share some of the minor elements of their author's biography, but also can stand for phases in the development of the Young Culture artist who was Kieślowski himself. He concludes by stressing that the politicised description of Polish life given by other Young Culture artists is revised at the end of *Camera Buff* and in the 1981 prose manifesto, "Głęboko zamiast szeroko" ("Deeper Rather Than Broader"), which both argue that an honest description of reality requires initial description of the self. That shift in perspective is fundamental to the emergence of "late Kieślowski".

Charles Eidsvik demonstrates the extent to which Kieślowski's feature films preserved the working methods and aesthetics of the documentaries that began his career. The resultant tension between fiction and documentary, he argues, "allowed Kieślowski to create extremely abbreviated, highly suggestive stories that strike one as intimate documents on the human condition". Eidsvik's fine-grained comparison of the short films about killing and love and their shorter versions in *The Decalogue* gives a fascinating insight into Kieślowski's editorial responses to the different contexts of television and film (the latter permitting more extreme and intense images and emotions), and allows one to plot the limits beyond which abbreviation reduces empathy. For Eidsvik, the two "short films", having more time to develop involvement, are more successful than their shorter companion-pieces.

My own "The curse of the law: *The Decalogue*" alludes to Galatians 3: 13 and works around the films dealt with by Eidsvik. It, too, considers the effects upon the features of the documentary aesthetic, linking the enigmas and problematic causality of *The Decalogue* to Erich Auerbach's account of biblical aesthetics, and juxtaposing the series' imagistic translations of the prohibitions of the original Ten Commandments with Kenneth Burke's theorisation of their negativity. My film-by-film analyses insist that each merits independent reading and judgment, and seek to demonstrate that the strongest episodes lie in the work's numerical centre.

Although it is often remarked that a shift in emphasis characterises the films of "late" Kieślowski, it is usually described in terms of an abandonment of Polish and political concerns for more universal, emotional and even mystical ones. Alicja Helman, however, defines it primarily in terms of the changed role of women in Kieślowski's work. Consequently, for her, its major caesura is not *The Decalogue*, but *The Double Life of Véronique*. *The Decalogue* may mark the depoliticisation of Kieślowski's work, but it retains the predominantly negatively-charged female figure of his earlier films. Whereas, earlier, the driving agent had been male, the French co-productions show Kieślowski's dialectical evolution towards an embrace of the intuitionist attitude so often culturally coded as "female", and here symbolised by female protagonists – although this does not entail his becoming a "feminist" director. Previously incidental, Kieślowski's women become protagonists and even *portes paroles*, particularly in the films with Irène Jacob. Perhaps, in this context, the recurrence of the negative female in *Three Colours: White* bears out the rule of "two steps forwards, one step backwards"?

In her essay on *The Double Life of Véronique* and the *Three Colours* trilogy, Janina Falkowska reassesses Kieślowski's explicit renunciation of politics in his late works. Considering each film in close detail, she nevertheless argues that, despite their complex treatment of such universalist themes as love, betrayal, forgiveness and helplessness, their evocations of human alienation amidst the technological paraphernalia of the late-20th century constitute a challenge to our culture's selfish mercantilism – one that still merits the name "political".

III.

Writing of Philip Kaufman's *The Unbearable Lightness of Being* (1987) and its reiteration of Ingmar Bergman's use of a juddering glass to suggest a tank's approach in *Tystnaden* (*The Silence*, 1963), Kieślowski stated that to track the wanderings of such a motif would be a fitting way to mark cinema's centenary.[24] His choice of example is perhaps significant, since a whole study of his work could revolve around its use of glass (milk bottles, glasses, windows, mirrors and other reflecting surfaces), with finally, in *Three Colours: Red*, the broken glass and glasses that undergo sublimely utopian metamorphosis into indestructible plastic, the two equally-full, equally-empty coffee cups of Valentine and the judge standing side-by-side, bringing the trilogy full circle to true equality. At the heart of these interconnections of glass lies the window become a mirror: an aesthetic of realist transparency become one of the reflexive. But if Kieślowski's work can seem finally to resemble a hall of mirrors, it is nevertheless devoid of narcissism: the mirror is the place of *transformation*, and to face it is to find oneself becoming somebody else. Thus, the characters' frequent reflection on first appearance indicates the depth of their desire for brotherhood. Nevertheless, the mirror offers them no exit from essential isolation, but merely confirms it. Hence, Kieślowski both becomes his characters and remains separated from them by the actor's or actress' difference, by the glass that only shatters at the end of *Red*, as Vincent Amiel notes.[25] The final broken window may permit the judge's reincarnation as Auguste, and certainly permits Kieślowski's own step outside the bounds of his work.

Although, in *Camera Buff*, Kieślowski himself renders homage to Ken Loach and the Czech New Wave, discussions of his work tend rather to invoke the great European auteurs with known – and even notorious – spiritual preoccupations: Bresson and Bergman. The main commonalities with Bresson are a terse, sometimes almost disdainful cutting (think of the montage linking the kidney operation and the break-in in *Decalogue 10*) and a concern with the spirit's hardbitten survival in a cold modernity. But whereas modernity's impersonality encases Bresson's non-professional actors, Kieślowski's work nurtures strong performances in his professional ones (their use having been customary in People's Poland, with its state professionalisation of all the arts). His films radiate his often-voiced respect for them, his willingness to permit them – and other collaborators – to co-create the work. Might not the late features be "really" documentaries about their performances? (That *tour de force, Klaps* [*Slate*, 1976], testifies to that admiration, as they step unruffled into character again and again, despite the continual insect-like irritation of the clapperboard clicking alongside their heads.) That intensity and authenticity of performance, in turn, validate comparison with Bergman, whose close-up focus on the face Kieślowski shares. However, where Bergman deems the whole face essential, Kieślowski's frame habitually cuts across the forehead,[26] yielding greater closeness and accentuating the eyes. (In *Curriculum Vitae*, this also emphasises their shading: the critique of authority shows the control board's members as having lost a portion of their individuality.) The closeness is that of love, a word that figures increasingly prominently in Kieślowski's late works, but is already present in the documentaries, illuminating Jadzia's plain features in *First Love* in particular. Kieślowski's framing suggests a documentarist's sense that reality does not offer itself harmoniously to – is not staged *for* – the camera, as the presence of whole faces would misleadingly suggest.[27] For many, however, Bergman and Bresson represent an all-but-spent tradition: critics bent on periodisation might speak of the dying residues of cinematic modernism amid a growing hegemony of the postmodern. When, in the interview he gave me in late-1995 (a mere hour, alas, his health being no longer of the best), Kieślowski spoke of the thinning ranks of directors deserving the name "great", he clearly did not mean himself. Nevertheless, many would see his own departure – both the one he announced and seemed possibly about to revoke, and the unforeseen one – as concluding a certain tradition of writer-directors willing and able to investigate the difficult aftermath of the collapse of the grand systems, unafraid to "ask big questions". Kieślowski's generosity towards collaborators revitalised the auteurist project, combating the self-regard that so often precludes the writer-director's self-renewal. His studied, intense dissections of blocked relationships, the energy and integrity he himself radiated and transmitted to actors and other co-workers, his considered use of stylistic strategies both radical and traditional, and the crystalline suggestivity of the screenplays he forged together with Krzysztof Piesiewicz gave his work exemplary aesthetic and ethical force. When Tony Rayns responded to the announced retirement by saying that he would be missed, Kieślowski replied that others would come along.[28] It is the generous message of the characters' doubling in *The Double Life of Véronique* and *Three Colours: Red*. But they will not be Kieślowski, and they will not fill the space he has left.

Appendix: *Paradise, Hell, Purgatory*

A year after Kieślowski's death, *Dialog* published *Raj* (*Paradise*), his last completed script, the proposed first part of a trilogy on Heaven, Hell and Purgatory.[29] It begins with Regina desperately phoning Filipinka, a girl in her late twenties, warning her not to do something.

Filipinka's aim is to bomb the office of a man we later discover is a drug-runner. On arrest, she is devastated to learn that the bomb killed four innocent people, among them two children: a teacher, she had planted it out of concern for her pupils following a corrupt police force's shredding of information she submitted about the dealer. During her interrogations, Filip, a young police stenographer, sees her, realises her innocence, falls in love with her, engineers her escape, and helps her kill the dealer. Their flight finally becomes literal when they appropriate a police helicopter and vanish into the sky.

It is hard not to visualise *Paradise* as an extension of *Three Colours: Red*, with Irène Jacob in the role of Filipinka. The reasons are obvious: the bombing of a drug dealer's office recalls Valentine's hatred of the man who controls Geneva's drug world, the cause of her brother's addiction; and her status as teacher echoes *The Double Life of Véronique*, as does the doubling between her and Filip (they have the same name and birthday). The concern with doubling appears only in Kieślowski's Jacob films, and even a trivial detail such as the proposed shot of the Adam's apple as Filipinka and Filip quench their thirst echoes Valentine's doing so in *Red*. Where Valentine enters a church in pursuit of Rita and – in the published screenplay – crosses herself, Filipinka goes to the confessional. Part-way through her confession, she discovers it to be empty. The detail is surely significant, and religion's privatisation is emphasised when Filip hears the confession's remainder, and they later marry by sucking blood from each other's fingertips and "go to Heaven" in a helicopter whose achieved height dumbfounds its erstwhile pilot. This conclusion recalls *Thelma and Louise* (1991), although this time the fugitives appropriate the helicopter. *Paradise* would have been in many respects an "action film", a new departure for Kieślowski, which is perhaps why the screenplay is ironic about its closing spectacle: "the effect of spectacle is completed by the helicopter touching down with dust flying and a loud racket".[30] Perhaps the knowledge that he would not film it himself freed him to imagine greater spectacle. The very last moment, however, is as richly poetic as any of his endings. "The helicopter, still visible for a moment, melts into the sky. The light beneath it now looks like one of the stars hung high above the people looking upwards."[31]

The last two parts of the trilogy were to have been written by Krzysztof Piesiewicz alone, although obviously developing themes, ideas and situations discussed with Kieślowski. *Piekło* (*Hell*),[32] set in Paris, begins with a father's departure from jail and return to his wife and three daughters Greta, Zofia and Anna: he has to force his way in. As his wife jeers at him, claiming to have let the children watch her intercourse with other men, and even to have solicited their

13

participation, the enraged man attacks her then jumps through a window to his death. Piesiewicz's story documents the effects of an accusation of child abuse which a boy fabricated for a dare. Children constantly weave in and out of the background, and when Anna and Fryderyk, her lover, sit in a café as children play outside, the juxtaposition may recall a key scene from that earlier depiction of Hell, *A Short Film About Killing*. After its shocking opening, the script shows the father's one-time accuser, Sebastian, drawing nearer to the daughters, twenty-odd years later, to disclose the truth. Like many other Kieślowski-Piesiewicz collaborations, *Hell* is punctuated by telephone calls, beginning with Sebastian's attempt to contact Greta, Anna's call to Fryderyk, who hangs up on her, and the guilty replacing of the phone by Zofia's husband. When a man frustratedly exits from a booth exclaiming "you can ring everywhere, you just can't talk to anyone", a Kieślowski-Piesiewicz motif is formulated perhaps too explicitly. Communication machines cannot repair relationships so strained that neither party really exists for the other. In this hell, the energy of the characters' steps only underlines the emptiness of the space they traverse. They feel they neither exist in themselves nor are seen – confirmed – by others. Thus, the father's self-immolation haunts his daughters, who are all alone in their relationships: Zofia's husband betrays her; Anna's lover is married; and Greta misconstrues Sebastian's interest in her as amorous. The past recurs infernally, as Zofia's argument with Piotr, watched by their children, replays the opening scene.

The characters encounter several symbolic objects, Zofia being associated with a billiard table and Greta with a kaleidoscope – two Kieślowskian images of arbitrariness and chance. The most important, however, accompanies Anna: a partly transparent sheet overlays a photograph of the Parthenon, supplying its missing parts. Below the paper-thin reconstruction lies a ruin. In much of *Hell*, sunlight blinds the protagonists. Rain falls when the truth has been told, but the relief is merely meteorological, not symbolic of any human restitution. The church where Zofia seeks refuge from the rain is locked on all sides, and, on learning of her husband's innocence, the girls' forbidding mother shows no regret. The lights that come on at the end are not heavenly ones, seen from Earth, but earth-bound, like the characters, kaleidoscopically shifting from the helicopter's perspective.

At the time of writing, Piesiewicz's script for *Czyściec* (*Purgatory*) – initially scheduled for publication in the July 1997 edition of *Dialog* – had not yet been completed, but negotiations for a possible filming of this trilogy's first two parts were underway.

[1]   The pressure which institutional religion exerts upon Poles is, of course, enormous, and, for Kieślowski, the fact that the Roman Catholic Church alone among Polish institutions remained stable during the 1980s is "nieszczęście Kościoła i nasze nieszczęście, polskie nieszczęście" ("the misfortune of the Church and our, Polish, misfortune"); he endorses an interviewer's suggestion that the Church actually hinders contact with God. See Tadeusz Szczepański, "Drzewo, które jest" ["The tree that exists": interview with Kieślowski and Piesiewicz], *Film na świecie* 385 (November-December 1991): 17. See also, for instance, his statement to Danièle Heymann ("Les portes s'ouvrent sur un sourire d'exil", *Le Monde* 16 May 1991: 24) that in France "la foi est une possibilité. En Pologne, c'est une obligation" ("faith is a possibility. In Poland it is an obligation").

[2]   Iris Murdoch, *The Time of the Angels* (London: Chatto & Windus, 1966): 183-187.

[3]   Tadeusz Szyma, "Bez końca", *Tygodnik powszechny* 28 July 1985.

[4]   See Mirosław Ratajczak, "Bez znaczenia?" ["Without meaning?"], *Odra* 10 (1985): 81. The question of this film's reception and Kieślowski's reaction to it merits closer consideration. Mirosław Przylipiak has drawn attention to Kieślowski's description of that reaction as "cios w nie przygotowany żołądek" ("a blow to an unprepared stomach") (interview with Urszula Biełous, "Artysta należący do świata" ["An Artist Belonging to the World"], *Wiadomości kulturalne* 17 September 1995, quoted in Przylipiak, "Monter i studentka, czyli jak to było naprawdę z niszczeniem Krzysztofa Kieślowskiego przez polską krytykę filmową" ["The Fitter and the Student, or How It Really Was with Regard to Krzysztof Kieślowski's Destruction by the Polish Film Critics"], *Kino* 31: 3 [March 1997]: 6-9, 50), and has expressed surprise that "the director and his scriptwriter enter the very centre of the ring in what was then perhaps the greatest and most momentous socio-political conflict in Europe, with their stomachs unprepared!" (private communication to the author, 4 April 1997). Kieślowski's point of reference here seems to be Houdini and the blow often deemed primarily responsible for his death. Thus, "unprepared" may perhaps be readable as "not hardened": the stomach may have been bared to receive a blow, but the recipient may still have been caught partly off guard, like Houdini. What surprised Kieślowski may have been the *degree* of opposition which the film aroused – something for which the largely positive reception of his earlier works indeed had not prepared him. Reviews in the most important metropolitan newspapers and journals were certainly almost all negative, although not necessarily violently so.

[5]   Marianne Moore, *Collected Poems* (New York: Macmillan, 1968): 41.

[6]   Przylipiak: 6-8.

[7]   Tadeusz Sobolewski, "Te same pytania" ["The Same Questions"], *Film*

5 (May 1995): 69.

8   Whence Antoine de Baecque's tart enquiry whether entry to "the church of Kieślowski" is compulsory: "Faut-il entrer dans l'église de Kieślowski?", *Cahiers du Cinéma* 429 (March 1990): 32-33.

9   Georgia Brown, "Too Beautiful for You", *The Village Voice* 29 November 1994: 64.

10   Danusia Stok (ed), *Kieślowski on Kieślowski* (London; Boston: Faber and Faber, 1993): 79.

11   Raymond Williams, *Culture and Society 1780-1950* (London: Chatto & Windus, 1958): 291-292. Emphasis in original.

12   Ibid.

13   Ibid.

14   Charles Thomas Samuels, "Interview with Jean Renoir", in his *Encountering Directors* (New York: G. P. Putnam's Sons, 1972): 210.

15   Eco argues that "every text presupposes and constructs always a double Model Reader – a naive and a 'smart' one, a semantic reader and a semiotic or critical reader. The former uses the work as semantic machinery and is the victim of the strategies of the author who will lead him...along a series of previsions and expectations. The latter evaluates the work as an aesthetic product and enjoys the strategies implemented in order to produce a Model Reader of the first level. This second-level reader is the one who enjoys the seriality of the series." (Umberto Eco, *The Limits of Interpretation* [Bloomington and Indianapolis: Indiana University Press, 1990]: 92.)

16   Sylvia Swift, "The Series in Kieślowski's Work", paper delivered to the Kieślowski panel at the Society for Cinema Studies Conference, Dallas, TX, 1996. See also the comments of Adam Mars-Jones in "The judge, the dog and the woman in *Red*", *The Independent* 30 November 1994, Film: 25: "It was also dangerous for the director to announce the themes of the films in advance, since when you know what the theme of something is supposed to be, it will seem unnecessarily obscure if you don't then notice it, and unduly obvious if you do".

17   Przylipiak: 50.

18   Rainer Maria Rilke, "Auguste Rodin", in *Sämtliche Werke*, fifth volume (Frankfurt am Main: Insel, 1965): 141.

19   Tony Rayns, "Glowing in the Dark", *Sight and Sound* 4: 6 (June 1994): 8.

20   Thus, when Goethe describes red as both dignified and charming, and

hence equally suitable for age and youth, it is hard not to think of *Red*, while his remarks on the manner in which blue's retreating quality invites pursuit may recall *Trois couleurs: bleu* (*Three Colours: Blue*, 1993). See Johann Wolfgang von Goethe, *Theory of Colours*, translated by Charles Lock Eastlake (Cambridge, MA; London: The M.I.T. Press, 1970): 310-316. I considered the question of colour in *Red* at greater length in a paper entitled "Kieślowski, Goethe and the Colour that Changed the World" delivered at the University of Aberdeen's Film/Culture/History Conference in August 1996.

[21] That lack of a clear ending is a leitmotif of Kieślowski's work. Even the night porter, in one sense so clearly "named" as a "Fascist", is left "unnamed" at its end: when a teacher asks her children what the smiling, uniformed man is called, no name follows. As always, Kieślowski's final gesture – as in the film of the same title – is *Nie wiem* (*I Don't Know*, 1977). For some useful reflections on the relationship between open-endedness and Kieślowski's use of serial form, see Vincent Amiel, *Kieślowski* (Paris: Rivages, 1995): 53-54.

[22] Bogusław Zmudziński, "Rezygnacja Krzysztofa Kieślowskiego, czyli życie jest gdzie indziej" ["Kieślowski's Resignation, or Life is Elsewhere"], *Universitas* 11 (1994): 68-70.

[23] Tadeusz Sobolewski, "Solidarność grzesznych: O *Dekalogu* Krzysztofa Kieślowskiego", *NaGłos* 1 (1990): 91-101.

[24] Krzysztof Kieślowski, "Milczenie Bergmana" ["Bergman's Silence"], in Janusz Wróblewski (ed), *Magia kina* (Warsaw: Tenten, 1995): 57.

[25] Amiel: 150.

[26] Some relevant remarks about the face, drawing on the philosophy of Levinas, may be found in Véronique Campan's *Dix brèves histoires d'image* (Paris: Presses de la Nouvelle Sorbonne, 1993): 119.

[27] Moreover, Kieślowski gives the face a social context, as Robert Phillip Kolker complains that Bergman fails to do. See *The Altering Eye: Contemporary International Cinema* (Oxford; New York; Toronto; Melbourne: Oxford University Press, 1983): 185. Nevertheless, this is not a criticism which Kieślowski himself would make, and one of his finest pieces is an admiring essay on *The Silence* (in Wróblewski [ed]: 53-57).

[28] Rayns: 10.

[29] Krzysztof Kieślowski and Krzysztof Piesiewicz, "Raj", *Dialog* 3 (1997): 5-33.

[30] Translated from the Polish: "a efektu widowiska dopełnia lądujący wśród kurzu z głośnym warkotem helikopter". Ibid: 32.

[31] Translated from the Polish: "Helikopter widoczny jeszcze przez chwilę,

stapia się z granatem nieba. Jego dolne światło wygląda teraz jak jedna z gwiazd zawieszonych wysoko nad zapatrzonymi w górę ludźmi". Ibid: 33.

[32] Krzysztof Piesiewicz, "Piekło", *Dialog* 5 (1997): 5-31.

Ultimate concerns

Tadeusz Sobolewski

TRANSLATED FROM THE POLISH BY PAUL COATES

The interview book *Kieślowski on Kieślowski*[1] by Danusia Stok allows one to view Kieślowski's cinema in the light of his biography. It appears that the director of *Amator* (*Camera Buff*, 1979) littered his films with many coded references to his personal situation, and to such key facts in his life as his father's sickness and death, his mother's death in a car crash, his own youthful spell in the theatre, the beginnings of his filmic career, the duel with the authorities and the censors, the birth of his child and – finally – his own heart ailment and weariness of cinema, which, instead of being part of life, had become its competitor.

Do the "fairy tales about people" – Kieślowski's own joking definition of feature films[2] – conceal the director's own inner memoirs? They certainly constitute a symbolic documentation of his own private reckoning with life. Except for Jerzy Skolimowski, no other Polish director has presented so complete a testimony concerning himself encrypted within his films.

Kieślowski's refusal to permit Stok's book's publication in Poland during his lifetime may be attributed to the director's particular secretiveness, or perhaps to his long-standing feud with the Polish critics. The disjunction between Kieślowski and the Polish critics (but not the public) stemmed from our age-old habit of dealing with artists as spokesmen for the community, promulgators of ideas, prophets pointing out the way to others. From the very outset, Kieślowski's films were viewed within Poland as part of an intellectual campaign. We began by viewing him as a leader of the so-called "Cinema of Moral Anxiety", that 1970s term for a series of films about contemporary reality that were interpreted in political categories, as expressions of a critique of the system. Later, in the 1980s, a religious aura surrounded the readings of these films (although the religiosity was paradoxical, deriving from a revolt against God and finding no other sanction for goodness than the human conscience). Kieślowski shrugged off the political and religious roles written for him. And, for better or worse, we in Poland failed to find an approach to Kieślowski's work that would have allowed us to grasp its specific, integral quality as an individual act, rather than a function of social aspirations – as a unity, not an expression of a political or religious conversion.

It is traditional for Polish critics to compel the artist to answer "social" questions, condemning all manifestations of "nihilism" (as in the poetry of Tadeusz Różewicz). Kieślowski's strategy, however, was to seek a dialogue with the viewer over the heads of "society", beyond the bounds of current conventions and intellectual fashions, with which he was permanently at odds. One could state outright that, as of *Spokój* (*The Calm*, 1976) and *Camera Buff*, Kieślowski did not so much underwrite wider social aspirations as strive to free himself from them.

The astonishment aroused by the second stage of his œuvre, after martial law, lay in the way this born activist, the reputed leader of his generation, began to display a programmatically apolitical position at a time when Polish life had become thoroughly steeped in politics. As Wisława Szymborska (a poet Kieślowski quoted on occasions, as he did Różewicz) wrote ironically in one of her poems of the 1980s:

Whatever you mention has a resonance,
Whatever you pass over in silence, an import
That is political, one way or the other.[3]

It was his lot to work in an era of systemic crisis and great hopes for life's renewal. This was the era of Solidarity, of martial law, of Communism's departure and society's eventual repolarisation by divisions within the Solidarity camp. Throughout this period, Kieślowski blatantly turned his back on politics, like a person stripped of all illusions. Phrases such as "locking one's door from the inside" and "I am less and less interested in the world, more and more in the individual" began to recur in his interviews. In 1994, during a meeting with the public in Lvov (Ukraine), he stated that he "disliked the Catholic Church", "would not vote, so as not to be responsible for what was all around him", and that "one reason for abandoning cinema was his aversion to playing a public part, his yearning for privacy". Asked how he would answer the question he himself posed to people in his 1980 documentary, *Gadające głowy* (*Talking Heads*) – "What do you want from life?" – he replied with one of his own films' titles: "Peace". How much resignation, tiredness caused by illness and disappointment with life was there in those replies, how much lofty aspiration to "an inner peace"?

Viewed today, Kieślowski's old documentary, *Siedem kobiet w różnym wieku* (*Seven Women of Different Ages*, 1978) – a backstage view of the art of ballet – appears to be an artist's unwitting commentary on his own life, especially at those points where the director underscores the sheer physical effort that accompanies dancing practice, the struggle against weariness, which later yields the effect of lightness. As he observes the artiste during practice, Kieślowski distils beauty from the hard labour of the exercises, and spectacle from her preparations. But when he comes to show the moment of the première, the triumph gives way to melancholy. Here is the on-stage kiss of two lovers, symbolising love: lips that approach without touching. The effect is beautiful but brief – diminished and somehow hollow. Seen in the context of Kieślowski's own road, the film is brim-full of bitter knowledge: art is a life's vocation, but fulfilment is fleeting and momentary, and may even be non-existent.

During the first – realistic – phase of his work, Kieślowski behaves as if he wants to abolish the disparity between art and life. In the later esoteric works, as he achieves formal mastery, Kieślowski obsessively stresses the disparity between them, so that in the end he betrays art in the name of life – he rejects it.

Is not *La Double Vie de Véronique* (*The Double Life of Véronique*, 1991) a self-commentary on these dilemmas? Drawn by the illusory (and frankly somewhat kitschy) beauty of the music of Zbigniew Preisner, the Polish Weronika gives her life for art. Her French double renounces art for life, wins love and returns in the finale to "her father's house".

Art, which the camera buff had treated at first as a vehicle for telling the truth about the world, proves no more than one for telling the truth about oneself, a field for the harmonisation of self and world. None of Kieślowski's heroes achieves this harmony, however. And as for self-knowledge – its conclusion is the tear in the eye of the judge, the last frame of Kieślowski's last film. Thus, his esoteric films do not say anything that had not been said in the previous ones, do not yield any new hope or "clutch God's ankles", as the Polish proverb ironically puts it.

After *Dekalog* (*The Decalogue*, 1988), Bolesław Michałek remarked that Kieślowski did not treat life's conundrums in the traditional manner of Polish Romanticism, which resolves them with a single stroke. He shows that one lives with the conundrums – that there is no escaping them.[4]

On his release from prison, Antek Gralak, the hero of *The Calm*, seeks to put down roots in life. His needs are few: to find a job, a flat, a wife. He finds all three, but the state of equilibrium is short-lived. Gralak is caught in the middle of a dispute between the workforce at the construction site where he works, and its directors. Those high-up treat him as their man, and think they have bought him. His colleagues demand solidarity from him and see him as a traitor, a blackleg. He himself wants to be faithful to both sides, to play the part of mediator. It proves impossible.

The Calm was seen as a political film. It was made during a year that saw workers' strikes and the formation of the first postwar opposition, the Komitet Obrony Robotników (Workers' Defence Committee; KOR). The scenes of striking workers were the first of their kind in modern Polish cinema. This was doubtless why the film was shelved. Censorship caused it to be read in a revolutionary spirit. But the meaning of the film was a different one. To speak in the language of ideas, its defence of personal freedom was carried out in the spirit of individualism, not Socialism, and from the viewpoint of the individual who falls victim to society. A socially activist stance would have led rather to a critique of non-commitment. In Kieślowski – in *The Calm*, as later in *Blind Chance* – non-commitment proves a luxury, something unattainable, particularly within a totalitarian system.

The Calm had to wait four years for its première. *Przypadek* (*Blind Chance*, 1981), whose significance is apolitical, was also "detained" for political reasons, and had to wait six years. Evidently greater social freedom is needed for the apolitical than for calls to revolt! *Blind Chance* was written before August 1980, shot before martial law, and premièred before the round-table talks in 1989. The times were revolutionary, but Kieślowski made a film about the arbitrariness of every choice of world-view. On the other side of the barricades are people just like us!

The hero of *Blind Chance* experiences the same stretch of time three times over. Whether he joins the ranks of the regime's organisations or those of the opposition depends on whether or not he catches a train. He stands with the Communist reformers (who turn out to be cynical manipulators) or converts to Catholicism (despairingly praying to a God in whom he does not believe: O Lord, be there!). In each incarnation, an accusation of treachery awaits him – something no one in Poland can avoid.

The first two variants of Witek's life are recounted in the conditional tense. Only the third variant, which ends in death, is real. Witek misses the train, avoids internal division, and abandons the social race. He becomes a doctor – joins no Party, signs no oppositional protest letter. He seems to be happy and fulfilled, or as much so as is possible in life. The fullness of his experience lies in his openness to the world of human suffering, which is no longer veiled from him by politics. Watching the scene with the old lady dying may remind one of Gombrowicz's sentence: "you speak of victims of the system? Go to the nearest hospital – there are people dying there too."[5]

Like Kieślowski, Witek rejects political engagement. His choice prefigures Kieślowski's own:

> Twice in my life I tried my hand at politics and twice I came out very badly. The first time was then, in 1968, when I took part in a students' strike in Łódź...And then they interrogated me...They wanted me to say something, sign something, which I didn't do. Nobody beat me up, nobody threatened me...What was worse was the fact that they threw people out of Poland [Kieślowski is referring to the anti-Semitic campaign.]...I knew that I couldn't do anything about it, that nobody could do anything about it, and that, paradoxically, the more I shouted against the authorities, the more I threw those stones, the more people would get thrown out of the country.[6]

His second excursion into politics – at a higher level, although, as it turned out, without any real influence – was his vice-presidency of the Stowarzyszenie Filmowców Polskich (Association of Polish Filmmakers) between 1977 and 1980:

> We were trying, as an Association, to fight for some sort of artistic freedom...Nothing came out of it...I had a painful feeling of having walked into a room where I absolutely shouldn't have gone, that the compromises which I had to make – and I was constantly having to make compromises, of course – that those compromises embarrassed me because they weren't my own private ones: they were compromises made in the name of a number of people. This is deeply immoral because, even if you can do some good for somebody, achieve something which people need, there's always a price to be paid. Of course, you pay with stress but it's the others who really pay...I don't want to be responsible for anybody else. And that's what I realized, despite the fact that I'd got myself mixed up in this Association affair. When Solidarity came along, I simply asked the Association to dismiss me.[7]

Compromise was immoral and ineffective. On the other hand, hatred left a bad after-taste. The generation of '68, disillusioned with the slogans of the Socialist system, did not yet question the slogans' value. In turning its backs on one ideology, it did not propose one of its own. It merely discovered that what went by the name of "real Socialism" was founded on a lie that was not even believed by the rulers themselves, who viewed ideals as screens for their exercise of power.

As Kieślowski remarks in his book, there were two ways of acting with regard to the regime of the time. The first was to enter a life-and-death struggle against it. His own approach was different: perceiving the evil, but understanding people's motives and their entrapment in the system.[8]

In *Życiorys* (*Curriculum Vitae*, 1975), which combines documentary and fiction, a genuine Party Control Commission investigates the case of a certain Antoni Gralak, who has been dismissed from the Party in which he believed – on grounds of insubordination. What interests Kieślowski is the phenomenon of the Party inquiry:

> I'm frightened of anybody who wants to teach me something or who wants to show me a goal...That's why I'm afraid of psychoanalysts and psychotherapists...I'm just as fanatically afraid of those therapists as I am of politicians, of priests, and of teachers. I'm frightened of all those people who show you the way, who know...I'm convinced that Stalin and Hitler knew exactly what they were to do. They knew very well. But that's how it is. That's fanaticism. That's knowing. That's the feeling of absolutely knowing. And the next minute, it's army boots. It always ends up like that.[9]

Does Kieślowski demonise power in his early works? On the contrary, he strips it of the demonic, removes it from its pedestal. Standing to one side, a political outsider attached to no ideology or faith (he said of himself: a man without roots), he is fascinated by the psychology both of the Party's functionaries and of its faithful servants. His vivisection of Communism bears no trace of ressentiment, presupposes the good faith of committed people and observes the crisis of their faith, the disintegration of the ideal, which had failed to satisfy the basic human longing for community, solidarity and social harmony.

In *Robotnicy '71: nic o nas bez nas* (*Workers '71: Nothing About Us Without Us*, 1972), the scene of an electoral meeting at a big enterprise (a shipyard?) succeeded in showing how far removed the "worker's authorities" were from the workers themselves – what feudal respect they arouse in the workers, how those who had protested not too long before now stand on ceremony. They were still a long way from "founding their own committees", as in 1980.

In the films he made in the 1970s, Kieślowski worked to reduce the distance between the people and the authorities – to reduce it, not add to it. While living in an undemocratic state he acted like a democrat. At the same time, a note of scepticism about the mediating role of the artist began to seep into his films. There was a growing sense of the paradoxicality of social life. And all the time Kieślowski respects all forms of the belief of simple people, whether it is religious or Socialist. The director of *Personel* (*Personnel*, 1975) treats the prevailing system like the weather, viewing it less as an "enemy" than as a hindrance to the achievement of "peace and quiet", goodness, harmony or simply community – all the things for which his protagonists yearn.

Kieślowski was thus able to grasp the innocent consciousness of the citizen of the Polish People's Republic. For the young man entering life in 1968, the system – although founded on lies – was a part of reality, just as crime is part of power in Shakespeare's world. For us, citizens of People's Poland, the authorities stood on an unattainable height. The First Secretary of the Party looked down from the pictures on the front page of the newspaper and on the television screen as if from an altar. His speeches were widely mocked, even parodied in cabarets, and the books that contained them gathered dust in the newspaper kiosks, alongside the combs. But, at the same time, the authorities were Father. They functioned as such even when they beat the students in 1968. The students mocked them and, at the same time, were amazed: how could they be capable of such injustice? The oppositionists of the Polish People's Republic tormented the authorities with the Socialist ideals they were traducing. The Marxist-Leninist Church was still standing and we all remained within its walls. No one even dreamed of a universal privatisation (even at the end of the 1980s, most Poles saw it as unrealistic). We inhabited a Socialist world, a communal one. Although viewed in the perspective of time, it seems to have been a community of "proles", petitioners crowding in front of office windows, as in Kieślowski's early documentaries – *Urząd* (*Office*, 1966) and *Refren* (*Refrain*, 1972). Kieślowski marvellously captured the mood of this shared proletarian fate, with its proletarian joys, in his first professional documentary, *Z miasta Łodzi* (*From the City of Łódź*, 1969).

The paradox of that world, which our generation entered as the only one available, rested on a double recognition of reality. It awoke in people both an urge to mock and one to affirm. The opposition to "the Commune" fostered within family walls, the view of the authorities as "Them", and the widespread spirit of dissent and resistance somehow went hand-in-hand with a desire that found its simplest expression in the diary of a female writer who still recalled the first recovery of independence in 1918: "I wanted that Poland to be a success".[10] People listened to Radio Free Europe *en masse*, but the People's Republic was their only reality. Young people sought a refuge from the omnipresent ideology – and found one. For some, it was the hippie movement; for others, the worlds of art and – last but not least – religion.

There was a massive intermediate zone, an acceptance of reality "despite everything", different from political acceptance. "For it's our country", as Birkut says in *Człowiek z marmuru* (*Man of Marble*, 1976) on release from a Stalinist jail. People "didn't want anything to do with the Commune", but they availed themselves of the privileges the system had created. Life had the form of normality, the system was assimilated, and even those who disagreed with it counted on it lasting. The road Kieślowski took during the 1970s led from amazement at the ill-management of the social world to a complete disinterest in politics. In the closing scene of *Personnel*, the young tailor from the opera is singled out by the youth organisation to denounce his firebrand colleague. Faced with a blank piece of paper, he twirls his pen round and round, as if hesitant. We are sure that he will not sign. But why does he waver so long? Why does he not give the manipulators a piece of his mind? Out of sheer politeness?

He takes their proposal at face value. He is living inside the system, and innate honesty is his only compass. The Witek of the third part of *Blind Chance* will be bolder – which does not mean that he revolts. He simply knows that one must not get involved. The film begins with a cry of "No!" and a close-up of Witek's mouth as he screams, knowing he will die in the plane in a second's time. The whole film unfolds under the aegis of this "No!", which concerns more than a political system.

Here the political revolt becomes a metaphysical one. In terms of Camus' distinction, "[t]he rebel slave affirms that there is something in him which will not tolerate the manner in which his master treats him; the metaphysical rebel declares that he is frustrated by the universe".[11] At this moment, the cinema that had described the world of the People's Republic as diverging from the one shown in newspapers or on television becomes a cinema with metaphysical aspirations. And by "metaphysical" I mean an ability to present the world from a distance, as if from the wings.

Perhaps *Blind Chance* – a film on the border of two aesthetics (realistic description and philosophical fable), and made on the border between two eras, in fact – deserves to be called "metaphysical", especially since it is so deeply immersed in a concrete historical reality from which at the same time it distances itself. In telling of life's restriction by a political system, Kieślowski does so from the vantage point of non-existence. He sets the system's shortcomings alongside the absurdity of death. And it is only from the perspective of the last things – albeit a negative one lacking religious meaning – that Witek's choices acquire higher meaning, that the whole of reality is raised to a higher level, one shot through with empathy. It permits one to view People's Poland from a perspective beyond the political – as a fragment of the world, rich and multilevelled, obeying the rules of probability.

Blind Chance – Kieślowski's key film – broke radically with the system, not just on the level of politics and ideology, but in its very way of conceiving man and his destiny. It expressed a philosophical disenchantment with life as such, not the system. The road to *The Decalogue* lay open. Paradoxically, Kieślowski needed the experience of martial law along the way to free himself of the last vestiges of political engagement. Adam Zagajewski, the author of a volume of essays published abroad, in emigration, under the pregnant title of *Solidarność i samotność* (*Solidarity and Solitude*), underwent a similar evolution during the 1980s. Kieślowski, like Zagajewski, chose solitude, did not want to "sway in time with the others", to manifest his resistance. Ten years earlier, the selfsame Zagajewski, in his famous youthful manifesto, had called for a "description of the unrepresented world". At that time, realism had had a revolutionary meaning. Kieślowski's work was part of the same wave. But, as the years passed, his revolutionary position (apparent, for instance, during the student revolt of 1968) gave way to a species of nihilism behind which lay an active compassion with a world of the absurd, subject to the logic of chance, with the "toiling masses, worn out with suffering and death", as Camus says.[12]

The Decalogue arose in opposition to the Polish culture of those years. Martial law had driven Poles back once more into the sphere of Romantic martyrology. There was a resurgence of patriotic poetry and Romantic messianism. So there was all the more need to view life in its raw state, even absurdity, in order to distil all the more powerfully those values that do not inhere in society, history and the idols to which the collectivity genuflects, but in human beings themselves. Previous Polish cinema had found no way to present sin and virtue as possibilities which everyone always confronts, rather than in terms of caricature and apotheosis. Kieślowski was the first to do so, although his "decalogue" – to use Gombrowicz's language – is "interhuman" in nature.

Apparently, in the initial conception of *The Decalogue*, all its protagonists were to have been inhabitants of a single housing block which blew up in a gas explosion. Such a finale would have parodied a Last Judgment that condemned the majority. And yet, Kieślowski and his co-scriptwriter Krzysztof Piesiewicz do not adopt the position of judges. Here there is a fundamental difference between Kieślowski and Hitchcock (despite the similar construction of suspense in *Krótki film o zabijaniu* [*A Short Film About Killing*, 1988] and *Krótki film o miłości* [*A Short Film About Love*, 1988]). In Hitchcock, as in a traditional morality play, what is at stake is a conflict between good and evil. Kieślowski's theme is not evil, however. What concerns him is man, man as a whole, caught up in a situation that leads him to evil. In this trial, the director and scriptwriter assume the roles of the "sinner"'s defendants. They stand close by him and compel the viewer to stand equally close. When we watch *A Short Film About Killing* and *A Short Film About Love*, we participate, on the basis of cinematic identification, in an act of murder and in one of voyeurism. In each case, we are its seconds. An orphaned boy undertakes a "sinful" experiment: armed with a telescope he observes a female neighbour, pursuing a form of pornography to find out what love is. He never does so. With a pedantry akin to that displayed by the voyeur, Kieślowski attempts to "photograph love" broken down to its basic components – and finds a void. "There's no such thing". There is the need for love, however, symbolised by the gesture of putting one's eye to the telescope.

In *The Decalogue*, theft, adultery and murder occur out of lack of love – and hence "for love". A bridge links the viewer and the "sinner": we stand in solidarity with the criminal. That solidarity can have a Christian meaning, for it leads to the notion of a love that would embrace the whole man, with all his weaknesses, and even his crimes, as in *A Short Film About Killing*, which is Kieślowski's masterpiece.

"I hate! I hate!", the lawyer cries out after the murderer's execution, in *Decalogue 5*'s last scene. We do not learn who or what the lawyer hates. Is it the cold consistency with which the world eliminates a criminal it had earlier deprived of hope? Rebellion against the world's order (chaos?) here touches the border of faith, symbolised by the light that glows on the "field of Cain" viewed by the weeping, cursing lawyer. Kieślowski evokes the questions: Does God kill? Can God be against Man? Is there a God?

Why did *The Decalogue* encounter such a reserved response in Poland? For some it was insufficiently religious. Others reproached Kieślowski with entering a domain that was "not his". He posed fundamental questions, which were thus a provocation, launched from outside any and every tradition, as in Camus, who summed up his position regarding the last things in a paradox: "I do not believe in God and I am not an atheist".[13]

Similar questions are posed in *Decalogue 1* by the boy raised by an atheistic father and a pious aunt: Why do people die? Who is God? Where is he? Does he exist? One of Kieślowski's students at the Katowice Film School once remarked contemptuously: "he's asking the questions of an eight-year-old!". Yes, they are the questions of an eight-year-old – and those of a philosopher. People come to terms with them, calm down with age. The older Kieślowski became the more he broached these questions. He created dramatic situations that placed the issue of the meaningfulness of belief on a knife's edge. The viewer was always left responsible for the answer.

In *Decalogue 1*, the aunt (Maja Komorowska), answers the boy in her own words, which were not in the original script: "God is. It's very simple if you believe." There is no falsity in her words or in the gesture with which she hugs the child. But the aunt's reply is not the last word. It is not the author's own thesis. In *Decalogue 1*, belief helps no one. Believers and unbelievers alike suffer the same fate. An innocent child falls victim to it. Immediately after the conversation about God we see the frozen lake where a vigil is kept by the watchman – a mysterious, silent figure who appears in almost all the segments of *The Decalogue* at critical moments, when the heroes are threatened by death. The expression on this figure's face shows that this "guardian angel" knows everything that is about to happen but remains helpless. He simply and compassionately follows the action and the heroes, like the chorus in a Greek tragedy. And here a third element enters – that of fate. Before dying beneath the ice, the boy takes part, together with his father, in a chess tournament held by a chess mistress with an unpleasant expression, who plays simultaneously on many boards. The boy will be the only one to checkmate her. The figure of the chess-player arouses disturbing associations, representing the death against which one cannot win.

In this film, Kieślowski plays a cruel game with the viewer. He puts us to the test, activating our cinematic belief – and then extinguishing it. He orders us to believe that the boy has been saved, then gradually removes that belief. He introduces into the action a miraculous, omniscient computer – and it, too, fails. Belief and reason lose to the actual state of things. Has Kieślowski left us helpless? The believing aunt cannot but doubt providence. The atheist doubts his own atheism, runs to the empty, incomplete church and overturns the altar. There follows the famous scene with the icon of the Madonna, and waxen tears flow down her cheeks.

The meaning of this scene remains open. It contains both nihilistic revolt (it is merely an image painted on a board down which wax is dripping) and symbolic meaning (if there is a God, he suffers along with men). The director does not know the answer to any of the questions he raises, and does not impose any on us.

The Protestant theologian Paul Tillich once asked if there is a kind of faith compatible with doubt and a sense of meaninglessness.[14] He replied that such a faith does indeed exist and is characteristic of the modern West. Perhaps its existence goes some way towards explaining the worldwide success of Kieślowski's late films. Tillich uses the notions of "secular humanist faith" and "ultimate concern".

Even negations of faith can be forms of its expression – as, in fact, is the case with the father in *Decalogue 1*. The theologian of "ultimate concern" states that acceptance of one's own despair is a form of faith. Discovering the arbitrariness of our fate, the absence of Providence and the omnipotence of chance, absurdity and death need not issue in nihilism, but rather in "the courage to be".[15]

Asked by a group of Katowice upper-level grammar school students, in his last interview, whether he "believes in God, or just himself, perhaps in other people, some idea, goal, fate – anything", Kieślowski replies in all seriousness: "I think all those things are bound up together, in fluid, ever-changing proportions. And if life is interesting it is precisely because those proportions are always changing."[16] In his introduction to the Polish edition of one of Tillich's books, Jan Andrzej Kłoczowski states: "man poses the question of the meaning of the world and of being, and in asking discovers that he himself is the question about the meaning of his ultimate concerns".[17] As an artist and as a man, Kieślowski embodied just such a question for us. His greatness lay in unveiling his questions in front of us.

If, for all their agnostic message, Kieślowski's films invigorate their viewers, it is because they build a link of solidarity between us that excludes no one.

Notes

[1] Danusia Stok (ed), *Kieślowski on Kieślowski* (London; Boston: Faber and Faber, 1993).

[2] Tadeusz Sobolewski, "Bajka o ludziach" ["Fairy Tale About People"], *Tygodnik powszechny* 12 April 1993.

[3] Translated from the Polish: "O czym mówisz, ma rezonans/o czym milczysz, ma wymowę/tak czy owak polityczną". Wisława Szymborska, "Dzieci epoki" ["Children of the Epoch"], in *Widok z ziarnkiem piaska* (Poznań: Wydawnictwo a5, 1996): 122.

[4] Bolesław Michałek, "Kieślowski: lo sfondo e la diversita", in Małgorzata Furdal and Roberto Turigliatto (eds), *Kieślowski* (Turin: Museo Nazionale del Cinema, 1989): 44.

[5] Witold Gombrowicz, *Dziennik* [1953-56] (Paris: Instytut literacki, 1971): 250, 270.

[6] Stok (ed): 38-39.

[7] Ibid: 39.

[8] Ibid: 59.

[9]   Ibid: 36.

[10] Translated from the Polish: "[Dąbrowska i jej najbliżsi] chcieli, żeby Polska teraźniejsza się udała". Maria Dąbrowska, *Dzienniki 1958-1965*, selected by Tadeusz Drewnowski (Warsaw: Czytelnik, 1988): 340.

[11] Albert Camus, *The Rebel*, translated by Anthony Bower (London: Penguin Books in association with Hamish Hamilton, 1962): 29.

[12] Ibid: 267.

[13] Albert Camus, *Notatniki 1935-1959*, selected and translated by Joanna Guze (Warsaw, 1994): 228.

[14] Paul Tillich, *Dynamics of Faith* (London: George Allen & Unwin, 1957).

[15] Paul Tillich, *The Courage To Be* (Welwyn: James Nisbet and Company, 1952).

[16] Translated from the Polish: "Myslę, że to jest wszystko razem, w stale zmieniających się płynnych proporcjach. I w ogóle, jeśli życie jest ciekawe, to właśnie dlatego, że te proporcje się zmieniają". Jacek Błach and Agata Otrębska, "Wymykamy się Bogu z ręki", *Gazeta wyborcza* 23-24 March 1996.

[17] Translated from the Polish: "Człowiek stawia pytanie o sens świata i bytu, a pytając odkrywa, że on sam jest pytaniem o sens swojej troski ostatecznej". Jan Andrzej Kłoczowski, "Introduction" to Paul Tillich, *Dynamika wiary [Dynamics of Faith]*, translated by Adam Szostkiewicz (Poznań: "W drodze", 1987): 22.

Kieślowski and the crisis of documentary

Paul Coates

I. Concealed autobiography

For all the breaks in his career – the triple life of documentarist, political director, and extraterritorial feature-maker that might parallel that of Witek Długosz, the protagonist of *Przypadek* (*Blind Chance*, 1981) – Kieślowski's work has a profound unity; it seems at times as if all his films' figures are speaking with his voice, as even his documentaries' subjects echo his interview statements. That sense of the other as a possible self later inoculates the features against the binarisms of melodrama, causing them to take everyone seriously, imbuing fiction with the documentarist's passionate dispassion. Rimbaud's "Je est un autre" becomes a possible motto for his whole work – conjugated realistically at the outset, modernistically in the end. Even in his early documentaries, a dialectic of apparent impersonality masks and mediates the deeply personal, since it alone renders expression possible.

The work is autobiographical in two senses and at two levels. Firstly, it is so at its surface, where certain themes which the director chooses to broach and concurrent events in his life correspond. An example of this is given by Jacek Petrycki, the cameraman on several of Kieślowski's early films: Petrycki remarks that Kieślowski chose his films' subjects from his own most immediate experience, as if wishing to examine them and understand them for himself:

> Kieślowski spent his childhood in trains, apart from which he and his mother travelled to see his father, who had TB. This became the inspiration for the film *X-Ray*. He had a daughter... and that stirred his imagination and gave rise to the film *First Love*.[1]

In a similar vein, Tadeusz Lubelski comments that "it is remarkable how close is the connection between Kieślowski's works – even the early documentary ones – and the director's personal experience", and mentions, among other things, the parallels between Romek Januchta's work in *Personel* (*Personnel*, 1975) and Kieślowski's own training as a theatre dresser.[2] Documentary masks autobiography with Kieślowski's characteristic modesty, the "talking heads" format being particularly useful because the assembled mass of material permits the selection of those voices that, in a subtle ventriloquism, will echo his own seemingly silent one, while at the same time concealing the personal nature of the selection. Kieślowski's frequently-expressed passion for editing is, among other things, one for the hunt for a voice to echo his own. The moment of that voice's selection may be the terminus of a whole film, as of a real hunt – as occurs, for instance, in *Nie wiem* (*I Don't Know*, 1977), where the dismissed manager of the leather works finally concedes that, although he once thought his policies right, they may not have been; "nie wiem" are his last words, and those of the film itself. When characters in *Byłem żołnierzem* (*I Was a Soldier*, 1970) or *Prześwietlenie* (*X-Ray*, 1974) speak of life's difficulty and their exclusion, it is as if Kieślowski has chosen their remarks to express his own feelings. The indirection of suffering's expression is the precondition of its being voiced at all. Perhaps the most richly polyphonic and complex example is *Gadające głowy* (*Talking Heads*, 1980), whose every voice feels like Kieślowski's own, calling for less aggression in everyday life, for freedom and love. The lady near its end who says that she only wants peace – "spokój" – pronounces a Kieślowskian keyword. Since peace is associated with endings (is it any accident that the name of the key actress of Kieślowski's final films – Irène – means "peace"?), we know the conclusion is near, and everything comes full circle as we hear the voice of Kieślowski himself repeat the opening questions. His voice is now separate from the voices through which he has spoken, which he lays aside, like masks. He enters silence wittily and thoughtfully as the last speaker, aged 100, mentions her desire to go on living. It is a modest wish, yet the fact of the film's ending here (doubtless no older speakers could be found) combines with our sense of the weight of the epochs it has traversed, of ever-older lives and ever-deeper layers of time, to evoke the difficulty and poignancy of something so seemingly simple. That desire for continuance will haunt Kieślowski's works – *No End* being his most characteristic title – lending depth to its commitment to the series, which here distends into an epic collection of variant responses to the same questions. And yet, mere survival will be insufficient: it must be accompanied by transformation, a resurrection to clothe the sad present flesh in a happier body, in a happier country or time – as is most fully apparent in *La Double Vie de Véronique* (*The Double Life of Véronique*, 1991) and *Trois couleurs: rouge* (*Three Colours: Red*, 1994). Inasmuch as *Three Colours: Red* itself reincarnates *The Double Life of Véronique*, which itself reworks a small portion of *Dekalog 9* (*Decalogue 9*) as part of its theme of enlargement and miniaturisation, it shows the films themselves as reincarnations of one another.

To speak of a movement into depths is to reach the second level of autobiography – one that is "deeper" in the sense of embodying feelings, rather than events, feelings probably rooted in the childhood that may well have impressed them at a level below Kieślowski's own conscious awareness. The shift from documentary to feature-making represents an explicit step towards these feelings – "Deeper Rather Than Broader", to quote the title of Kieślowski's famous 1981 personal manifesto. At the same time, however, the two forms of filmic expression are linked by the Chekhovian aesthetic mentioned by Zbigniew Benedyktowicz, which evokes Kieślowski's own advocacy of the superiority of "reality's dramaturgy" to that of any fiction: "Why do we have to present images that evoke laughter or tears on the stage? Why not simply present images of everyday life, which do not provoke laughter or tears but rather reflection on and analysis of life's phenomena".[3]

To speak of this deeper level both is and is not indiscreet. It is, for Kieślowski consistently resisted all efforts to read his films as autobiographical, to state "which characters he stood behind", a resistance whose strength may be gauged by his prolonged refusal to sanction a Polish translation of Danusia Stok's *Kieślowski on Kieślowski* (1993), believing that he had said more than he wished a Polish audience to know. Not until 1995 did he make similar statements available to them, in Krzysztof Wierzbicki's *I'm so-so...*,[4] even going further at points – as when he mentioned his fear of his father. Yet, to speak of this level is also not indiscreet, for it respects Kieślowski's privacy. I have not interviewed his friends and relatives in an effort to disclose "the man behind the mask", but have merely reflected upon the material Kieślowski himself chose to place within the public sphere: his films and interviews. The documentarist might seem deeply wedded to impersonality, but the case of T S Eliot indicates the possibility of its functioning as a strategy for giving form to otherwise inchoate emotions. My aim is not to make a perversely novel, paradoxical contribution to the burgeoning secondary literature on Kieślowski, but to do justice to his work's depths. It seems to me that his films derive their resonance from being autobiographies *deep down*: that is, from the subtle play of concealment and revelation involved in ferrying private material into the public sphere while simultaneously, tactfully, leaving it in the depths of privacy, where it belongs and always remains lodged as the unconscious, whose dredging – as Freud finally conceded – may prove interminable. If Kieślowski's work progresses through its repetitions, it may be in the growing consciousness and self-consciousness with which this operation is performed.

In *Blind Chance*, Kieślowski makes of one character three persons. To argue that superficially different *curricula vitae* can belong to "the same" person is virtually tantamount to stating that multiple characters can have the "deep structure" of a single one. Whence Kieślowski's passion for the series and alternative version. Thus, it can be said, for instance, that Magda reincarnates Witek in *Krótki film o miłości* (*A Short Film About Love*, 1988) when she, too, crumples, overwhelmed, to her knees. When, in *Blind Chance*, Adam says he could easily have been in Werner's shoes, the implication is that he could, in a sense, have *been* Werner. Meanwhile, in *Życiorys* (*Curriculum Vitae*, 1975), Gralak, the Communist hauled over the coals by the Party control board, paradoxically bears the same name as the apolitical protagonist of *Spokój* (*The Calm*, 1976). Gralak says that baptising his son did not make him in any way less a Communist: essence is not expressed or altered by action, but remains occulted within the individual, like the soul Kieślowski says he sought to film in *The Double Life of Véronique* – like Kieślowski's own autobiography within all his films. The multiplicity of *portes paroles* which critics have discerned in his films is indicative less of their incompetence and fabled disagreement than of the omnipresence of concealed autobiography in the work. His career comes full circle when the documentary interviewer becomes the interviewee – and yet still remains, in a sense, the director, remarking on whether objects are properly lit – in *I'm so-so...*, a move prophesied when Filip Mosz turns his camera on himself at the close of *Amator* (*Camera Buff*, 1979). The entire late work draws conclusions from this gesture by Filip, the only image-maker among Kieślowski's protagonists, and so perhaps his most credible double. After all, did Kieślowski not say "if I'd known that they were going to confiscate my film the night we filmed those lockers while making *Station*, then, just like Filip, I'd have opened the cans and exposed the film",[5] and "[t]here were many documentaries which I didn't make. I managed to put a few of them into *Camera Buff*"?[6] Thus, that film, its final gesture and the questions of doubling and the persistence of documentary in the features deserve closer consideration. Firstly, however, one needs to consider more closely the nature of Kieślowski's conception of documentary.

II. "The dramaturgy of reality"

Kieślowski often stated that his work's primary aim was to describe reality. It is possible and appropriate to correlate this statement with ones by the new wave poets Adam Zagajewski and Julian Kornhauser, and assimilate Kieślowski's project – as several critics have done – to the generational, political post-'68 one of giving voice to an unrepresented, unofficial reality. Documentary viewing may well be fuelled by an "epistemophilia" analogous to the "scopophilia" from which many theorists derive film-going in general, but only in oppressively centrally-controlled countries, whose authorities seek to monopolise all accurate report, does that "desire to know" become a burning popular passion. Initially, during his Łódź Film School studies, Kieślowski's notion of description was somewhat rudimentary. His diploma thesis, whose supervisor was Jerzy Bossak, discerns something like a recovery of cinema's mission in Warhol's six-hour placement of a camera opposite the Empire State Building entrance.[7] (Warhol's static, impassive work does indeed recall some of the very earliest silent films, albeit massively extended.) Kieślowski himself amusingly recounted the practical consequences of such a *parti pris* in his last public meeting, held in Poznań:

I made a film about a milk bar. Old ladies arrive and eat up other peoples' left-over dumplings, and in front of the bar sits a violinist, scraping out the Polish anthem wonderfully off-key. And this seemed terribly meaningful to me. I shot all that and showed it to Karabasz, who said: 'you know, even if Eisenstein came along he wouldn't be able to do anything with this'. And he was right, since all the things I've mentioned were there – the old ladies, the dumplings, the violinist and the anthem – but they didn't add up to any broader concept. There was just the sense that here we are describing what some milk bar looks like – that is, that here we are with this one old lady eating up dumplings, and that it means nothing more than that, that it cannot be transposed into the kind of suffering shared by anyone else.[8]

This critique of the material's shortcomings is not just technical, for the issue of wider resonance – "the kind of suffering shared by anyone else" – is the central documentary one of the degree of an individual's typicality. A key aporia of Lukácsian aesthetics, which exalted 19th-century realism yet deciphered its characters as class allegories, the question returns with a vengeance through the frequent yawning gulf between the generality of a work's idea ("a film about the working class") and its particular instance (why *this* worker or group of workers? How representative are they?). Kieślowski would attack the problem in various ways: in *Krótki dzień pracy* (*Short Working Day*, 1981) or *Curriculum Vitae*, documentary and fiction fused to yield a character whose representativeness was underwritten by his "model" status, while the person's partial derealisation into a model – at least in theory – simultaneously insulated him from unwanted private repercussions. Kieślowski's most frequent solution, however, was the serial alignment of voices expressing the same, or cognate, feelings, individual instances massing into the "statistically significant proportion" that validates generalisation. Each person is permitted his or her individuality, but each echoes another to some degree. It is thus hardly surprising that his documentary work should culminate in a version of the opinion poll, *Talking Heads*. In this most vertiginous series – to my mind, Kieślowski's most haunting documentary – the interview's reduction to the short questions, "Who are you?" "What do you wish for?", permits a sample of exceptional length and hence representativeness. The talking heads become those of a whole society.

Kieślowski's use of the series is part of his broader practice of juxtaposition. His critique of his own milk bar footage could be read as one of Direct Cinema or *cinéma-vérité* aesthetics. He later told the Poznań meeting what was missing: a sense of "why they are doing this and perhaps how they came to do so, what happened before".[9] Traditional Griersonian documentaries would supply such additional information through commentary. But, since a voice-over would subvert Kieślowski's almost Bazinian early project of allowing reality to speak for itself,[10] something else had to be found. In the documentaries that would earn him his fame, Kieślowski would often achieve the "broader concept" through juxtaposition – either of two contradictory realities, or of various statements reinforcing one another to disclose shared aspiration or suffering.

One form of juxtaposition simply presents series of responses to several specific but fundamental questions (*I Was a Soldier, Talking Heads*). These works are a form of what Bill Nichols terms the "interactive documentary", where "[t]extual authority shifts toward the social actors recruited: their comments and responses provide a central part of the film's argument".[11] Kieślowski's juxtapositions often seem to "follow reality" by progressing chronologically past temporal markers given in intertitles: tracking the doctors of *Szpital* (*Hospital*, 1976) round the clock; moving through a week aligned allegorically with the stages of life in *Siedem kobiet w różnym wieku* (*Seven Women of Different Ages*, 1978), so that the girl taking dancing lessons on day one is conceivably reincarnated as the instructress of day seven, life's circle completing and renewing itself. The chronological movement can even run backwards, as in *Talking Heads*, where ever-earlier dates give the birth-year of the ever-older respondents to the same questions. Elsewhere, juxtaposition may underscore the serial nature of bureaucracy. *Urząd* (*Office*, 1966) shows successive petitioners shuffling past a window, so, although "what did you do all your life?" may be an individual instruction for filling out a form, the series and the recurrent shots of files piled high clearly answer the question: one filled out forms. Similarly, *Refren* (*Refrain*, 1972) evokes the process of applying for graveyard plots with multiple shots of IDs, stamps descending on forms, and reiterations of the various services which the funeral parlour offers. Black humour links birth and death in the end: Vivaldi's music wells up on the soundtrack, as it had earlier as a man cycled through a cemetery, and the numbered rows of hospital cots containing babies grimly prefigure the time of their arrangement for their final rest. The most political form of juxtaposition links the separate worlds of workers and management. Kieślowski's *Fabryka* (*Factory*, 1970) alternates shots of management discussions of supply problems with ones of workers toiling. The last shot, of completed tractors being driven out, is a deadpan epiphany: the pandemic production problems give the completion of anything a near-miraculous air. In the film *Robotnicy '71: nic o nas bez nas* (*Workers '71: Nothing About Us Without Us*, 1972), meanwhile, the classification of different spaces and times devolves into a pointed underscoring of the *class* differences within a supposedly unified People's Poland – the oxymoron of a worker's state whose workers have little or no say. Here reality "speaks for itself" with the irony so characteristic of later Kieślowski. His ability here to dispense with the traditional documentary "voice of God" becomes a reflex of the historical conjuncture that allows him to do so: the contradictions are so patent that one need not spell them out.

The political realities of People's Poland also "speak for themselves" in several films that record the extended reminiscences of figures who experienced its underside: *Murarz* (*Bricklayer*, 1973), *Z punktu widzenia nocnego portiera* (*From the Point of View of the Night Porter*, 1977) and *I Don't Know*, the latter two being among Kieślowski's longest documentaries. Not surprisingly, these works often suffered official shelving.

The protagonist of *Bricklayer* may remind one of Mateusz Birkut in Wajda's epoch-making *Man of Marble* (*Człowiek z marmuru*, 1976), which also analyses Socialism's construction through the exemplary disillusionment of one who laid down its actual building-blocks, as well as taking up documentary's "truth-telling" brief. The man speaks of how he could have gone to the top – his colleagues are now all in ministries – but has no regrets. "We thought we'd made a revolution, but theory is one thing and practice another", he says. When the early 1950s Party campaign against "hooliganism" antagonised the young, he asked to return to the building trade.

Admirably free of bitterness, sunny and besuited, he arrives at a May Day procession. He comments that "we seem not to notice the mistakes people make at work". The camera floating above the streets embodies his satisfaction in seeing things he helped make, "a sign you didn't waste your life". There is no condescension in Kieślowski's evocation of his continued pleasure in 1950s Związek Młodzieży Polskiej (ZMP; Union of Polish Youth) songs, and his decision to "return where I came from" is clearly endorsed. The bricklayer is a paradigmatic Kieślowskian protagonist: as Tadeusz Sobolewski notes, he is someone whose initial belief in the system is shattered.[12] Sobolewski argues that Kieślowski himself had hoped that his own documentation of the burdens of everyday Polish life would help bring workers and rulers together.[13] Perhaps that is why the documentaries have no commentary to point out contradictions; the director will not present himself as superior. If the documentaries' shelving chipped away at hopes for reform, martial law crushed them. The ghostly hero of *Bez końca* (*No End*, 1984) becomes the logical outgrowth of the director whose refusal to comment had rendered him always already spectral. After *No End*, there can be no more documentaries: the system is no longer reformable.

The monologue of *From the Point of View of the Night Porter* is that of a subject *selected* to illustrate the authoritarian mentality Kieślowski privately described as "fascist".[14] The subject is not the Fascist, whom the *soi-disant* Socialist authorities claimed loudly to combat, but, in fact, authority's mainstay, making sure everyone clocks in, confiscating the tackle of fishermen without permits, writing reports on children who skip school, advocating public hanging. "Rules are more important than people", he states, as Wojciech Kilar's lyrical music evokes his repressive idyll. Nevertheless, Kieślowski, worried about the film's apparent tendentiousness, forbade its television broadcast, fearing it might harm the man. He wished to skewer a *type*, not an individual – something so much harder to do in documentaries than in features, which do not showcase real people, that his worries about this film arguably set the stage for his move to feature-making. Thus, the film stops short of labelling Marian Osuch a Fascist or "authoritarian personality", its last moments hesitating over how to name him. A teacher asks a group of children what the smart, smiling man in the cap is called, and their response is not given. As always, Kieślowski's final response is that of the protagonist of *I Don't Know*, with whom he sympathises most deeply when he speaks those three words. (One may be reminded of *Decalogue 1*, in which Krzysztof, Irena and even the computer all come to say "I don't know", as if in solidarity with Kieślowski himself, with his "je doute, je doute toujours".)[15]

Kieślowski prefaces *I Don't Know* with a title emphasising the potential typicality of its subject's experience: "A certain man tells of his life. Irrespective of the subjectivism and fragmentary nature of his account, this man and his condition exist objectively. One has to take account of these facts, since their multiplication is a social phenomenon." Seated in his home, shot face-on, the man stresses at the very outset how he "felt he had become 'an awkward customer'". His narrative concerns his managerial efforts in the late-1960s to eliminate corruption from the "Renifer" leather works. Although 80% of its employees had been sacked for theft at least once, the militia obstructed him and helped set him up: stolen leather was to be planted in his car boot, an anonymous tip off told him. A Council of State award in 1969 did not end the local campaign against him; he was shot at while hunting, beaten up three times, and received threatening telephone calls. In the end, he concludes: "I do not know how one should live". Calmly filmed and delivered, the man's indoor monologue is punctuated by occasional dissolves and shots of the house's exterior as the day slides by. The final sombre repetition of the opening title may indicate Kieślowski's own uncertainty over whether the film has sufficiently brought home the account's representativeness. As in the case of *From the Point of View of the Night Porter*, an ending that may be read as placing a question mark next to the film extends into a refusal to sanction its television screening, reflecting Kieślowski's growing doubts regarding the ethics of documentary filmmaking.

The majority of Kieślowski's documentaries are very firmly *punctuated*, broken up and sectioned, apparently for two reasons. One is analytical: the material is to be ordered in accordance with an idea. Indeed, Kieślowski told Stok that his films' strengths lay more in their ideas than in their action[16] – a characteristic that persists in such abstract feature titles as *The Calm*, *Blind Chance* and *Krótki film o zabijaniu* (*A Short Film About Killing*, 1988), or the alignment of the *Trois couleurs* (*Three Colours*) trilogy (1993-94) with "liberty, equality and fraternity". The simplicity, elegance and rigour of the punctuation dissolve the problems of construction that bedevil so many post-*vérité* documentaries. A second reason is the desire for relief and release. Films focusing on suffering (*X-Ray*) or bureaucratic routine (*Office*; *Refrain*) may require interruption by the image of an elsewhere, a place where suffering and oppression disappear. A world outside may become visible, whether it is through cutaways to the forest around a TB clinic (*X-Ray*) or a window which the camera sweeps past (*Refrain*). Its utopian quality emerges in song that concludes *Z miasta Łodzi* (*From the City of Łódź*, 1969), a dream of a town that may not be the real Łódź, but is nevertheless related to and prefigured by it, with its often bizarre and strangely innocent pursuits (playing with a voltmeter in the park) and its love of music. In *Dworzec* (*Station*, 1980), by way of contrast, the punctuation has a certain menace as ominous drum taps accompany intermittent shots of the surveillance camera recording the random goings-on about the station. The film ends by entering the surveillance officer's room and viewing his screens, to lyrical music. It is an utopian moment of demystification and relief. A similar moment concludes *I Was a Soldier*, when one of the blind soldiers voices his longing for peace and quiet for all people. At the same time, since fades to white punctuate the film, its final fade to black poignantly underlines the blindness of these soldiers, their past hopes (one mentions a one-time ambition to be a painter) crushed into dreams. Since Kieślowski maintains that the dramaturgy of reality exceeds what any work could devise, the works often end with signs of endlessness, life's prolongation beyond the bounds of a sign to which it is not reducible. Such endlessness is itself utopian, signifying the impossible. One may think in particular of the circular, self-renewing close of *Seven Women of Different Ages*, the wizened last speaker's desire to go on living in *Talking Heads*, or the endless files at the end of *Office*. Endlessness may seem difficult to suggest in works that are almost all shorter than an hour, but in these – and other – cases Kieślowski does so consummately.

When Kieślowski described his films as stronger on ideas than on action, he did so *à propos Blizna* (*The Scar*, 1976) perhaps because its unsatisfactoriness – which is genuine, albeit exaggerated by Kieślowski himself – reflects the difficulties of the transition from documentaries to features. Later films would be more successful, partly because stripped down to the more manageable dimensions of the "short film", a form which is nevertheless also part of the documentary's afterlife in the features:[17] expressing ideas in a few brief strokes was part of the documentary legacy transmitted to Kieślowski by his mentor, Kazimierz Karabasz (whose editor, Lidia Zonn, and cameraman, Stanisław Niedbalski, he also inherited).[18] The extent to which even Kieślowski's features follow documentary principles is well caught by Charles Eidsvik in his comments on *A Short Film About Love*:

[T]he objects (as in documentary) do not seem planted for effect but just part of the clutter of reality. The camera continually reframes, refocuses, and then cuts to a new, better vantage point. As in a documentary, Adamek foregrounds the struggle with real locations, with the impulsiveness that makes real people so hard to document, with the contingencies that give documentary-like presence to a moment.[19]

Since Kieślowski's features retain many documentary-like elements, one may wonder why he abandoned the form. When discussing the matter with Stok, he gave two reasons: when police confiscated footage shot during *Station* in search of casually snapped evidence of a known murderer's movements, he realised how he could be serving the authorities unwittingly; at the same time, the documentarist's moral responsibility towards his subjects was beginning to restrict the kind of material he could deal with:

> If I'm making a film about love, I can't go into a bedroom if real people are making love there. If I'm making a film about death, I can't film somebody who's dying because it's such an intimate experience that the person shouldn't be disturbed. And I noticed, when making documentaries, that the closer I wanted to get to an individual the more the subjects which interested me shut themselves off...I'm frightened of those real tears. In fact, I don't know whether I've got the right to photograph them.[20]

A documentarist doubting the ethics of documentary work was unusual in the era of Direct Cinema and *cinéma-vérité*.[21] (Rouch and Morin's remarkable *Chronique d'un été* [*Chronicle of a Summer*, 1961] is one of the few precedents.) More exceptional still was his courageous willingness to abandon the form in which he had done his apprenticeship, the one he had never thought to leave. Kieślowski's renunciation surely also reflected a sense that, by 1981, documentary and quasi-documentary exposés of the system had done all they could for Poland: the "race" had caught up with the truth-telling artist which Ezra Pound described as its antenna; Solidarity had emerged. Thus, Kieślowski's turn away from documentary, although one *towards* the personal, was not simply personally or existentially motivated, but turned on the same hinge as history. Subsequently, "documentary" would become an attitude, rather than a genre: a non-hierarchical world-view, open to the unpredictable, as Eidsvik has shown. But Kieślowski's remarks about tears also allow one to correlate the move to feature-making with a desire to plumb suffering more deeply. It pervades the eloquent final paragraphs of the 1981 manifesto, "Deeper Rather Than Broader", where the linkage of deprivation and the milk bar resurfaces:

> Irrespective of the themes and issues with which my films deal – and this is not the time for that – I am seeking a way for the people watching them to have feelings akin to my own: the feelings of helplessness, compassion and regret which stab

through me when I see a man weeping at a tramstop; when I observe people who would like to be so close to others and are so distant; when I watch someone eating dumplings left on another's plate in a snack bar; when I catch sight of the first liver spots on the hands of a woman who did not have them a year earlier and know that she is looking at them too; when I see the terrible and irreversible injustices that score people's faces so visibly.

I want my viewers to feel this pain too, want the fleshliness and distress it seems to me I am starting to understand well to seep into what I am doing.

So I sit and labour to find a way. Apart from a very few individuals – and I am not sure they are a happier few – today we are all in the same situation.[22]

Is it any accident that the very title of his first feature should have been a sign inscribing suffering, *The Scar*?

Fear of the documentarist's responsibility and a desire to fathom suffering more deeply were clearly central. But another factor may have overdetermined Kieślowski's renunciation of the form: his response to the often impassioned Polish debates of the 1970s over "creationism" in documentary. If documentary always oscillates between the poles contained uneasily within Grierson's paradoxical "*creative* treatment of *actuality*",[23] these debates concerned the extent of permissible "creativity", of directorial interference in the material. Whereas such documentarists as Wojciech Wiszniewski, Piotr Szulkin and Grzegorz Królikiewicz utilised formal devices previously associated with fiction, Kieślowski – who had never seen documentary as a mere stepping-stone to features, and remained committed to documentary as description – seems to have seen attempts to marry the forms as irrevocably compromised: fictional strategies required a fictional context. Fidelity to the traditional documentary notion that – as Mirosław Przylipiak puts it – "one is not allowed to make a documentary against its protagonists"[24] seemingly precluded such quasi-expressionist stretching of the form. It was surely also a fidelity to the teachings of Kazimierz Karabasz, whose *Muzykanci* (*The Musicians*, 1960) he would term one of his favourite films. Kieślowski met the crisis of Karabasz's model of documentary by removing the commentary that so often duplicated and tautologously neutralised the image, by employing serial structures and by splicing together the *cinéma-vérité*-derived documentary modes which Nichols classifies as "observational" and "interactive",[25] thereby distinguishing his work from the traditional forms that had begun to be appropriated by and identified with television. However, all this can be seen as a last-ditch beleaguered stratagem. And yet, Kieślowski himself may also have felt some of the impulses animating his documentarist contemporaries. But, whereas they contained fiction within documentary, in his work the long-denied fictional element, in what may well be a "return of the repressed", finally shattered the documentary mould, engulfing the entire form.

III. Documentary's death and transformation

The phrase "the death of documentary" has double resonance in relation to Kieślowski's work, recalling both his renunciation of the form in the early 1980s and his general proclamation of its death. By the end of his career, Kieślowski had come to feel that occasional worthwhile documentaries were merely exceptions confirming the rule. Documentary as a form had given way to reportage: "not films about life, people and events but about harried reporters content to have arrived somewhere and seen something".[26] Kieślowski's move into fiction preceded the doubts in the form's evidentiary function sown by digitalisation and postmodernism, but may well tempt more and more documentarists. (Thus, Brian Winston has argued that documentary now needs to legitimate itself on grounds other than the "will-to-knowledge" of the past,[27] an argument impressively illustrated by Errol Morris' *The Thin Blue Line* [1988].) But, although Kieślowski proclaimed documentary dead, one should recall that nowhere is death more likely to be code for "transformation" than in the work of the director of *The Double Life of Véronique*.

I noted earlier that Filip Mosz, the documentarist of *Camera Buff*, being the only image-maker among Kieślowski's protagonists, was probably his most credible double. In the classic scenario of doubling, self and reflection meet in simultaneous face-off. In *The Double Life of Véronique*, however, the only Kieślowski film explicitly to raise the theme, the heroine's two lives do not parallel and confront one another, but are successive: Weronika's death shifts the narrative from Poland to the France of her *alter ego*, Véronique. The succession is also a form of learning, however: Véronique benefits mysteriously from Weronika's experience, abandons her own singing lessons, and survives. In Kieślowski's own double life, the documentary ethos has an afterlife in his feature films – in their modes of production (non-hierarchical), shooting (the documentary-style camera behaviour which Eidsvik describes) and conception (organisation around ideas). His concern with duality in *The Double Life of Véronique* may be related to what Nichols has termed the "indexical" bind in documentary: since "the photographic *image*...shares in the being of the model...It is the model but it is not the model".[28] It is, as it were, both Weronika and Véronique – as well as the saint's handkerchief, whose relationship to its alleged prototype is highly controversial, despite her name's common explanation as meaning "true image".[29] The photographic image's simultaneous identity and non-identity with reality can either frustrate both documentarist and viewer or prompt mystical attempts to efface the distinction, like that of André Bazin.[30] Beyond these aporetic alternatives lies reflexivity, self-conscious thematisation of the disparities of images and things. For Kieślowski, however, doubt in documentary yields neither abandonment of the "naïvely truth-telling" forms of traditional documentary, nor adoption of a more sophisticated reflexive one, but a fictional dramatisation of the ironies of the documentarist's position that – surely significantly – incorporates some of his own documentaries, thereby explicitly tinging with autobiography the film in which it occurs.[31] Just as Winston has argued that the crisis that befalls a documentary confronted with postmodern critiques of representation can be resolved by its relocation closer to art than to science,[32] so, for Kieślowski, the crisis of documentary issued in a shift to a form of filmmaking less identifiable with "epistemophilia" – to the making of features. Thus, *Camera Buff* studies the documentarist's discovery of the ambiguities of the Ibsenian truth-telling role which the specific needs of late-1970s Polish society generated for its leading filmmakers. Whereas the left-wing theorist Nichols casts history as the documentarist's "rebuker",[33] Kieślowski – doubtless disenchanted with Marxist categories which the bitter 40 years of "People's Poland" had only debased – grants that role to *context*: on discovering the repercussions of showing his film of an idle brickworks – its workers' possible loss of their nominal jobs – the documentarist Filip exposes his negative and trains his camera on himself. A similar discovery underlies Kieślowski's stated rationale for the renunciation of documentary: militia confiscation of footage shot at the Warsaw central station caused him to drop an activity that could aid the powers that be, however unwittingly.[34] Kieślowski may have used this incident as a personal myth – after all, official seizure of an earlier film's soundtrack did not turn him into a silent filmmaker – but it clearly marked the crisis of a long-incubating doubt. It was the moment at which a second Kieślowski was ready to step out of the shadow of the first. It also embodied a leitmotif of his self-assessment: realisation of the ease with which one's work can be put to malign use.[35]

In locating the transitional moment around the time of *Camera Buff*, Kieślowski sanctions the drawing of parallels between himself and Filip Mosz. But there is also a key difference. Conceived as more successive than simultaneous, the relationship between self and double becomes positive: not agonistic, not the mimetic struggle for one, limited space which René Girard describes,[36] but the unconsciously cooperative passing of a baton. It can be so because the double who walks away is less the self's rival than its reincarnation. A decade later, *The Double Life of Véronique* transposes to another key – gives a gloss on – the veiled autobiographical renunciation of *Camera Buff.* The rivalry of self and double requires mutual awareness. But, in the encounter of Weronika and Véronique on the Kraków Rynek, it is only one-sided; as so often in legend, Weronika's glimpse of her double foreshadows *her* death. The theme of one self's submergence in another conjugates the self-effacingness of a man so open to others' suggestions, so fascinated by the work of actors (the fiction films becoming as much documentaries of actors working as anything else, a theme explicitly raised in the acting school sequence of *Decalogue 4*) as finally to draw conclusions from the documentarist's humble secondariness before reality and *its* dramas, and simply, sublimely, abandon filmmaking altogether. Kieślowski's consummate ability to tap co-workers' resources arguably modulated gradually into a will to absent himself from the set entirely.

Where a director proves capable of the radical change involved in renouncing documentary for feature film (not just alternating between them, like Wenders or Herzog, or starting with one, trying the other – possibly under duress – then reverting to the first love that is fiction, à la Leni Riefenstahl), his still more radical abandonment of filmmaking itself should not be totally surprising. Kieślowski's generosity towards collaborators – his willingness to share the writer-director's mantle with Krzysztof Piesiewicz, for instance – may seem to have represented the best way of revitalising the auteurist project. Nevertheless, renewing auteurism by diluting the author's authority may well presage its end in a postmodern culture averse to "grand narratives". Like the great withdrawals of Rimbaud, of Kafka ordering Brod to incinerate his work, of Hermann Broch's Virgil, who actually does so, Kieślowski's follows the logic of modernism, albeit perhaps as its last gasp. For, if the factors mentioned earlier played a role in the move, another may well be the documentarist's acutely modernist sense of the variability, and hence arbitrariness, of his or her work (something that reaches its apogee in Musil and in Joyce's multiple styles). For the documentarist, this is primarily an effect of the way in which the frequent lack of a meticulously scripted starting-point – the dependence on the frequent vagaries of external events – entails the film's discovery *during* the production process. Documentarists enjoy a particular freedom when arranging and selecting footage. Whereas, in fiction films, selection usually occurs beforehand during scripting, and the later concern is primarily with the *how* of representation (where to put the camera, who to cast, and so on), documentary's proclaimed openness to life and frequent commitment to chance (a keyword for Kieślowski) often render selection almost entirely retrospective. The occupational hazard of numerous false starts can cause heavy deletion of footage, a characteristic of documentary work accentuated when distribution requires further cuts (Lanzmann's *Shoah* [1985] – where 350 hours shot became 9½ in the cinema – is only the most extreme example). Indeed, the film which the documentarist seeks may only precipitate in the cutting room: it is thus hardly surprising that Kieślowski deemed editing filmmaking's most enjoyable part, or that his sense of the variability of footage should have culminated in the quixotic proposed fashioning of about twenty "hand-made" versions of *The Double Life of Véronique*. Shearing away vast narrative slabs is not only perfectionism, but also the documentarist's ruthless freedom *vis-à-vis* his own footage – a freedom whose luxuriousness becomes particularly apparent when exercised, as he declared it was, irrespective of a scene's cost. That freedom's application to fiction creates the omissions, and hence the mysteries, so dear to "late" Kieślowski.

Where narrative structures are lacking, rhythmical ones offer an alternative. Hence, such otherwise incompatible documentarists as Riefenstahl, Lanzmann and Resnais[37] describe their works' composition in musical terms, and early documentarists sometimes shaped city life as "a symphony", a tradition continued, for instance, in Chris Marker's *Sunless/Sans soleil* (1982), which deems Tokyo something "to be deciphered like a musical score", the "subtle cycles" of its inhabitants' movements "as different and precise as groups of instruments".[38] Unfortunately, much recent theorisation of documentary conceptualises it primarily *vis-à-vis* mainstream fiction film, and construes the need for structure primarily as one for story.[39] Signs of events' staging – for instance, in *Nanook of the North* (1921), *Night Mail* (1936) or *Triumph des Willens* (*Triumph of the Will*, 1935) – are taken to demonstrate the form's greater proximity to fiction than its truth-telling brief concedes, and thus to undermine it. Such postmodern critiques of fact/fiction binarisms are apposite, but seemingly unaware of the European traditions of more associative, essayistic and even poetic documentary practices that overlap with the avant-garde (as in the "city symphonies", Marker's films, and even Riefenstahl's *Olympiad* [*Olympia*, 1938]). Rhythmic structure, in its turn, need not be merely "musical", but can underpin a structure of argument, as in so many of Kieślowski's works. The binarism of "the musical" and "the rhetorical" (a form of the "art/science" one) also demands deconstruction. Rhythm is clearly of enormous importance to Kieślowski, *Blind Chance* and *The Double Life of Véronique* being only the most obvious instances of works whose sections are edited differently,[40] a quasi-musical sense of counterpoint validating music's thematic presence in the later film. The double life of the documentarist is paradoxical: a career that began with proclamations of reality's primacy can conclude in esoteric musicality, *symbolisme*. Witek's hand held against Werka's on the other side of the train window is a realistic detail in *Blind Chance*, but the realism becomes symbolic in *Three Colours: Red*, when Valentine presses her hand against the judge's on the other side of his car window.

It is in 1981 – in *Blind Chance* – that Kieślowski draws conclusions from the documentarist's passion for editing and the multiple lives one body of footage can lead, thereby discovering the theme of his remaining work: the variability of one life, which dissolves the distinction between the real and the fantastic (where the fantastic is, by definition, compensatory, here everything compensates – counterbalances – everything else). Kieślowski's practice here can be seen to react piquantly to André Bazin's antipathy towards cutting. Bazin argues that "montage presupposes of its very nature the unity of meaning of the dramatic event. Some other form of analysis is undoubtedly possible but then it would be another film".[41] Since, for Bazin, "montage by its very nature rules out ambiguity of expression",[42] he denigrates the "manipulation" of reality in a Soviet montage that is, of course, merely the extreme case of all filmic editing. Kieślowski, however, renders editing itself ambiguous by providing that "other film" whose necessity Bazin mentions – either within one work (*Blind Chance*) or through variation between works (*Decalogue 5* and *A Short Film About Killing*) – while the principle of varying themes dominates the mutually-echoing features, which continually shrink and enlarge each others' elements. His art's transformation into a hall of mirrors may have caused his final uneasy sense of having come to inhabit fiction, rather than the world.

When the protagonist of *Blind Chance* chases a train three times, a different life results on each occasion. The film takes Kieślowski out of the watershed which *Camera Buff* had entered. But only a small step separates recognising a story's arbitrariness from deeming it pointless: a step as small, perhaps, as the one that determines whether or not Witek catches the train and enters a different life. Thus, an alternative motto to Rimbaud's "Je est un autre" might be the "nic nie musisz" ("you don't have to do anything") spoken by Witek's father. Kieślowski's later films may be fictions, but their commitment to freedom and variability displays a documentarist's afterlife, as does his whole career. At first, the surface of the world is revelatory: merely to film it is to find meaning yield itself up. But "merely filming" soon becomes problematic: footage needs structure, which is arbitrary, while the documentarist's responsibility to his subjects causes, firstly, their transformation into the "models" of a documentary-fiction hybrid, and then the move into total fictionality. It is as if Kieślowski is following Jean Rouch's precept that "[f]iction is the only way to penetrate reality".[43] In the end, once-transparent surfaces become opaque, like those Kieślowskian windows so often overlaid with reflections: Auguste may not look like the judge's double, but he is; and a sketch for the unrealised "Raj, czyściec, piekło" ("Heaven, Purgatory, Hell") trilogy emphasises that "Hell" will look like "Heaven", and vice versa: "the external is opposed to the heroes' inner states, which means, for instance, that the action of *Heaven* unfolds in Moscow or a deepest dungeon, while the heroes of *Hell* live very nicely thank you in Sienna".[44] Kieślowski's "je doute toujours"[45] ends with the final doubt of all appearance. A visual sphere now emptied of self-evidence can only be abandoned. The image has become (that keyword of *Kieślowski on Kieślowski*) a trap.

Notes

[1]   Translated from the Polish: "Dzieciństwo spędził Kieślowski w pociągach, poza tym jeździli z matką do sanatoriów do ojca chorego na gruźlicę. Okazało się to inspiracją do filmu *Prześwietlenie*... Urodziła mu się córka... uruchomiło to jego wyobraźnię i tak powstał film *Pierwsza miłość*". Maciej Parowski, "Kieślowski Life", in Stanisław Zawiśliński (ed), *Kieślowski bez końca* (Warsaw: Skorpion, 1994): 76.

[2]   See Tadeusz Lubelski, "From *Personnel* to *No End*: Kieślowski's political feature films", in this volume.

[3]   Translated from the Polish: "Dlaczego musimy koniecznie dawać na scenie obrazy, które wywołują łzy albo śmiech? Dlaczego nie dawać po prostu obrazów z życia codziennego, które nie skłaniają ani do śmiechu, ani do łez, tylko do refleksji i analizowania zjawisk życia?". Anton Chekhov, quoted in Zbigniew Benedyktowicz, "Długi film o miłości", *Kwartalnik filmowy* 4 (1993/94): 110.

[4]   Krzysztof Wierzbicki, *Krzysztof Kieślowski: I'm so-so...* (1995).

[5]   Danusia Stok (ed), *Kieślowski on Kieślowski* (London; Boston: Faber and Faber, 1993): 112.

[6]   Ibid: 208.

[7]   Krzysztof Kieślowski, "Dramaturgia rzeczywistości", *Film na świecie* 388-389 (3-4: 1992): 8.

[8]   Translated from the Polish: "Zrobiłem film o barze mlecznym. Przychodzą staruszki i wyjadają innym leniwe, a przed barem mlecznym siedzi skrzypek i przedziwnie fałszując rzępoli polski hymn. I wydawało mi się, że to jest strasznie znaczące. Nakręciłem to wszystko, pokazałem

Karabaszowi, a on powiedział: – Wie pan, nawet jakby tu Eisenstein przyszedł, to by z tego nic nie zmontował. I miał rację, ponieważ było w tym to wszystko, o czym mówię: były staruszki, były leniwe, był skrzypek i była 'Jeszcze Polska...' – tylko że nie budowała się z tego żadna szersza myśl. Było tylko poczucie, że oto opisujemy, jak wygląda jakiś bar mleczny – to znaczy, że tak jednostkowo jesteśmy już przy tej staruszce z kluskami, że nic to więcej nie znaczy, nie przenosi się to na rodzaj cierpienia wspólnego komukolwiek innemu". Marek Henrykowski and Mikołaj Jazdon (eds), "Fragmenty spotkania z Krzysztofem Kieślowskim (24.11.1996) Teatr Ósmego Dnia, Poznań", *Kino* 29: 5 (May 1996): 12.

[9] Translated from the Polish: "dlaczego wyjadają i być może dlaczego doszło do tego, że wyjadają, co się stało przedtem". Ibid.

[10] Kieślowski: 7-9.

[11] Bill Nichols, *Representing Reality: Issues and Concepts in Documentary* (Bloomington and Indianapolis: Indiana University Press, 1991): 44.

[12] Tadeusz Sobolewski, "Droga Kieślowskiego", *Odra* 10 (1986): 30.

[13] Ibid: 31.

[14] Stok (ed): 78.

[15] "Je doute, je doute toujours" [interview with Claude-Marie Trémois and Vincent Remy], *Télérama: La Passion Kieślowski* [hors série] September 1993: 90-96.

[16] Stok (ed): 102.

[17] Arkadiusz Cencor and Waldemar Wilk, "Uważam się za rejestratora", *Świadomość społeczna w filmach Krzysztofa Kieślowskiego* (Wrocław: D.K.F. Politechnika, 1986): 3-8, where – among other things – Kieślowski discusses the Polish tradition of the *brief* documentary.

[18] Stanisław Zawiśliński, "Zbliżenie I: Jeden na jednego", in Stanisław Zawiśliński (ed): 17. Later in the same interview (21-22), Kieślowski contends that, although individual powerful documentaries continue to be made, the genre as a whole is now defunct.

[19] Charles Eidsvik, "Kieślowski's 'Short Films'", *Film Quarterly* 44: 1 (autumn 1990): 54.

[20] Stok (ed): 86.

[21] As Alan Rosenthal notes in his introduction to the "Documentary Ethics" section of his *New Challenges for Documentary* (Berkeley; Los Angeles; London: University of California Press, 1988), such doubts were "not at the forefront of discussion in the early 1970s" (245).

[22] Translated from the Polish: "Niezależnie od tematów i spraw w moich filmach – o czym nie teraz – szukam sposobu, żeby oglądający je ludzie mieli uczucia podobne do moich: uczucia bezsilności, współczucia, żalu,

które przyprawiają mnie o fizyczny ból, kiedy widzę mężczyznę płaczącego na przystanku tramwajowym; kiedy obserwuję tych, którzy chcieliby być tak blisko z innymi, a są tak daleko; kiedy widzę człowieka wyjadającego zostawione przez kogoś kluski w barze mlecznym; kiedy dostrzegam pierwsze plamy wątrobiane na rękach kobiety, która jeszcze rok temu nie miała ich na rękach, i wiem, że ona też na nie patrzy; kiedy widzę krzywdę straszną i nieodwracalną, która wybija na ludzkich twarzach tak widoczne znaki. Chciałbym, żeby ten ból stał się udziałem moich widzów, żeby cielesność i męka, które – wydaje mi się – zaczynam dobrze rozumieć, przedostały się do tego, co zrobię. Siedzę więc i mozolnie szukam drogi. Poza nielicznymi i nie jestem pewien, czy szczęśliwszymi jednostkami, wszyscy jesteśmy dzisiaj w tym samym miejscu." Krzysztof Kieślowski, "Głęboko zamiast szeroko", *Dialog* 1 (1981): 111.

23   Quoted in Paul Rotha, *Documentary Film* (London: Faber and Faber, 1936): 68. Emphases added.

24   Translated from the Polish: "nie wolno robić filmu dokumentalnego przeciw jego bohaterowi". Mirosław Przylipiak, "Od konkretu do metafory: zarys przemian polskiego filmu dokumentalnego w latach siedemdziesiątych", *Kino* 1 (1984): 14.

25   Nichols: 32-44, in particular.

26   Translated from the Polish: "To nie są filmy opowiadające o życiu, ludziach, wydarzeniach, lecz o zaganianych reporterach, zadowolonych z tego, że gdzieś tam dotarli i coś zobaczyli". See Stanisław Zawiśliński (ed): 21-22, or his interview with Danièle Heymann ("Les portes s'ouvrent sur un sourire d'exil") in *Le Monde* 16 May 1991: 24: "Le documentaire est mort de nos jours. Il a cessé d'exister, complètement" ("the documentary is dead in our time. It has ceased to exist, completely").

27   Brian Winston, "The Documentary Film as Scientific Inscription", in Michael Renov (ed), *Theorizing Documentary* (New York; London: Routledge, 1993): 55-57; and Brian Winston, *Claiming the Real: The Griersonian Documentary and Its Legitimations* (London: British Film Institute, 1995): 251-259.

28   Nichols: 151. Emphasis in original.

29   Donald Attwater, *The Penguin Dictionary of Saints*, second edition, revised and updated by Catherine Rachel John (Harmondsworth: Penguin Books, 1983): 324.

30   See, for instance, André Bazin, "The Ontology of the Photographic Image", in *What Is Cinema?*, essays selected and translated by Hugh Gray (Berkeley; Los Angeles: University of California Press, 1967): 9-16.

31   For some reflections on the status of the autobiography in this film, *Camera Buff,* see my *The Story of the Lost Reflection* (London: Verso, 1985): 43-46. It might piquantly be compared with Andrzej Wajda's astonishing *Wszystko na sprzedaż* (*Everything for Sale,* 1968), which also fuses fiction and autobiography. See 35-37.

[32]   Winston (1993) and Winston (1995).

[33]   Nichols: 142.

[34]   See Stok (ed): 79-86.

[35]   See, for instance, his comments on the events of 1968 in the Łódź Film School in Krzysztof Krubski, Marek Miller, Zofia Turowska and Waldemar Wiśniewski (eds), *Filmówka: powieść o łódzkiej szkole filmowej* (Warsaw: Tenten, n.d.): 193: "Zostałem użyty w grze amoralnej, a wówczas odbierałem świat prosto. Wydawało mi się, że jeśli zajmuję stanowisko zgodne z sumieniem, wszystko jest w porządku, nikomu nie szkodzę. Wtedy właśnie się okazało, że należy zajmować stanowisko zupełnie odwrotne, lecz tego nie wiedziałem." ("I was used in an amoral game, and at that time I had a simple notion of the world. It seemed to me that if I just adopted a position in accordance with my conscience, everything would be in order, and I would not harm anyone. It then turned out that the position one should have adopted was diametrically opposite, but I didn't know that.")

[36]   See his tremendously fecund *Violence and the Sacred*, translated by Patrick Gregory (Baltimore: The Johns Hopkins University Press, 1977): 143-192, in particular.

[37]   Kieślowski's abandonment of documentary might usefully be compared with that of Resnais. In Resnais' case, fiction emerges out of documentary's perceived inability to represent "Hiroshima", which either may be seen as an implicit criticism of his own *Nuit et brouillard* (*Night and Fog*, 1955), or may simply imply Japanese suffering's resistance to conceptualisation by a Westerner. In Kieślowski's case, the emergence is more gradual, not precipitated by the crisis of a single project (the documentary Resnais had committed himself to make, but came to feel he could not deliver).

[38]   Quotations from the soundtrack of the film.

[39]   See, for instance Michael Renov, "Introduction: The Truth About Non-Fiction", in Renov (ed): "Documentary filmmakers since the days of Flaherty's *Nanook of the North* have frequently chosen to build stories around the heroics of larger-than-life figures plucked from their 'real' environs – in short to narrativize the real", or Brian Winston, "Documentary: I Think We Are in Trouble", in Rosenthal (ed): 21: "Audiences in the 1890s required of the new medium what they expected of older media – stories... And it was the fiction film that was to provide for this age-old want. Only when Flaherty began to structure his actuality material so that it, too, might satisfy those needs could Grierson and others detect a new form and name it 'documentary.' But the need for structure implicitly contradicts the notion of an unstructured actuality."

[40]   For a description of the different editing strategies in the three sections of *Blind Chance*, see my "Exile and Identity: Kieślowski and His Contemporaries", in Graham Petrie and Ruth Dwyer (eds), *Before the Wall Came Down: Soviet and East European Filmmakers Working In the West* (Lanham; New York; London: University Press of America, 1990): 110-111.

[41] André Bazin, "The Evolution of the Language of Cinema", in Bazin: 36.

[42] Ibid.

[43] Winston (1995): 182.

[44] Translated from the Polish: "zewnętrzność jest w opozycji do wewnętrznego stanu bohaterów. Tzn. że np. akcja RAJU toczy się w Moskwie lub ciężkim więzieniu, a bohaterowie PIEKŁA żyją sobie jak u Pana Boga za piecem w Siennie". Stanisław Zawiśliński (ed), *Kieślowski* (Warsaw: Skorpion, 1996): 119.

[45] Trémois and Remy.

From *Personnel* to *No End*: Kieślowski's political feature films

Tadeusz Lubelski

TRANSLATED FROM THE POLISH BY PAUL COATES

This essay considers a group of seven feature films shot by Krzysztof Kieślowski during the decade of 1975-84: *Personel* (*Personnel*, 1975; the first full-length television feature), *Blizna* (*The Scar*, 1976; the first full-length cinema feature), *Spokój* (*The Calm*, 1976), *Amator* (*Camera Buff*, 1979), *Przypadek* (*Blind Chance*, 1981); *Krótki dzień pracy* (*Short Working Day*, 1981) and *Bez końca* (*No End*, 1984).

I. Seven features in ten years

The decision to isolate a portion of an œuvre in this way is, of course, an arbitrary one. After all, *Personnel*, the first film in this group, was not Kieślowski's first film. It had been preceded by numerous documentaries, some of which – for instance, *Fabryka* (*Factory*, 1970) or *Robotnicy '71: nic o nas bez nas* (*Workers '71: Nothing About Us Without Us*, 1972) – contain themes that will later return in new variants in the political features, particularly in *The Scar*. It had also been preceded by Kieślowski's first small-scale features: his film school effort, *Koncert życzeń* (*Concert of Requests*, 1967), and the television work, *Przejście podziemne* (*Pedestrian Subway*, 1973). There is a further complication: throughout the decade of 1975-84 the director continued to make documentaries (eight in total) which have various relations with the decade's features, either supplementing them or prefiguring certain themes.

One might also question the interruption of the uniform sequence of features just after *No End* and before *Dekalog* (*The Decalogue*, 1988). After all, this cuts short a natural developmental sequence: an œuvre always constitutes a unity, and, in Kieślowski's case, it is an exceptionally integral one. Admittedly, a break occurred in it at some point. But may it not have occurred earlier, even before *No End*, which inaugurates a new poetics in Kieślowski's work, an abandonment of realism, and at the same time a new stage of cooperation with subsequently inseparable partners – co-scriptwriter Krzysztof Piesiewicz and composer Zbigniew Preisner? Or perhaps it happened even earlier, before *Blind Chance*, which laid to rest any illusions about the system's reformability, and for the first time privileged an essayistic discourse over the dramaturgical order of cause and effect. But did not the first intimation of an abandonment of realism appear even before that, in *The Calm*, in the form of those memorable horses thrusting through the television test card?

Let us assume, nevertheless, that there are significant grounds for remaining within the proposed limits. The seven works mentioned earlier constitute a series of films revolving around political issues. Admittedly, it would be an oversimplification to call them "political films": not one of them – with the possible exception of *Short Working Day* – is truly dominated by a political theme. Nor does Kieślowski himself accept their generic classification as such: "Even when my films were about people involved in politics, I always tried to find out what sort of people they were. The political environment only formed a background. Even the short documentary films were always about people, about what they're like."[1] And yet, it is difficult to picture their heroes without that political backdrop: in each work, the protagonist's actions are defined by the specific social situations of Polish life. Not until *The Decalogue* does that begin to change.

Moreover – and this argument has particular weight for the Western viewer – the pre-*Decalogue* Kieślowski remains the less well-known one, Kieślowski before his discovery by Western Europeans. Thus, a description of this stage of his feature work has the merit of presenting his artistic background.

II. Seven steps towards a description of the world

On many occasions, Kieślowski stated that his work's point of departure lay in a need to describe the world in which people live: "Only when you describe something can you start speculating about it. If something hasn't been described and a record of it doesn't exist – it doesn't matter what form the description takes: a film, a sociological study, a book, or even just a verbal account – then you can't refer to it. You have to describe the thing or situation before you can deal with it".[2] Years later, he urged a French journalist: "You cannot really grasp what it means to live in a world that cannot be described. It is characteristic of your world, the West, that it is continually described and discussed. To inhabit a world that is neither named nor described is to live in a ceaseless abstraction. One cannot tell where reality begins."[3]

When Kieślowski entered adulthood, the world of People's Poland was still an undescribed one. Propaganda falsified the picture of everyday life, and art was busy with other things: tradition, the past, conventional games with the audience. The fact that their world was undescribed became a basic finding of Kieślowski's contemporaries, who made their debuts towards the end of the 1960s. That generation would soon focus its own artistic programme on correcting their predecessors' error in this respect.

The first years of the 1970s – after the assumption of power by Edward Gierek in December 1970, a moment connected with the last brief upsurge of hope in People's Poland for a degree of normality in national life – saw a new generation of artists clearly establishing themselves in Polish culture. They were called the "Young Culture generation", after the periodical they tried to publish in Kraków, albeit – due to the Communist authorities' decree – unsuccessfully. They were also "the generation of March 1968", for that shared experience had opened their eyes to the realities of life in their own country (Kieślowski himself graduated from Łódź Film School in March 1968 and was politically active as never before). The manifesto of this generation was a book of essays by two Kraków poets, Julian Kornhauser and Adam Zagajewski, *Świat nie przedstawiony* (*The Unrepresented World*, 1974).

"To exist means to be described in culture" was the main slogan of Adam Zagajewski's article, "Rzeczywistość nie przedstawiona w powojennej literaturze polskiej" ("Unrepresented Reality in Post-War Polish Literature"),[4] an article that was a generational manifesto. Of course, the author realised that diagnosing reality is not the only, nor even the main, task facing culture. It is, however, its "degree zero", the precondition of its effective functioning as a whole. He and his peers called for a description of "that which is": the whole of the reality in which it was their lot to live, however unassuming and even drab it might be. And less so as to accept it than in order to understand it and – at the same time – understand one's own life within it. Zagajewski wrote:

> There is a reality of people, things and thoughts, meetings and children's summer camps, a reality of duplicitous belief, lies and hopes, a reality of Party meetings and football matches, of the Peace Race and political jokes, of hospitals and banners, death and new investment projects, pensioners and personnel, Houses of Culture and brawls at village weddings, youth songs and young scholars, libraries and beer booths. That which secretes its own interior under the forms of tragedy and comedy, liberty and slavery, truth and falsehood, hypocrisy and courage – hides within itself conflicts as old as civilisation itself and as young as People's Poland. It is a complete reality completely lacking a culture interested in it.[5]

That everyday reality of the Polish People's Republic, that "reality of

Party meetings and football matches", once passed over in embarrassment or served up in propagandistic tones, began to seep into the texts of the Young Culture artists. Described in the poems of Stanisław Barańczak and Ryszard Krynicki, in the songs of Wojciech Młynarski, in the repertoire of the "Salon des Indépendants" Warsaw student cabaret, and in the satirical cartoons which Andrzej Krauze and Andrzej Mleczko published in the capital's weeklies – this reality began to be viewed in terms of an ethical task, as a field of choice.

The same conception also appeared in the cinema. The first Polish filmmaker to describe the world of People's Poland in the spirit of Young Culture was Krzysztof Zanussi, born in 1939 – two years before Kieślowski. *Struktura kryształu* (*The Structure of Crystal*, 1969), his debut film, and a whole series of films about the choices facing the young intelligentsia – up to and including *Barwy ochronne* (*Camouflage*, 1976) – were a revelation to the Polish public of the time. It is no accident that it is Zanussi who becomes the hero's intellectual guide in *Camera Buff*, a master suggesting motives for pursuing this difficult profession.

Kieślowski himself, however, began with the documentary, having long been convinced that – as he wrote in 1968 in his diploma thesis – "*the dramaturgy of reality*...with its lack of climaxes, its simultaneous order and muddle, is the most modern and truest of structures".[6] As a documentarist, he worked in a group. This was not only because – as a natural leader – he felt good within a group, but also because it represented a more effective means of bringing pressure to bear on the institutions that funded filmmaking – the Wytwórnia Filmów Dokumentalnych (Documentary Film Studios) and Polish Television. At the beginning of the 1970s, he and his colleagues set up their own production unit, the S.F. im. Karola Irzykowskiego (Irzykowski Studio), to make films describing reality. Incidentally, one of the studio's four co-founders was the very Andrzej Jurga who would be Filip Mosz's second mentor in *Camera Buff*.

Kieślowski's success in Poland as a documentarist can be gauged by the fact that in 1976 the *Polityka* weekly awarded him what was then a very prestigious prize, the "Drożdże" ("Ferment") prize "for work that stimulates thought". The prestige was of a special, "system-internal" kind. *Polityka* – whose editor was Mieczysław Rakowski, a future First Secretary of the ruling Communist Party – was an organ of the Party opposition. Its prize was reserved for achievements that were genuinely outstanding but nevertheless did not overstep the bounds of the existing system's reality.

When Kieślowski received the "Drożdże" prize, the public was already acquainted with *Personnel* and his two best-known early documentaries, *Pierwsza miłość* (*First Love*, 1974) and *Życiorys*

(*Curriculum Vitae*, 1975). It did not yet know the recently-completed *The Scar*. In the interview he gave upon receiving the prize, the director stated: "Making fiction films has not been and is not my goal. If I do so it is because too many doors are closed where documentary is concerned." Here he doubtless had in mind both the restrictions of censorship and – something he felt even then – the recalcitrance of the documentary material. Nevertheless, he emphasised that, for him, the differences in technique were not essential: "If I say that fiction films have never been my goal it is because I make fiction films in exactly the same way as I do documentaries". Plot and "actors instead of people playing themselves" – just add these two elements, and a documentary becomes a feature.[7] The goal remains unchanged: describing reality to discern its problems in need of solution.

It is significant that three of Kieślowski's first seven films are adaptations, and these three are also works of reportage. Romuald Karaś, the author of the book *Puławy – rozdział drugi* (*Puławy – The Second Chapter*, 1967), from which *The Scar* was derived; Lech Borski, the author of the novel which provided the material of *The Calm*; and, finally, Hanna Krall, without a doubt the best-known of the three, the author of the reportage *Widok z okna na pierwszym piętrze* (*The View from the First-Floor Window*, 1980), on which *Short Working Day* was based – all three were journalists and reporters, not "storytellers". The director himself wrote the scripts of the three most personal of the films, *Personnel*, *Camera Buff* and *Blind Chance*. Reality also indubitably provided the material for the construction of these screenplays – but reality as lived and felt, rather than as observed. Even the last of the seven has its roots in reportage, except that, in this case, the director needed the personality of his co-scriptwriter to activate it: "Kieślowski offered me work on a text about martial law and its climate, which I experienced daily", Krzysztof Piesiewicz recounts. "That was how *No End* came into being. It tells of my most personal and dramatic experiences."[8]

III. A Young Culture artist

It is astonishing how close the link is between Kieślowski's works – even the early documentaries – and the biography of their author. For a long time this went unremarked. Tadeusz Sobolewski, the Polish critic most faithful to Kieślowski, first pointed it out: "the dilemmas experienced by the heroes of his early features", he wrote, "are his own".[9] The same applies to those of the documentaries, one might add. The theme of *Prześwietlenie* (*X-Ray*, 1974) – patients being treated for tuberculosis – is linked to his father's illness. The heroine of *First Love* even gave birth to her daughter in the very hospital where the director's own wife had earlier had their daughter Marta. However, the autobiographical element expresses itself most directly in two features from the 1970s: *Personnel* and *Camera Buff.*

Personnel is the most evidently autobiographical of all Kieślowski's works. It is appropriate to call this typical, since it is his feature debut. The story it tells stems from the personal experience of the director himself, who was first a pupil of the Państwowe Liceum Techniki Teatralnej (College for Theatre Technicians) (1957-62), and then, after graduation, was employed for a year in the costume section of the Teatr Współczesny (Contemporary Theatre) in Warsaw. (He sewed actors' trousers.) Romek Januchta in *Personnel* is thus a self-portrait by Kieślowski. He takes his first job just as seriously as Kieślowski once did – indeed, he takes it more than seriously, as something sacred. The sense of service in the performance of his daily duties is linked to delight in the theatre, to youthful fascination with art.

Even so trivial a motif as the role connections play in getting a job has an autobiographical underpinning. In the film, Romek is helped by the opera stage-manager, a friend of his aunt. In life, Krzysztof Kieślowski's uncle was the director of the College for Theatre Technicians, which was why he encouraged him to study there. There are other interchanges of the same kind – indeed, the film's plot is set at the time of its making, that is: a dozen or so years after Kieślowski's own experiences. Since, in the meantime, the school had been closed, Romek Januchta did not manage to complete it. However, it remains a cult object for its old pupils, as was really the case. At times, the tailor's conversations revolve around current affairs, such as the famous England-Poland match at Wembley which, in autumn 1973, saw the English team's elimination from the World Cup finals. The plot was transposed from the Warsaw theatre to the Wrocław opera, which had the reputation of being the best in Poland during the first half of the 1970s.

Autobiography is, without a doubt, less directly present in *Camera Buff.* Kieślowski had never been as camera-struck as his hero, nor had he ever had links to the amateur film movement, unlike Zanussi. But the central question Filip Mosz confronts, that of professional ethics, was his own concern at this time. Kieślowski has often explained that his main reason for abandoning documentary was the way it exposed his subjects to various dangers in their lives. The motif of the firing of Filip's close friend because of Filip's work in film is a projection of the author's own fears regarding his own documentary work. It is also significant that the subjects of two of Filip's documentaries – a pavement and a dwarf – were those of two of Kieślowski's own earlier, subsequently-abandoned documentary projects.[10]

The important thing, however, is that *Personnel* and *Camera Buff* can be viewed as the metaphorical manifestos of an entire generation. The hero of each is a model of the Young Culture artist recognising his goal. Seen in this light, they even form a whole: the hero of *Personnel* undergoes the first phase of Young Culture, and *Camera Buff* the second. Twenty-year-old Romek Januchta recognises his own true position, while Filip Mosz – who is ten years older – draws artistic conclusions from that recognition.

The recognition Romek Januchta achieves in the course of *Personnel* involves a loss of illusions about the operatic world in which he starts work. Romek's initial wide-eyed view of everything is that of the enchanted apprentice. He has the naïve youthful belief that contact with real Art will yield some initiation into higher things. Meanwhile, the content of his initiation is quite the reverse. The world of the people who concoct artistic spectacles proves inferior to, uglier and worse than, Romek's idealised image. At first, Romek is prepared to accept the separate "artiste's entrance" of which he learns in the very first scene of the film. Gradually, however, as the scenes unfold, it emerges that this privilege is unmerited: the artists are no better than the opera's tailors. Their conversations, jokes and – above all – the effects of their work are on no higher a level. It is no accident that Romek starts wearing glasses during the film. He first dons them while visiting the office of the head of the Communist youth organisation. "I can see better", he says. The glasses that permit "seeing better" are a clear metaphor for intellectual illumination.

The experience Romek gains nevertheless does not issue in disillusionment. Neither then nor later – never – did Kieślowski deprive the viewer of any of his films of the hope that the world's higher meaning, dreamt of in youth, may really exist. "Does that art really exist?", Romek asks his mentor, the elderly cutter Sowa. "Of course it does". Sowa is far from leading Romek to a shallow disillusionment, from telling him "abandon your belief in the way you thought things are". He helps him grasp that it is the theatre of which they are part that falls short of these high, youthful demands. That perceptive critic Konrad Eberhardt noticed this at once, after the television première of *Personnel*: "The heart of the matter is that Sowa has realised that he is working in a bad theatre. And that he has infected Romek Januchta with that view."[11] During a crew meeting, Sowa says it outright: "This theatre is a corpse. It no longer has anything to say to anyone."

Nevertheless, it is not Sowa who stands for the Young Culture artist. His function in the film is limited to that of "opening up" Romek. He reinforces his critical faculties, as well as showing him that one can have one's own view and defend it – that one's own personal opinion is all that counts. He is the one to point out that Mr Wilhelm, their colleague in the tailors' workroom who spouts clichés by day, is secretly writing a play: "He showed me it once, it's very good, he writes terribly sincerely...". But it is Romek who takes the next step and proposes the launch, on the opera's own premises, of a youth cabaret as an outlet for "the technicians".

The interpretation of this motif prompted by *Personnel* – in accordance with the rules of the "Aesopian reading" unofficially practised in People's Poland – is a "systemic" one. The existing opera and the future cabaret are two models of Polish culture in the 1970s. The opera is a model of official culture which, unable to describe the world, has forfeited its power to heal. The future cabaret is a model of the Youth Culture which Zagajewski had proposed in *The Unrepresented World*: its role will be to describe the world.

It is worth noting that the opera house in which Kieślowski chose to set his film is, in fact, preparing to stage *Aida*. Verdi's work is particularly difficult to stage, and calls for elaborate sets and monumentalism. For this particular troupe to stage *Aida* is the acme of artificiality and misconceived aspiration. Admittedly, we do not see the dramatic end result of this labour – we have to rest content with following Romek's reactions to the beginning of the opening night. However, his evaluation of *Aida* translates into his later decisions. And it is no accident that cabaret – a non-required, open cultural form asserting spontaneity and sincerity – should become the main protagonist's field. In Poland at that time – in the mid-1950s, as at the end of the 1960s and the beginning of the 1970s – it was often, in fact, in the cabarets and student theatres that the prevailing model of culture began to change.

After cabaret it was time for film, which is dealt with by *Camera Buff*. Of course, on a higher level of reception, the film is a universal one about the birth of an artist, the discovery of one's calling. "Happiness died, the creator was born", wrote Jean Gili in his analysis.[12] But here, too, the film's documentary concretion encourages a reading "in the context of People's Poland". Filip Mosz incarnates the Youth Culture artist who sets out to "represent the world". *Camera Buff* is a protocol of his victories, defeats and – above all else – the traps laid for him along the way.

This time, the artist's point of departure is not a higher aspiration or idealistic delusion regarding Art. His discovery of his own aspirations occurs gradually. It begins, however, with a modest, primitive goal: he buys a camera to film his daughter "being born, and as the months go by". He soon learns that filming others can make him and his camera indispensable. The chance capture on celluloid of Piotr Krawczyk's mother, who dies unexpectedly shortly thereafter, leads to a near-metaphysical experience Filip could not have foreseen.

Piotr's emotion becomes the most unshakeable eulogy of Filip's passion for film: "What you're doing is beautiful, lads. Someone dies and yet they're still here."

Filip gains his first real awareness of what he is doing while making his first film off his own bat, to his boss' commission, about his firm's anniversary. Here he discovers the filmmaker's freedom, realising that, even while executing a banal commission, one can turn one's camera to one side and capture on film a pigeon on a parapet or make off to the neighbouring room in which – having carried out instructions – the artists collect their fees. When an older fellow camera buff asks Filip after his film's festival screening, "So you film what's there, that's quite an idea!", it is a jokey direct reference to the above-mentioned article by Zagajewski. "What's there" is one of his subtitles.[13]

The next stage is one of revelling in the camera's seemingly boundless ability to "represent the world". Just as the cutter Sowa had guided Romek, so at this stage Filip's guides are real filmmakers playing themselves: Jurga and Zanussi. Jurga's comments on the verdict of the amateur film festival's jury cause Filip to grasp his own responsibility to choose the subjects of his filmic statements. And, during a meeting that follows a screening of *Camouflage*, Zanussi opens his eyes to the question of a director's social responsibility, of which he had previously been unaware.

Here Filip flings himself into a whirl of filmmaking: he develops the amateur club, carries out new ideas, accepts television commissions. The bright side of all this activity is embodied in his colleague Witek, an unbridled camera buff. Tadeusz Bradecki, still a novice actor at that time, whose role this is, plays off against the performance of Jerzy Stuhr, thereby accentuating the main protagonist's reflectiveness and hesitations. (Incidentally, both actors are now themselves fine directors, and for several years Bradecki was director of Kraków's Stary Teatr [Old Theatre].)

During this selfsame stage, however, Filip also experiences the darker, disturbing aspect of "representing the world". It is not only that, following the television broadcast of his documentary unmasking municipal authority waste, an old colleague of Filip – responsible for the firm's "cultural sector" – loses his job. It is more a matter, first and foremost, of Filip's coming to feel that he is not up to shouldering the responsibility for his own films. He is hampered not by a lack of civic courage, but by his failure completely to think through the issues they raise. And he had not done so because he did not know himself well enough.

So, when Filip decides to destroy the freshly-shot film before it can be posted to the television, it is by no means out of cowardice – for instance, out of fear of further disciplinary measures by his boss. No – and in this respect Kieślowski does not simplify his own task. Despite appearances, the boss is far from obtuse, while Osuch, the colleague who has lost his job, bears Filip no grudge, but, on the contrary, behaves with rare generosity, encouraging him not to take to heart such effects of his artistic work. "You have to realise that from now on this sort of thing will happen to you frequently. But you have to go on. Something has stirred inside you – hang on to it!"

Thus, Filip's unexpected decision was not dictated by cowardice, but by his realisation that the process of describing the world has to begin with oneself. That is the hidden meaning of Filip's famous final scene, in which he trains the camera on himself and begins to tell his entire story, which the viewers of *Camera Buff* already know. There have been various interpretations of this scene. Zygmunt Kałużyński, the well-known, intelligent but often superficial *Polityka* critic, read it as expressing the hero's defeat: "The camera buff turns his equipment on himself – so perhaps he gives up and devotes himself to his private self, as his boss had exhorted him to do?".[14] And yet, in the light of the whole film, this scene calls for a different reading: self-knowledge is a necessary step on the way to an honest description of the external world. Only then will the description be truly valid and sanctioned.

Echoes of the Young Culture programme also make themselves felt in several of the incidental figures of the earlier *The Scar*. The television journalist – played, significantly, by Michał Tarkowski (Sowa from *Personnel*) – and the group of sociologists Bednarz employs are further representatives of the younger generation, translating the theses of *The Unrepresented World* into their own professional work. While preparing his material, the journalist (Tarkowski) makes no attempt to manipulate Bednarz. Honesty, not ringing declarations, is what he wants from him. When the director asks him about the old, incomplete material – "was it intended as a film against me or against a method, an idea?" – Tarkowski replies, "I had something far less equivocal in mind. It wasn't meant as facile journalism. It was meant to be a film about you, as you are."

Kieślowski himself would doubtless have subscribed to such an outline of the project, as well as to the sociologists' formula in *The Scar*: "what concerns us is truth. And reducing the number of errors". There can be no doubt that the essay-programme of Young Culture found its richest and most varied development in Kieślowski's work.

IV. Ethical choice

The above example shows that to advocate truth "about that which is" is to make a choice that is not in the first instance epistemological or artistic, but ethical, for it requires consistent opposition to anyone who either wishes to conceal that truth (for "public life cannot always be open", as the director explains in *Camera Buff*), or to postpone its telling (for "this is not the right time", as another director – Bednarz – maintains in *The Scar*). It is easy to see that both directors appear as representatives of the authorities. The authorities have no desire to reveal the truth about themselves, but guard it closely. That is why finding it out can be so dangerous.

The dangers connected with "truth-telling" or "being oneself" and describing "how things are" are, of course, quite obvious (if unofficial). A copybook example of such a situation – as it were, straight out of the "fearless journalism" of the time – appears in *The Scar*. The journalist records a statement by one of the rebel workers at the "badly-sited" large chemical plant in Olecko. "Truth always gets you the chop", the worker says. A moment later, the director's assistant (Jerzy Stuhr – cast for the first time in a negative role by Kieślowski, one in line with his stereotypical appearance as "top dog") confiscates the journalist's tape and bans any discussion with workers not on a "vetted" list. And the worker who has offended the authorities will probably meet the same fate as Osuch in *Camera Buff* – dismissal.

Sometimes, however, the danger is hidden, the devil – disguised. Such is the case in *Personnel*, for the process whereby Romek Januchta acquires self-knowledge – described above – does not proceed smoothly and automatically. Romek is tempted by the system, as embodied in the glib secretary of the youth organisation (played by Tomasz Zygadło, Kieślowski's friend and the co-director of the banned documentary, *Workers '71: Nothing About Us Without Us*). The overcritical Sowa is someone whom the system would gladly do without. Romek, still innocent and with a bent for "constructive criticism", is quite another matter. He perhaps could be bought, and his proposed cabaret controlled, turned into a "safety valve". Thus, the first proposal is that he join the youth organisation ("with us you can't but gain"); then – in the film's last scene – he faces a fundamental test of character. The director urges Romek to denounce Sowa, his mentor and friend. If he writes as required, it will mean that he has sold himself. If he refuses, he will save himself, but certainly also forfeit access to the privileges which the system offers. The viewer is kept in doubt to the very end: the hero first tightens then unscrews the pen. "I deliberately left it like that", Kieślowski comments.[15]

Pointing out the ethical nature of one's choice of artistic method was something in which Young Culture specialised. *Etyka i poetyka* (*Ethics and Poetics*) was the title given by one of the movement's key authors, Stanisław Barańczak, to a volume of essays published in 1979

– the year *Camera Buff* was released. To describe honestly "how things are", how people really live and think, meant a basic decision accompanied by genuine risks.

In *Personnel* and *Camera Buff*, this conception of the link between ethics and poetics featured within the represented world itself. Things were different in *The Calm*, where Kieślowski performed a sort of narrative experiment with the characteristics of a parable. Using the example of Antek Gralak, he tried to determine the likelihood of an average person finding fulfilment in life in People's Poland, even when that person's aspirations went no further than the simplest, most basic needs. Antek Gralak, whom we meet in the film's first scene in prison at Christmas, listening to carols with his cellmates, sharing his dreams with them, wants nothing more from life than the "peace and quiet" of the title.

Antek expounds his programme in life during a drinking bout with colleagues. "A woman, children, a place of one's own. Dinner always at home, no canteens, no milk bars, no sir. After all, I can earn 2 or 3000 anywhere. I don't need any more than that, Mietek. I'll give my pay to the wife, keep just enough for cigarettes for myself. Work, after work – go home, kids off to school. Television, the first programme, the second programme, I'll watch everything." Jerzy Stuhr's performance as Antek not only lends credibility to so limited a programme, but also defends the character. His playing suggests that the hero has a right to such self-limitation, and that defence matches the concept of the entire film.

It turns out, nevertheless, that even this minimalist programme cannot be achieved. This is because the "peace and quiet" programme presupposes remaining on good terms with everyone. Antek wants to gain the approval of his colleagues on the building site; he feels stronger within a group. But he also wants to have the site's boss on his side, particularly because he is genuinely grateful towards him: despite Antek's prison record, the boss saw no problem in taking him on. Antek is not worried about the dishonesty of the boss, who uses legal loopholes to sell construction materials on the side, for personal gain, laying his employees open to standstills and loss of bonuses. When the workforce rebels against the boss, Antek cannot adopt a clear position. He wants to join in the strike, but he also wants to be "the boss's man". However, this proves impossible, and Antek loses the trust of both sides. "Peace and quiet" are now out of the question.

Of course, the viewer is at liberty to read the film's message from a radical standpoint: one has to make choices and cannot be on both sides in a dispute. Nevertheless, Kieślowski suggests that the viewer endorse his hero's "non-commitment". Because the viewer sees more than any of the figures in the represented world, he alone knows in all certainty that Antek behaves decently in every situation. After all, he is no coward: he is capable of rebelling against the boss in the end, although, before doing so, he makes a goodwill gesture. As the author of *The Calm*, as in all his other political features (with the possible exception of *Short Working Day*), Kieślowski will defend his heroes' right to non-commitment, the only requirement being that they are honest.

This is how it will be right up to *No End*, where the interned worker Darek – like Antek – does not want to choose either of the extremes. Both the pragmatism of the old lawyer Labrador ("Get it into your head that this isn't a time for winning. If you've decided to live, you have to be able to endure a lot") and the radicalism of his assistant ("Tougher, more definite times are on their way. If you have to do time, do it for something") are alien to him. What best suited Darek was the intermediate position of the dead lawyer Zyro, who "spoke of clarity, saying that both sides should wipe their spectacles, that everyone has to find his own way". This last position was surely closest to that of the film's author.

The figure of Filip Mosz in *Camera Buff* is particularly interesting in this context. He is, as it were, Antek Gralak, one stage on. The element of continuity between Stuhr's character and the previous figure is obvious. "I've seen that I need more than just peace and quiet", Filip explains to his wife, who is loath to accept his new passion for filmmaking. Meanwhile, that passion inevitably brings public activity in its wake, requiring one to take a stand, come out on behalf of one side or the other – and Filip, unlike Antek, does so. However, this does not bring him satisfaction either, but rather deepens his disquiet. The remedy which the film's construction suggests does not stress "commitment", but internal work, a self-reflection sufficiently profound to permit one to monitor one's own honesty. Where Filip's new social role is concerned, what matters to the author is not the effectiveness of his actions, but the internal yardstick that allows him to assume responsibility.

The film that most fully develops this complex of issues is *Blind Chance*. Here the human right to err and to make independent ethical judgments of one's own behaviour is taken furthest. The work's equivocal reception in Poland stemmed from a misunderstanding. Even serious analytical studies reproached Kieślowski with ethical relativism. For instance, Mariola Jankun-Dopartowa believed that Kieślowski failed in the film to create an existential space that would bring home to the viewer man's ability to determine his own fate. The critic sees this as an inheritance from the "false consciousness" of the "Cinema of Moral Anxiety", which was convinced that man does not shape reality by himself. Thus, the only conclusion to be drawn from

Blind Chance would be that "naïve youth will support any and every idea".[16] And yet, the film by no means justifies wrongdoing. Quite the reverse: it demonstrates that an inwardly decent and mature person will shrink from wrongdoing even in the worst and least favourable circumstances. This is just what happened in the case of Witek in the first variant of *Blind Chance*. Moreover, it had occurred earlier with Antek, and will recur with Darek.

The film's hypothetical structure – three versions of the fortunes of Witek Długosz according to whether he catches the Łódź-Warsaw train, misses it and is locked up, or misses it without being taken in by the militia – arose from a sense of the Young Culture programme's inadequacy to the new political situation. During the unforgettable "season of Solidarity" in 1980-81, when the boundaries of free expression suddenly expanded, mere description of the world became insufficient: a need for diagnosis began to be felt. At that time, Kieślowski himself published a famous article calling for an enrichment of the realistic conventions hitherto adopted by the "Cinema of Moral Anxiety". He recommended that it now develop "in depth rather than breadth, inwards rather than outwards".[17]

Blind Chance implements this new programme, for it strives to view the hero from within. This is not just a matter of showing him in more intimate moments than in the previous films, during decisive conversations, confessions and erotic scenes. It is primarily one of the author attempting to puncture as thoroughly as possible the superficial political labelling of the Poland of the time ("as a ZMS[18] activist, he's on the authorities' side"; "that one belongs to the opposition"; "the other guy avoids politics completely"). Kieślowski shatters such superficial distinctions, showing that people from these warring milieux can be basically the same.

He does so by developing a certain narrative concept (one inspired, incidentally, by Krzysztof Zanussi's television film, *Hipoteza* [*The Hypothesis*, 1972]) based on the question: what would have happened had the protagonist's later life followed a completely different course, simply by chance? The fictional deliberation on the various possible fates here has many of the features of a self-analysis. No one seems to have noticed that Witek Długosz, the hero of *Blind Chance*, has the same birthday as the film's author – 27 June – albeit fifteen years later, in 1956. Kieślowski, too, as a chronicler of the authorities, had had a flirtation with them, and in 1970 was selected to carry out just the sort of "Pole of the Year" survey that Witek organises in the first variant of *Blind Chance*. He, too, had sympathised with the opposition: a number of his films, headed by *The Calm*, had been shelved for years. But the variant basically closest to him was the third – that of the man who stands on the sidelines.

He said as much outright on more than one occasion.[19]

That is why only the third variant is marked as real in the film. The narrative's framing suggests that this one "really" took place: *Blind Chance* begins with Witek's terrified scream on the aeroplane, which is headed towards the disaster of the third ending. The first two versions are recounted in the conditional tense. This was pointed out by Tadeusz Sobolewski: "Only the third variant seems to be real – it alone ends with the death in the air disaster that constitutes the framing situation. In the final variant, as in a game, Witek succeeds in avoiding the traps that would lie in wait for him if he led a life of engagement" – although it is only here, in the third variant, where he has a normal career, loves his wife and does not sign any protest letters, that the final trap awaits him.[20] It is the one from which there is no escape.

The construction of *Blind Chance* adds a message already outlined in the early films: that the famous "choice", the necessity of which is taught by ethical rigorists, is not necessary at all. One can live honestly and well on either side. In essence, a person's intellectual and spiritual background – his parents, education and reading – chooses for him. In each variant, Witek strives to be as honest as he possibly can. The essential thing – what he is – is not determined by chance. Accidents come from social life; that is the source of danger.

V. The people in power

If the goal of the Polish filmmaker of the 1970s was the description of reality, that description had to include those people who determined the fate of the mass of society – the politicians. It is thus logical that Kieślowski was the Polish director most eager to shoot political documentaries. In the mid-1970s, between the films *Workers '71: Nothing About Us Without Us* and *Personnel*, Kieślowski presented the Documentary Film Studios with a plan for a film, many hours long, to be based on conversations with the rulers of the past, pre-Gierek era: Gomułka, Cyrankiewicz, Moczar. But not one of them gave his consent.[21]

Making documentaries with lower-level representatives of the authorities in its turn became an extension of a certain tangled web in which the films' heroes were caught. For many years, the director of the large industrial plant presented in *Nie wiem* (*I Don't Know*, 1977) felt that he had been wronged by Kieślowski,[22] while, in any case, the film was shelved. Even making a documentary about a night porter and his totalitarian views – a successful, prize-winning film – troubled Kieślowski's conscience, and he would not permit its television broadcast.[23]

Making feature films about the people in power was thus very clearly a substitute, *taking the place* of documentaries that were either impossible or inappropriate. Both *The Scar* and *Short Working Day* were based on reportages, their plots deriving from specific prototypical events that were widely known in Poland. The first case involved the construction in Pułway – a beautiful historic small town surrounded by woods – of a large nitrous fertiliser plant, which became operational in 1966. The plant's director, a Party appointee, was the model for the hero of *The Scar*. The second case was the explosion of collective hatred in June 1976 in Radom, a large industrial centre, following the announcement of further price rises. Here the prototype was the First Secretary of the Party's Voivodship Committee. For several hours that June, the building where he worked, besieged by workers, was the country's hottest flashpoint.

Kieślowski declared these films the "most unnecessary" of all the ones he had made.[24] His judgment seems overcritical, particularly in relation to *The Scar*. The film demonstrated the process of the authorities' detachment from society, the mechanism of their degeneration – namely, one of the central issues of life inside a system without democratic procedures. The picture Kieślowski drew had the merits both of incisiveness (made possible by, among other things, the documentary working method) and – above all else – objectivity. The director avoided caricature when portraying representatives of the authorities, although, in some cases, his critique of the mores prevailing at the "Party managerial" level rang true – as in the scene of the Party dignitaries' nocturnal feast in the "hunting lodge" (with the famous offer of a cigarette to a deer), or the element of staged "pressure of public opinion" during the deliberations about whether or not to award the town the industrial plant.

Generally speaking, however, the film eschews a tone of outright criticism. The *gravitas* of the tone flows in the main from the central figure, director Bednarz. He is the apparent dream choice for director of a large industrial investment project: a fine expert, energetic manager and, at the same time, a fair and decent human being. Franciszek Pieczka, who plays the part, is an actor specialising in the role of noble people's hero. In Witold Leszczyński's *Żywot Mateusza* (*Life of Matthew*, 1967), he had played the personification of spiritual innocence, and that famous role determined his speciality.

In *The Scar*, too, Pieczka plays a man of pure intentions. However, the film depicts the mechanisms that translate these intentions into diametrically opposed results. Firstly, there is the decision-making process itself. The decision to site the chemical plant on this particular spot is taken without consulting the local population or listening to its views, while the decision-makers are then switched to other regions, confronting the people left behind with a *fait accompli.*

Director Bednarz found himself in just such a position, although, when interviewed by a television journalist, he generously stated that he had been included in the decision-making from the very outset. We see that this is not true. Certainly, he had believed that, given time, people would come gradually to accept the plant nevertheless – that, in other words, the gains (thousands of local jobs; development of the regional infrastructure) would outweigh the losses (damage to the environment; relocation of many home-owners to tower blocks; the transformation of the former small town's natural social ties into a soulless agglomeration of multiple thousands of newcomers).

However, this does not happen. Years pass and the people's discontent grows. Bednarz realises this – indeed, from the very start, he had sought access to the reality of public opinion. But the authorities' higher echelons have no desire to take account of that opinion, and demand that Bednarz pursue the goals previously set. The result is that the director, sensing his own impotence, increasingly shuns human contact, a socially vicious circle is established, and no one's aims are achieved – neither those of the upper-level politicians, nor the personal ones of Bednarz himself.

The film conveys a very suggestive picture of the social impotence of an undemocratic system, something clearly visible today. It does so despite Kieślowski's failure fully to pursue either one of two intersecting formulas: that of the "paradocumentary" about a particular region (only one scene, of an open meeting, breathes the air of authenticity of *Workers '71: Nothing About Us Without Us,* and censorship causes the film to founder among vague hints, leaving unmentioned the original sources of decisions), and that of the political drama (the conflict within the works is not drawn sufficiently clearly, while tne strands from Bednarz's private life – his relations with wife and daughter – do not go beyond the stereotypical).

The shortcomings of *The Scar* recur five years later in *Short Working Day.* Moreover, the later film lacks the trump cards the actors' performances dealt the first one. Nevertheless, *Short Working Day* also has its virtues, first and foremost those of an unusual, close-up view of a high-level representative of the authorities, and – to boot – one in an exceptionally dramatic situation. And this is shown in a double perspective, both from within and from without. For we are witnesses both to the Party Secretary's actions on that remarkable "working day" and – no small thing – often see him alone, when nobody else does, and hear his interior monologue in the voice-over. We "get inside his skull", something we remember had always been Kieślowski's filmmaking ideal.

The primary value of this tactic is to satisfy the viewer's curiosity.

After all, it is interesting to be able to observe with impunity how a Party Secretary behaves when alone while a crowd storms his office. A reception situation of this kind evokes an instinctive spectatorial sympathy for the Secretary: after all, we always side with the lonely and endangered. However, all the director's rational arguments are marshalled against him, and although the actor – Wacław Ulewicz – defends him, he does so unconvincingly. Everything the Secretary does and – in particular – thinks when in danger compromises him completely. Trapped by the crowd, he is scared to make a decision. He has no grasp of the situation, neither at the national level nor at the local level. Slogans from Party "newspeak" substitute for genuine analysis: "Is it working-class, a justified protest? We'll have to promise them something, anything – words are cheap." So great is his ignorance of the people that he does not even know how to address them. Testing the megaphone, he uses successive formulas: "Comrades! Citizens! Ladies and gentlemen!".

Like such earlier film heroes as Antek Gralak and Filip Mosz, the Secretary wants "to be on good terms with everyone", on both sides of the conflict at once. On the one hand, he fears offending the authorities (one monologue after a telephone call to Warsaw: "He spoke quite harshly to me! Could they be setting me up for a fall?"); but, on the other, he wants to please the crowd ("After all, I did stay with them even though Warsaw told me to get out"). In this case, however, the author is not on the protagonist's side, for the latter's indecision stems not from the natural urge to harmony but from the opportunism which the system's falsity imposes. Thus, the Secretary is a victim – and it is as such that the viewer identifies with him. We are, of course, relieved that the workers do not throw him out of the window, as seemed likely at one moment. For the crowd, like all crowds on such occasions, is hostile and alien. Since we are watching it from the perspective of the ruler (from "the first-floor window"), it is hard to sympathise with it, and not even the "flashes-forward" – the shots of the authorities' future revenge, the "health run" on which a gauntlet of baton-wielding militiamen send selected "worker-troublemakers" – can generate it.

In effect, *Short Working Day* never achieved any public reception. It was first shelved by the authorities, and then – as of the end of the 1980s – Kieślowski himself, conscious of its weaknesses, refused to allow it to be screened. It was shown on television just after the director's death, and passed without echo.

Portraits of representatives of the authorities appeared one more time in Kieślowski, in *Blind Chance*. The duo of old Communist friends – Werner and Adam – is obviously tremendously important in the context of the protagonist's ideological dilemmas in the film's first variant, but, despite the use of two first-rate actors – Tadeusz Łomnicki and Zbigniew Zapasiewicz – it is restricted to the stereotypical contrast between the one who was principled and so lost power, and the corrupt one who retained it. In *No End*, the authorities are no longer present – neither their martial law representatives, nor their forceful attributes of the time.

VI. The people and the spirit

In the depressing circumstances of martial law, Kieślowski once again – for one last time – set out to describe reality. This time, too, his point of departure was a documentary project. He wanted to make a film in the one place that then seemed to embody most fully the conflict dividing society: a courtroom. At that time, numerous members of the intelligentsia frequented the courts to observe the trials being held there – trials of workers who had infringed the tightened rigours of martial law and continued strikes in their workplaces. Kieślowski had a well-advanced film project based entirely on the collision of two faces: that of the accuser and that of the accused.[25]

During shooting, however, it emerged that the presence of the camera was affecting the judges, so that whenever it ran they reduced their sentences and were even suddenly inclined to not-guilty verdicts. Once again, Kieślowski realised that a documentary would fail to convey the truth. Together with Krzysztof Piesiewicz, a lawyer he had met during the trials, he began to contemplate a feature film which would penetrate the deeper, hidden truth: not the world's behavioural outer skin, but its spiritual essence.

The resulting film, *No End*, of course contained a clutch of behavioural observations linked to the fact of the action's unfolding in autumn 1982. A voice intones "monitored conversation" from the telephone receiver; in the evening, a candle burns in the window (the way in which, at that time, on the thirteenth of each month, people expressed their mutual solidarity in grief); the heroine's son plays the tune of "Mury" ("Walls") on the piano – that of the most famous Polish opposition song of the time. All the same, one does not see such things as the Army's continual presence on the street, for the film primarily gives an account of a certain emotional nexus most typical of the prevailing mood: a sense of humiliation and hopeless lack of prospects going hand-in-hand with the duty to remain faithful, under the skin, to what, for the moment, had suffered defeat.

That emotional nexus colours the film's two main, linked strands: the love one and the legal one. The love theme is predominant, the legal one subsidiary, for it is as she is sucked into the case of the interned Darek that Ula – the beautiful widow – discovers the world of her recently-deceased husband Antek, of which she had known so little. Antek had been a lawyer and was to have defended Darek, one of the workers' strike-leaders.

But it is, in fact, Antek who is the most important character in the film, even though it is without a single flashback. In its very first scene, and on six subsequent occasions (it is the very first time in his work that Kieślowski selects such a high-risk solution) he appears as a ghost: in a black suit, as if dressed for a coffin, and invisible to the other onscreen figures. Antek watches over his nearest and dearest. He observes his son going to school; looks on sadly as his wife betrays him; wears a sympathetic smile as he studies his client asleep in his cell. And, even when personally absent, he intervenes via signs: he places a question mark after the name of the old lawyer, a pragmatist; and he forces his wife to halt her car suddenly and unexpectedly, thereby saving her from dying in a crash.

On one level of its reception, the ghost's presence has psychological import, connoting the persistence of the "beloved dead" in everyone's spiritual life. Not until Antek has died does Ula realise that she loved him far more than she knew during his life. It is thus understandable that Antek should feature in a world presented from her point of view – although his presence is only on a spiritual level. Ula's final decision to commit suicide should also be read as her decision to be with Antek, her final choice in favour of love.

But, on another level of reception, the ghost has a non-psychological dimension. The actor playing Antek (Jerzy Radziwiłowicz) had played the leading roles in the two key films in the Polish social cinema of the previous decade, *Człowiek z marmuru* (*Man of Marble*, 1976) and *Człowiek z żelaza* (*Man of Iron*, 1981). The Solidarity era, as it were, fulfilled the purpose of this screen character. What the viewer learns about the deceased Antek confirms that this hero, too, had thought and acted in line with that purpose. This lends Ula's fidelity to her dead husband another dimension, a far broader one than that of personal psychology. It is fidelity to the cause of Solidarity – which was dead, but not gone forever, in the general belief of the time. That cause had vanished from all life's outer circumstances, and even the word "solidarity" could not appear in the media. And yet people knew it would return. In the context of this belief, the importance of the posthumous meeting of Antek and Ula was matched by that of the moment when, during All Souls' Night, the son suddenly tore himself away from his father's grave and went over to another, "patriotic" one.

To judge by the available records, the film's reception could not have been worse. It had crushing reviews in the official press and received no prize at the National Film Festival in Gdynia. Meanwhile, reviews in the underground press were also unfavourable, disliking its defeatism and unconvinced by its poetics. However, I remember the very different experience of my own reaction to it as the only work to convey the truth about the prevailing mood in Poland. The director also recalled that neither before nor since had he met with so many private tokens of support from viewers – in letters, telephone calls and conversations.[26]

Perhaps those private signs of understanding served a purpose. They suggested to the director that – regardless of the external response – cinema does its work, living its secret, fullest life in the inner worlds of its viewers. Surely therefore, devoting oneself to this inner world is the best way to prolong a film's life? This is the road he would follow.

Notes

[1] Danusia Stok (ed), *Kieślowski on Kieślowski* (London; Boston: Faber and Faber, 1993): 144.

[2] Ibid: 58.

[3] Translated from the French: "Vous ne pouvez pas comprendre ce qui signifie vivre dans un monde qu'on ne peut pas décrire. Ce qui est propre à votre monde, l'Ouest, c'est qu'on l'a toujours décrit et raconté. Quand vous vivez dans un monde qui n'est pas décrit, pas nommé, vous vivez toujours dans une abstraction. Vous ignorez où commence la réalité et où commence le reste". Vincent Ostria, "Le hasard et la nécessité. Krzysztof Kieślowski parle à Vincent Ostria", *Les Inrockuptibles* 36 (June 1992): 79.

[4] Adam Zagajewski, "Rzeczywistość nie przedstawiona w powojennej literaturze polskiej", in Julian Kornhauser and Adam Zagajewski, *Świat nie przedstawiony* (Kraków: Wydawnictwo literackie, 1974): 43-44.

[5] Translated from the Polish: "Jest rzeczywistość ludzi, rzeczy i świadomości, zebrán i kolonii dziecięcych, rzeczywistość podwójnej wiary, zakłamania i nadziei, rzeczywistość zebrań partyjnych i meczów piłkarskich, Wyścigu Pokoju i dowcipów politycznych, szpitali i transparentów, śmierci i nowych inwestycji, emerytów i personalnych, domów kultury i bójek na wiejskich weselach, piosenek młodzieżowych i młodych naukowców, bibliotek i budek z piwem. To, co jest, kryje w sobie własne wnętrze pod postacią tragedii i komedii, wolności i zniewolenia, prawdy i kłamstwa, obłudy i odwagi, kryje w sobie konflikty stare jak cywilizacja i nowe jak Polska Ludowa. Jest to rzeczywistość kompletna, której do pełni brakuje kultury interesującej się nią". Ibid: 43-44.

[6] Translated from the Polish: "dramaturgia rzeczywistości, z jej brakiem point, z jej porządkiem i bałaganem jednocześnie, to najnowocześniejsza i najprawdziwsza ze struktur". Krzysztof Kieślowski, "Dramaturgia

rzeczywistości", *Film na świecie* 388-389 (3-4) (1992): 7.

7   Translated from the Polish: "artyści zamiast ludzi, którzy odtwarzają siebie". Zygmunt Kałużyński and Marian Turski, "'Zaglądać ludziom pod czaszkę.' Rozmowa z laureatem 'Drożdży' Krzysztofem Kieślowskim", *Polityka* 10 (1976): 1, 8.

8   Translated from the French: "Kieślowski m'a proposé de travailler sur l'atmosphère de l'état de siège, sur ce que je ressentais du climat ambiant. De là est né *Sans fin*. Il parle de mes expériences les plus personnelles et les plus dramatiques". Michel Ciment, "Entretien avec Krzysztof Piesiewicz, scénariste et avocat", *Positif* 346 (December 1989): 33-35.

9   Translated from the Polish: "Bohaterowie jego wczesnych fabuł przeżywają dylematy, które były jego własnymi dylematami". Tadeusz Sobolewski, "Gra z życiem", *Tygodnik powszechny* 36 (1995).

10   Stok (ed): 208.

11   Translated from the Polish: "Istota problemu kryje się w tym, że Sowa zdał sobie sprawę, iż pracuje w złym teatrze. A także, że poglądem tym zaraził Romka Januchtę". Konrad Eberhardt. "Głos niepowołanych", *Kultura* 47 (1975): 14.

12   Translated from the French: "Un bonheur est mort, un créateur est né". Jean Gili, "L'Amateur", in Michel Estève (ed), *Krzysztof Kieślowski* (Paris: Lettres modernes, 1994): 18.

13   Zagajewski: 43.

14   Translated from the Polish: "Amator skierowuje swój aparat na samego siebie – może więc zrezygnuje i zajmie się sobą prywatnym, do czego wzywał go dyrektor?". Zygmunt Kałużyński, "Przebudzenie z apatii", *Polityka* 28 (1979): 10.

15   Translated from the Polish: "Umyślnie tak to zostawiłem". Kałużyński and Turski: 8.

16   Translated from the Polish: "naiwna młodość opowiada się za każdą ideą". Mariola Jankun-Dopartowa, "Człowieczeństwo zawrócone. Trzy przypadki bohatera lat osiemdziesiątych", in Mariola Jankun-Dopartowa and Mirosław Przylipiak (eds), *Człowiek z ekranu. Z antropologii postaci filmowej* (Kraków: Arcana, 1996): 168.

17   Translated from the Polish: "głęboko zamiast szeroko, do środka nie na zewnątrz". Krzysztof Kieślowski, "Głęboko zamiast szeroko", *Dialog* 1 (1981): 111.

18   Związek Młodzieży Socjalistycznej (Union of Socialist Youth).

19   Maria Marszałek, "O mnie, o tobie, o wszystkich. Z Krzysztofem Kieślowskim rozmawia Maria Marszałek", *Kino* 8 (1987): 8-10.

20   Sobolewski: 8.

[21] Stok (ed): 208.

[22] Ibid: 73-74.

[23] Ibid: 75.

[24] Ibid: 208-209.

[25] Ibid: 126.

[26] Ibid: 136-137.

Charles Eidsvik

Krzysztof Kieślowski's films often are about lonely people, who, lost in their own worlds or in the grip of private obsessions, do unusual, irrational or shocking things. Two such lonely and obsessed people – Jacek in *Krótki film o zabijaniu* (*A Short Film About Killing*, 1988) and Tomek in *Krótki film o miłości* (*A Short Film About Love*, 1988) (and, of course, in the television versions of these films) – commit the transgressions around which the stories evolve. With a great deal of premeditation, Jacek seeks out the opportunity to murder a taxi-driver – any taxi-driver – and steal his car. We never really know Jacek's motives, and in *Decalogue 5* we do not even know his name until he is sentenced to death. Tomek's obsession is less shocking, and his motives are easier to understand. So that he can somehow come into closer contact with a young woman across the courtyard on whom he has a crush, he not only steals a telescope, but also begins directly to interfere with the woman's life.

Tomek's story is far simpler than Jacek's. Tomek's theft allows him to see closely enough so that he can witness not only the young woman's sexual frolics, but also her wistfulness, her anguish at her love troubles, and her own solitude. This leads him to try to get closer to the woman, firstly by cruel pranks, and finally by confessing to his voyeurism and love. We watch Tomek as he suffers the consequences: a beating by the woman's lover and sexual humiliation by the woman. The woman, guilt-stricken by what she has done to Tomek, now becomes obsessed with him. But Tomek, now protected from her by his landlady who wishes to treat him as a surrogate son, is now the one out of reach.

In that making a fool of oneself after falling in love is fairly common, neither Tomek's motives nor his actions are that hard to understand. The premeditated murder of a stranger is another matter. In *A Short Film About Killing*, we cannot know why Jacek wants to kill. We can only follow the tough, alienated drifter. He strikes up conversations with friendly strangers – a cinema attendant, a street artist – and asks about a taxi-stand. If strangers are aggressive, he attacks. But he does not care whom he hurts, and he has a mean streak: he nudges a pavement chunk off an overpass, letting chance determine if, or on whom, it will fall. He refuses to give directions to an English tourist. He kicks a young man into a urinal. But he has a playful, human element too: he asks a photo-shop clerk to blow up a photo of his sister that he carries; he playfully interacts with two schoolgirls outside a café where he is waiting. But he carries a rope, and carefully prepares it for the murder he is set on committing. Although we also watch that day in the victim's life, and in that of a law student who later will become Jacek's attorney, the story is organised around the young would-be killer's day, the murder, and its consequences. We find out a great deal about the victim. He hates cats but likes dogs. He plays the lottery. He does not like people in general, and enjoys irritating people who want rides. He is carefully selective about whom he picks up. He has the bad luck to pick up Jacek. The law student is a sensitive idealist who hopes to make the world better by his work. He passes the bar exam. He happens to be in the café where Jacek waits. He defends Jacek. Then, in an interview before Jacek's execution, he befriends him, only to watch him die.

Thematically, these stories are not that unusual. Loneliness and obsession drive many narratives, and a fair fraction of the cinema's output has involved characters who broke the Fifth or Sixth Commandments. What makes Kieślowski's work special is that his stories are constructed so that we react personally and profoundly. The task of this essay is to try to explain how that is so.

Although it has long been unfashionable to describe films in terms of how they were made, the tensions built into Krzysztof Kieślowski's approach to film production account in good measure for the unique responses which films such as *A Short Film About Killing* or *A Short Film About Love* elicit. Trained as a documentary filmmaker at the Łódź Film School, he "escaped from documentaries" because "[t]he closer [he wanted] to get to somebody, the more that person shuts him or herself off".[1] Although he shifted to fiction, Kieślowski stubbornly maintained his documentarist habits of production. These included using subject specialists as collaborators. Needing partners to help him write scripts, Kieślowski settled on "amateurs" such as Krzysztof Piesiewicz, whose interest in "the intimate details of everyday life" and "private hopes and suffering" were grounded in his work as a lawyer.[2] Despite the feature film's traditionally hierarchical production structure, Kieślowski kept to the collaborative methods preached at Łódź. Rather than view the script or *mise en scène* as the basis of the director's art, he adhered to the documentarist credo that "a film really only comes into existence in the cutting-room. To shoot is only to collect material, create possibilities...the elusive spirit of a film, so difficult to describe, is born only there, in the cutting-room".[3] For Kieślowski, editing involved "directing attention" and "distributing tension". But it also remained what it must to a documentarist who wants to keep his audience awake, the art of abbreviation, of cutting so much out that the audience must fill in the gaps with their imagination. As he stated in an interview, in his early documentaries he often "said everything I had to say on a topic in ten minutes. Whatever was unnecessary was cut out; it takes only a small but essential part to set thoughts and emotions in motion...Between the cuts whole worlds can occur. This insight became second nature to me."[4] The tensions from using a documentarist's sense of the film medium but with fiction materials allowed Kieślowski to create extremely abbreviated, highly suggestive stories that strike one as intimate documents on the human condition.

But how far could his abbreviation of his materials go without diminishing returns? For most of his works, we will not know.[5] But, for what began as *Decalogue 5* and *Decalogue 6*, two episodes in his television treatment of the Ten Commandments, Kieślowski found the money to make film versions. The two films, each of which runs eighteen minutes longer than the 57-minute television stories, were made under the titles *A Short Film About Killing* and *A Short Film About Love*.[6] Although Kieślowski wrote and shot the television versions and their film counterparts to be separate pieces, in editing he borrowed materials from the television productions for the films, and vice versa. For all practical purposes, each of the two television and cinema pairings are different edits of the same fund of available footage. Thus, they offer us at least a rough idea of what Kieślowski did when working at the limits of compression, and what he could do with the few minutes more he allowed himself to use for cinema audiences.

The screenplays

The screenplays, collected and published as *Decalogue: The Ten Commandments*, illuminate Kieślowski's pragmatic sensibilities. As Kieślowski put it in an interview: "For me the script is key because it's the means to communicating with the people I work with. It may not be the skeleton, but it is the indispensable foundation. Later, many things can be changed: certain ideas may be eliminated, the end may become the beginning, but what's between the lines, all the ideas – that stays the same."[7] In form and style, the scripts are not at all like standard film script formats: they are prose treatments that delineate the sequence progression in the story. Unlike standard scripts, they give actors starting-points from which to build. For example, the young lawyer in *A Short Film About Killing* is described as "sympathetic, sensitive and perhaps even slightly too delicate sort of person".[8] Or the taxi-driver, taking the tarpaulin off his car, "carefully folds it up in his own pedantic fashion".[9] The screenplay for *A Short Film About Killing* pays attention to motives and feelings, as well as to actions: "Tomek pushes the telescope away: he is in no mood to watch this scene develop further. Besides, he has no choice – his landlady is calling to him from the other room."[10] Or: "He smiles helplessly – he really is embarrassed. He is probably even embarrassed to admit he is embarrassed. He returns to his room and looks reluctantly through the telescope. He knows what he will see and does not want to see it, but places his eye against the viewfinder nevertheless."[11] But at no point do the screenplays move from the generalised tone of being a story *précis* from which the filmmakers will work.

To be sure, bits of atmosphere are included that likely will be revised or replaced in shooting, or not shot at all: for example, in *A Short Film About Killing* the square has a Japanese tourist with an Instamatic camera shooting in all directions.[12] This suggestion of background detail and atmosphere serves as an invitation for collaborators to suggest other details. Often a screenplay incident seems primarily to be something on which to build on location. For example, in the scene with the painter,[13] in the screenplay of *A Short Film About Killing* the painter does tourist pieces of the local architecture. In the produced piece, he is doing a sketch portrait of a young girl. Bringing in the girl allows Jacek's eye to be caught, and allows his one "soft" or attractive quality – his close relationship with his now-dead sister – one more point of contact with the story.

Much of each screenplay gets cut. Usually cut parts are replaced by something else or are redundant: for example, the head examiner's "All that remains is for you to get married"[14] after Piotr has passed his exam. The "club" camaraderie of the legal profession is shown in other scenes; this is not necessary. Sometimes it is a matter of tone: in the script for *A Short Film About Killing*, Jacek ends his encounter with the photo technician who is to enlarge the snapshot of Jacek's dead sister by asking "You won't lose it, will you?".[15] This humanising moment for Jacek, like the decency which his victim, the taxi-driver, exhibits to the freezing prostitute,[16] may have created empathy for both killer and victim that Kieślowski tries so hard to avoid. At least in the final cut, Kieślowski seems intent on making *A Short Film About Killing* a piece about one scoundrel killing another, on making us sympathise with a victim not because we like him, but because he is a victim.

Other changes or shifts are of a type every film has: what is hard to do is changed; possibilities are built onto. In the script for *A Short Film About Killing*, there are several such changes. In sequence 18, the taxi-driver honks at a man with a poodle, which "cringes". In the produced piece, there are two sweater-wearing poodles, one of which gets out of its collar and runs off. It is easier to rig a collar to open than to train a dog to cringe at a horn; in terms of characterising the taxi-driver, the effect is the same. Kieślowski elaborates on the prankish interchange between Jacek and the two schoolgirls at the café, childishly splattering cream on the window. Kieślowski adds a train, a horse and a bicyclist to the background of the murder scene. He changes how Beata, the greengrocer clerk, lives. He makes the *E.T.* figure attached to the taxi window a more generic grinning gargoyle – perhaps to get a more grotesque facial expression, or perhaps to avoid problems of insurance coverage in international distribution that would come from using a copyrighted commercial image. Kieślowski also adds dialogue, especially to the execution scene (with the prosecutor reading the verdict aloud), and shifts action, making the execution more panicky and clumsy, and reducing the role of the decorator witness, replacing it with Piotr's attempt to recover from Jacek's execution.

Only two new scenes are added to those in the script. One is an encounter with another young man in a urinal: it replaces the script's first scene with Jacek and a panhandler in showing Jacek's toughness, but adds sadism to his portrayal. The second is the scene in which Jacek drops a chunk of concrete on a car passing below an overpass. He is trying to watch a taxi rank unobtrusively. He spots the chunk on the guard-rail. Without looking carefully, he edges it off the ledge, letting chance determine whether it will hit a car. It does, causing an accident. The scene reveals Jacek's indifference to the damage he causes, and, of course, is another example of Kieślowski's theme of the interplay of chance and intentions.

The script for *A Short Film About Love* is even more skeletal than that for *A Short Film About Killing*. Again, Kieślowski provides material on characterisation, for example, Magda's: "She looks the sort of person who is capable of looking after herself and who does more or less what she pleases, without too many qualms".[17] The final film follows the script's order quite closely for the entire middle section – sequences 20 to 31 of the script. But the beginnings and ends of both *Decalogue 6* and *A Short Film About Love* depart from the script markedly. Part of this may be due to Grażyna Szapołowska's suggestion that cinema viewers need a "story".[18] Part is due to an emphasis on showing how Tomek's mind works. For example, in scene 4 of the script, Tomek already is delivering milk. In filming, Kieślowski added a scene in which Tomek overhears Magda complaining of unreliable milk delivery and asks for the job – one assumes, as a way of getting into closer contact with her. Sometimes changes add drama. For example, In scene 8 of the script, Tomek buys a more powerful telescope, putting up with the seller's leering guess as to why he wants it. Kieślowski replaced this with a sequence showing Tomek breaking into a building to steal the telescope. Kieślowski also added visual touches and symbols at the shooting stage: in sequence 10, for example, Magda comes into her flat and cries. In the filming, she also spills a bottle of milk.

Scenes dealing specifically with Poland's situation (such as the power outage in sequence 1) were cut from the script for *A Short Film About Love*. In other cases, sequences are truncated, but one can only speculate why. For example, in sequence two, the revenge Tomek extracts by puncturing Magda's lover's tyres does not appear onscreen; neither does the lover's telephone call to someone else – his "betrayal" of Magda. In any Kieślowski film, script material missing from the film may just have been less necessary than what was left in. Kieślowski also said that he shot a large number of realistic scenes for *A Short Film About Love*, but ended up cutting it all out.[19] Neither the published script, *Decalogue 6* nor *A Short Film About Love* gives any clue as to what this material amounted to.

A comparison of *Decalogue 5* and *A Short Film About Killing*

As Kieślowski pointed out at the 1989 Berlin Film Festival, the viewpoint of *A Short Film About Killing* was primarily that of the young man Jacek, whereas *Decalogue 5* primarily takes the viewpoint of the lawyer Piotr.[20] This difference in viewpoint is most apparent in the two sets of beginnings and endings. *Decalogue 5* opens with 54 seconds of Piotr's arguments on freedom, responsibility and the fallacy of deterrent sentencing for criminals. *Decalogue 5* ends with Piotr repeating: "I abhor it, I abhor it". His is the mentality through which presentation of the scenes is filtered, although the bulk of the story centres not on Piotr, but on the killer, Jacek, and his victim, the taxi-driver. In contrast, *A Short Film About Killing* begins with an ambiguous object – it looks like an eye – in a gutter stream, followed by a dead rat and a cigarette wrapper – the detritus of urban life. This is followed by a shot of a hanged cat, with celebrating boys running away from it. *A Short Film About Killing* ends with the lawyer crying wordlessly. Thus, *Decalogue 5* is essentially an argument about the senseless cruelty of both a crime and capital punishment as a form of retribution, whereas *A Short Film About Killing* is not only a critique of capital punishment, but also a spectacle of urban rubbish, cruelty and despair, an outcry against ugliness in both its moral and its aesthetic dimensions.

Yet, this picture of the two versions of Piesiewicz's and Kieślowski's story makes the versions seem more radically different than they actually are. To have a perspective on the commonalities, as well as the differences, it is useful to compare the story at its 85-minute theatrical length with *Decalogue 5*'s 57-minute duration.[21]

The film contains scenes and sequences not contained in the television version. These scenes mainly add dimension to the characterisations. For example, the television version cuts out the taxi-driver's visit to a lottery (which takes 69 seconds), where he expresses his sense of hope, despite his record of just breaking even at gambling. Jacek's encounter with the gypsy storyteller and all of Piotr's celebration at passing his exam and his conversation with his fiancée are cut out; these cuts shorten the television version by over four minutes, but cut out much of our sense of Piotr's life outside his profession. Jacek's encounter with the English tourist takes 44 seconds; that is gone from the television version. So is Jacek's visit to Beata, the vegetable seller, after the murder; that sequence saves two minutes and twelve seconds. Some scene-shortening also occurs at the expense of characterisation: for example, the part of the scene at the beginning is cut just after the taxi-driver throws away a rag; the section of the scene in which the taxi-driver scares a cat away and says he hates cats because, like people, they are deceptive is cut: that saves 30 seconds (and is unneeded, because the hanging cat at the beginning is also cut). The conversation about talent between the portrait artist and Jacek in scene 7 of the script is cut. Apart from these, the scenes in *A Short Film About Killing* are very much like those contained in *Decalogue 5*.

The exception is in material that would make a television viewer especially uncomfortable: for example, the dead rat and hanging cat; and the clumsiness of Jacek's murder of the taxi-driver (with the rope going round the taxi-driver's mouth before it gets pulled down around his neck; then later with the taxi-driver's false teeth falling out; and, finally, with Jacek repeatedly bludgeoning the taxi-driver's blanket-covered head with a stone). Similarly, in *A Short Film About Killing*, the clumsiness of the execution of Jacek (with the guards having trouble getting the blindfold to cover Jacek's eyes) is lessened by substitution of a quicker, less clumsy and less panicked take. The film's high-angle shot of brown liquid dripping into the pan below the hanged Jacek does not appear in *Decalogue 5*. In the film, Jacek's murder of the taxi-driver takes seven minutes and twenty seconds; in the television version it take four minutes and 50 seconds. In the film, the execution takes half a minute longer than in the television version.

But it is not just the ugly shots that are cut or elided, but so are other shots that are memorable, although unnecessary to the telling of the story: for example, during the murder, a long shot of the car in the field seen through the undercarriage of the moving train; or another of the car door through which we have seen Jacek dragging off the taxi-driver, closing of its own accord. Other picturesque shots are shortened, but remain more briefly on the television screen than they remained in the film.

What do the above cuts amount to? In time, about half of the 25-minute difference between the film and the television version. The rest is harder to trace: shots begin later and sometimes end sooner in the television version; alternate, quicker takes replace longer ones. Often a shot from the television version and the cinema version will contain the same action; but, in the television version, the action takes less time. What appears to have happened is that Kieślowski sometimes had takes of different lengths. For the film version, he chose the one that would give more suspense or a better performance; for the television version, he took the shortest one. This kind of cutting is not inherently an issue of choosing a lesser take for the television version; the two versions have different rhythms, so a take suitable for one might have seemed too long or too short for the other.

Given the different jumps between story elements involved in crosscutting between the three main characters, one does not miss or even notice a good number of changes between the film and television versions, except subjectively: the film makes one more uncomfortable as the suspense builds and holds for a longer duration and sometimes with more extreme images. *A Short Film About Killing* lingers, playing on our dread and discomfort. We dislike the taxi-driver and Jacek more in the film than in *Decalogue 5*, and, viscerally, hate all the more what is done to them. The strategy in *A Short Film About Killing* is to make the viewer dread what will happen; the dread increases with duration. *Decalogue 5* cannot afford such strong images or emotions. The 57 minutes allowed on television do not allow a filmmaker to push too far.

Another difference between the film and television versions may also be a function of the lower commitment and concentration level of the television viewer. Up to the ride leading to the taxi-driver's death, the central principle of both versions is crosscutting from one of the lead characters to one of the two others. In *A Short Film About Killing*, up to the fatal meeting of Jacek and the taxi-driver, the film cuts from one character to another 42 times, with the lawyer present in thirteen segments, the taxi-driver in eleven, and Jacek in eighteen. In the television version, there are only 27 segments: the lawyer and taxi-driver are in seven each, with Jacek in thirteen. Often segments involving Jacek that were split into two sequences in the film are condensed into one for television. This results in a more coherent look at Jacek's steps towards becoming a killer. Most of the taxi-driver's segments are shortened. Other elements also de-emphasise the taxi-driver: for example, when Piotr says being a lawyer allows him contact with people he otherwise would not meet, the cinema version cuts to the taxi-driver, but the television version cuts to Jacek. From that point on, Jacek tethers the crosscutting, appearing in alternate scenes. The lawyer and taxi-driver share the other half of each crosscut pairing. Once Jacek begins preparing the rope, the cuts to him come with increasing frequency.

One cost of the simplified cutting in *Decalogue 5* is that the parallels between the three characters are lost. For example, when Piotr jubilantly tells a man in a Mercedes that he has become a lawyer, the taxi-driver, looking on, disapproves. Only a glimpse of this incident remains in the television version. The carefully laid-out cuts between characters in *A Short Film About Killing* follow the convention that the three stories are occurring more or less simultaneously. But, in *Decalogue 5*, Piotr learns that he has passed the exam while Jacek already is in the café preparing his rope. When Piotr later tells the judge that he was in the café when Jacek was, we have to take Piotr's word for it; we never see them together in the café. Except that we see the taxi-driver turn down half a dozen fares, only to pick up Jacek, who will kill him, the role of chance is foregrounded less in *Decalogue 5* than in *A Short Film About Killing*.

Two elements that differ from *Decalogue 5* and *A Short Film About Killing* are the cinematography and the music, but the differences, particularly in cinematography, are difficult to describe because they are differences in subjective response, rather than anything to which one can point concretely. Sławomir Idziak's heavily filtered images edge the television image towards greenish-yellows, which Idziak intended we should associate with urine.[22] The visual worlds of *Decalogue 5* and *A Short Film About Killing* are disgustingly ugly, particularly in outdoor scenes involving either the taxi-driver or Jacek. In *Decalogue 5*, the ugliness is not as disturbing as in the theatrical film, in part because we do not expect much of television images, but expect cinema images to be beautiful. (In the videotape of the cinema version, this ugliness is exaggerated further by increased contrast.) Additionally, the filters are used as a kind of mask, darkening parts of the image which Kieślowski and Idziak did not wish to show. On television, this masking effect does not make much difference, because there is too little expectation of visual information or beauty to make us attend to deliberate ugliness. But, on the film screen, to have large chunks smogged out feels like an affront. Idziak wanted the greenish-filtered images to avoid the possibility of inadvertently creating "a pornography of violence".[23] The sense of ugliness is also oddly increased in the cinema version by Idziak's trade mark shoulder-mounted camera, which in all his films increases the feeling of nervous vitality and participation. On the small screen of a television, however, a camera handheld as skilfully as Idziak's simply is not noticed. Similarly, on the television set, one hardly notices the three or four times Preisner's music kicks in. Once (in both versions) the music nervously raises tension during the first half of the taxi-driver's last drive. At the other times, it plays to a sentimental reading of Jacek's memory of his dead sister. In the film version, music is sparse, but there is perhaps twice as much, pointing not only to Jacek's memories, but also to the mood of quiet celebration of Piotr and his fiancée in the café.

A comparison of *Decalogue 6* and *A Short Film About Love*

Although *Decalogue 6* shares much with *A Short Film About Love*, the two differ more than *Decalogue 5* differs from *A Short Film About Killing* in that, in addition to added characterisation, stronger visualisations and stronger emotional elements in the cinema version, there is also a shift in tone. Kieślowski attributes the tone of *A Short Film About Love* to Grażyna Szapołowska, the actress who plays Magda, the free-spirited artist with whom Tomek, the 19-year-old postal employee, is obsessed. Szapołowska convinced Kieślowski that cinema viewers needed "story", a convention within which to see the film.[24] Kieślowski and Piesiewicz came up with a framing approach to the central story that partly removes the film from the straightforward realism of *Decalogue 6*. *A Short Film About Love* opens with Magda in Tomek's room while he sleeps. She sits in the chair from which he spied on her. The story itself then takes place, as if in flashback, but primarily from Tomek's perspective, until about two thirds of the way through. The film then shifts to her perspective and the film ends with her visit continuing, as she looks through his telescope and imagines spying on herself and Tomek, who now are friends who can comfort one another. This framing effectively makes the film a story of transgression, pain and a kind of spiritual reconciliation, whereas the *Decalogue 6* story, like most of the other episodes, is a story of transgression and its consequences.

Apart from the fact that the framing bookends change the context of the entire story, they do not account for most of the differences that one can point to between the film and the television story. The film's beginning and end do not take much time: Magda's opening takes only 83 seconds; and her new scene at the end is just under five minutes. Just as Kieślowski did for *Decalogue 5* and *A Short Film About Killing*, he edited *Decalogue 6* and *A Short Film About Love* in different rhythms, and had much more time to pay to characterisation and secondary characters in the film version. In *A Short Film About*

Love, the relationship between Tomek and his landlady is far more fully and complexly developed than in *Decalogue 6*.

Tomek's attitudes towards his own voyeurism are more fully developed. The cinematography – especially of voyeur scenes – is "artier", with longer lenses, lower angles and more modulated lighting used to observe Tomek as he observes Magda. The scenes with strong emotional reactions and tension – whether those of Tomek or Magda – take longer. (Because some of the scenes are reordered for the film, the use of different takes is masked.) Partly because of the cinema version's framing device, partly because of its slower rhythmic pace, and partly from different takes, *A Short Film About Love* comes off as a far more romantic film than anything in the *Decalogue*.

Viewer reactions, however, are not an entirely reliable guide to Kieślowski's work, because reactions stem from contexts that change with editing. Kieślowski clearly understands that context is the source of meaning. For example, *Decalogue 6* and *A Short Film About Love* share a scene in which Magda hears the sound of milk delivery in the hallway, opens the door, sees Tomek's landlady delivering the milk, and asks if Tomek is back yet. The landlady says, "Not yet". In *A Short Film About Love*, this scene occurs after we have watched Tomek return, but Magda remains unaware that he is back. She accepts the answer in pain, and looks away. In *Decalogue 6*, she has seen Tomek's and the landlady's shadows on the window; she knows he is back. The scene with the landlady is identical. But my notes on Magda's reaction (on first viewing the *Decalogue* tape) were that Magda turned away in anger at being lied to, whereas I had read the same reaction shot as turning away in pain in the film version. We read emotions in part by context, by what we expect – or project – expressions to mean.

Nevertheless, the above scene is an anomaly in that the general ordering of most of the story is (except for the opening and ending materials) similar in the television and film versions. A comparison of three scenes from *Decalogue 6* with their film counterparts is instructive in grasping how Kieślowski uses the extra time he has available in the film. *Decalogue 6* opens with Magda's first visit to the post office to cash in the money order for which she received a bogus notice sent by Tomek. The scene begins with Magda already talking to Tomek, and lasts 50 seconds. The film version goes a minute longer: it includes Tomek dealing with a pensioner, and includes more of Magda's hope for a financial windfall, as well as her anger when there is no money. Similarly, Tomek's theft of the telescope takes just over a minute and a half in *Decalogue 6*, and almost three minutes in *A Short Film About Love*. Here there are several differences. In the film, Tomek takes longer to find the telescope, and, once he has it home and has tested it, he carefully puts away the opera glasses which the telescope replaces; he is a voyeur who appreciates and respects the tools that have allowed him his pleasure. (Tomek always carefully covers and uncovers the telescope.)

More important is the scene in which Tomek awakens at the sound of tyres squealing outside. He looks out, sees Magda and a boyfriend quarrelling, and Magda running to her building. With the telescope, he watches her come into her flat, turn on the light, get milk, carry it to the table, accidentally spill it, sit down, and cry. In *Decalogue 6*, although the landlady calls for Tomek, they do not converse. The scene ends with Magda, seen through Tomek's telescope, sobbing while running a finger through the spilled milk. In *A Short Film About Love*, Magda's reactions take longer and are interrupted by a conversation between Tomek and his landlady. Tomek asks why people cry. The landlady gives some explanations, including "when they can't take it anymore". She explains how her son lessened pain: by creating a physical pain elsewhere. Tomek goes to his room and, in a game of "chance", closes his eyes, stabbing between his fingers with a scissors until he punctures a finger. Sucking his finger, he shares a separate, silent communion of pain with Magda. In *Decalogue 6*, the whole sequence takes three and a half minutes. In *A Short Film About Love*, the scene takes almost two minutes longer, but it allows Kieślowski better to modulate Magda's reactions, to show the intensity of Tomek's empathy for Magda, and to give a close glimpse of the complex relationship between Tomek and his landlady. In *Decalogue 6*, the sequence is important in that it motivates Tomek to put another money order notice in Magda's mail; that sets off her humiliation, his confession to her, and so on. In *A Short Film About Love*, the night-time sequence not only is among the more poignant in the film, but also allows us to grasp Tomek's dependence on his landlady and the motives that bring him out of a purely voyeuristic relation with Magda. It also prepares the Tomek-landlady relationship, so that after Magda's bearded lover punches Tomek out, it makes sense that Tomek's landlady places a cold cloth on his face, functioning as a mother. The discussion of pain, her helping him after he is hit, and the earlier scene in which she suggests that he can stay with her after her son returns together provide motivation for her wanting to protect him against Magda in the story's end sequences. The most important impact of length is on characterisation.

Emotional highs and lows are more extreme in *A Short Film About Love* than in *Decalogue 6*. When Tomek encounters Magda the morning after his beating, after he insists that he loves her but wants nothing from her, he rushes away from her. *Decalogue 6* shows him going down the hallway, turning, walking back, and then asking her to go for ice cream in a café with him. In *A Short Film About Love*, he runs to a roof, holds ice against his temples, and uses the pain and shock to get his head clear. Kieślowski cuts to him knocking on Magda's door. She opens it; he asks her to go for an ice cream date. The pain and despair make his elation at her acceptance seem all the higher, as he races his milk cart outside on the pavement (even though the elation footage is almost identical in the television and film versions). The extra footage in this sequence in *A Short Film About Love* takes just an extra minute, but changes the emotional terms of what follows.

The scenes between Magda and Tomek in the café and on the street afterwards are structured in the same way for television and film, although the film version spends a little over half a minute longer for more nuanced reactions from the two characters. The scene following, with Tomek in Magda's flat, runs a little over two minutes longer in the film than in *Decalogue 6*, again allowing longer, better articulated reactions from the characters and more footage of Tomek's landlady observing them through Tomek's telescope. The two extra minutes are two minutes of discomfort for the viewer, waiting for disaster and watching as it happens. Tomek's escape from Magda's flat is half a minute longer in the film. The actors use the time better to articulate the emotions of the two differently suffering characters, and to push the suspense and dread longer. The "commitment" which Kieślowski believed a cinema audience has[25] is in good part an acceptance of emotional extremes, and an acceptance of suspense, dread and similar narrative discomforts that are part of theatrical cinema's masochistic pleasures, which a television viewer is likely to be too distracted to appreciate.

Once Magda begins to feel guilty (basically from the moment Tomek rushes out) to the point at which she has seen that Tomek has returned takes fifteen and a half minutes in *Decalogue 6*. She encounters Tomek's landlady delivering milk, and then visits the post office, where Tomek bitterly tells her that he does not spy on her anymore (with the post office scene taking one minute and 41 seconds). In *A Short Film About Love*, Magda is allowed just over sixteen and a half minutes of unhappiness, to the point when she sees Tomek's silhouette in his room (but those minutes include the scene with the landlady delivering milk). Szapołowska uses much of the half-minute of additional footage to show Magda's wistfulness as she thinks about Tomek. In a few seconds, Szapołowska changes the film's mood considerably. What then follows is her visit to Tomek's room, her trying out of his telescope, and her remove to a satisfying fantasy. Overall, *A Short Film About Love* allows Magda, like Tomek, a far greater emotional range and a more likeable overall impression than *Decalogue 6* allows her.

One element that *A Short Film About Love* exploits is the relationship between viewing and voyeurism. In *Decalogue 6*, voyeurism appears in part as a moral transgression. The voyeur confesses, is humiliated, and becomes bitter; no matter that Magda now seems to want a human relationship with Tomek, the whole experience has made him bitter. In *A Short Film About Love*, voyeurism begins with a sexual connotation, but, in the crying scene, is transformed into a way of getting information about Magda's emotional dilemmas. It is Tomek's channel to other people. Voyeurism allows Magda to humiliate Tomek. But it also becomes his landlady's way of accessing what occurs when Tomek and Magda meet in her flat, and thus perhaps allows the old woman to intervene in Tomek's suicide attempt. Magda switches roles once she gets out her opera glasses; she begins to become "like" Tomek, and, finally, looking at her own flat window, can achieve her own fantasy relationship with the telescope to her eye – albeit with her eyes closed. As Kieślowski pointed out,[26] this story is always told from the viewpoint of the person who is loving, never the viewpoint of the loved one. That the loving person also is inherently a voyeur, a watcher of the beloved, becomes one of the film's central themes. The telescope and camera lens, of course, are closely related instruments, so the film viewer shares the practice of voyeurism with the characters and the filmmaker of *A Short Film About Love*. In *A Short Film About Love*, Kieślowski may well suggest that, even in a lonely society, we are, to some extent, united as a community of voyeurs, reaching out (however impotently) to see how others cope with their lives. Although that may not be a cheerful conclusion, it is far more optimistic – although less realistic – than the pessimism enforced by Tomek's reaction to Magda at the end of *Decalogue 6*.

Kieślowski believed that people go to cinema in groups, but watch television alone; lovers often hold hands in the cinema but almost never while watching television.[27] If that is true, the voyeurism in *A Short Film About Love* becomes a kind of loving, socially-acceptable counterpart to Adamek's moody cinematography and Preisner's romantic music. Preisner's music is particularly affecting in the scenes of wistful longing, firstly by Tomek and later by Magda. Preisner brings in his melody one guitar note at a time during Tomek's scenes, then adds a cello, violin or piano. For Magda's scenes, he more often begins with a one-finger piano melody, and then adds pizzicato violin and other instruments. The music celebrates loneliness and longing, but also suggests the possibility of simple ensemble harmony without any instrument losing the clarity of its voice. Preisner, no less than

Adamek and Kieślowski, conspires to romanticise *A Short Film About Love*.

Reflections

The two *Decalogue* stories strike one in the way that short stories often do, as compact vignettes wringing meaning from single predicaments. As such, 5 and 6 are remarkably well-structured and effective. Individually, however, each lacks time to establish complicity between a viewer and the filmmaker's vision. The two *Short Films* have sufficient time, but just barely. Sometimes the complicity which a film evokes is moral, as in the scene in which Tomek's landlady explains why people cry. Often it is aesthetic, in compositions such as the shot in which we see the taxi-driver's car through the undercarriage of a freight train. Sometimes it is a matter of seeing a pattern or images or symbolic elements which the filmmaker has set up for us to see. More often than we are aware while watching a film, aesthetic pleasure derives from music, such as the simple melodic motif that accompanies longing in *A Short Film About Love*. Perhaps the commonest invitation to complicity occurs when we become privy to well-acted private moments. Tomek buttering and eating his bread to accompany Magda's snack is one such moment. The cinema films have time for such moments, and thus for a kind of implicit relationship between Kieślowski and his viewers to form. It is precisely this implicit relationship that Kieślowski had to sacrifice to get his stories down to the 57-minute limit for a television hour.

How important is complicity or fellow-feeling between a filmmaker and his audience? This partly depends on one's view of Kieślowski. For Marin Karmitz, his producer on the *Three Colours* trilogy, Kieślowski was essentially a moralist working in the tradition of Rossellini, De Sica and Visconti.[28] As a moralist, Kieślowski perhaps reached the height of his powers in the *Decalogue*. But as a filmmaker? Here I think the feature films work far better, because there is more time for tension to develop between Kieślowski's documentary-based working methods and his subject-matter, and more time for his viewers to get our imaginations racing. As viewers, we need time to commit to a story, to become complicit with its people, aesthetic patterns and moral predicaments. We need time to watch, perhaps to judge, and then to understand the characters as we would perhaps ourselves like to be understood, even if only by strangers. How much time did Kieślowski need in order to utilise his talent to its fullest? I think the two *Short Films* stand at the border between just enough and too little. Even a master of compression needs time to work his magic.

Notes

1   Danusia Stok (ed), *Kieślowski on Kieślowski* (London; Boston: Faber and Faber, 1993): 86.

2   Miramax Films pressbook for *Blue* (New York, 1994). No pagination or sources of interview quotations listed.

3   Stok (ed): 202.

4   Pressbook for *A Short Film About Love* (Münich: Filmverlag der Autoren, 1989): 6. Quotations are from an interview by Frauke Hanck and from the discussion at the International Forum in Berlin in February 1989.

5   His producer, Marin Karmitz, said that he first cut of *Three Colours: Blue* (1993) came in at 140 minutes, and that successive versions trimmed it further until he finally reached 96 minutes. (Miramax Films pressbook for *Blue.*) In all probability, no record exists of any cut but the last one.

6   PAL VHS videotape copies of *Decalogue 5* and *Decalogue 6* from Artificial Eye, and PAL VHS videotape copies of *A Short Film About Killing* and *A Short Film About Love* from Tartan Video were used to determine scene lengths and cuts. Comments and times of 35mm prints are based on screenings of the Filmverlag der Autoren German release in 1989.

7   Miramax Films pressbook for *Blue.*

8   Krzysztof Kieślowski and Krzysztof Piesiewicz, *Decalogue: The Ten Commandments*, translated by Phil Cavendish and Suzannah Bluh (London; Boston: Faber and Faber, 1991): 115.

9   Ibid: 116.

10   Ibid: 154.

11   Ibid: 155.

12   Ibid: 120.

13   Ibid.

14   Ibid: 124.

15   Ibid: 126.

16   Ibid: 126-127.

17   Ibid: 152.

18   Stok (ed): 170.

19   Ibid: 166.

20   Pressbook for *A Short Film About Killing* (Münich: Filmverlag der Autoren, 1989): 3. Quotations are from an interview by Frauke Hanck and

from the discussion at the International Forum in Berlin in February 1989.

[21] Although the cinema version played at 85 minutes, transfer of footage to PAL video in Europe occurs at 25 frames per second, rather than 24, thus making a European video copy of the 85-minute film just under 82 minutes, with the picture without titles taking about 79 minutes. Thus, the film version runs about 79 minutes plus titles, against the television version's 56 minutes. The times to which I refer are from videotape copies. Although the *Decalogue* was also shot on 35mm, European practice is to shoot and transfer television materials at 25 frames per second, so no timing allowances need to be made for television. The video copies of the two *Short Films* do not accurately represent the visual qualities of the 35mm theatrical originals because, in copying to video from theatrical prints, picture contrast is increased. This is particularly problematic for *A Short Film About Killing*, which had a very "thin", contrasty and heavily filtered image to begin with. The tones in the two *Decalogue* versions look closer to the colour and contrast renditions of the theatre prints than do the video versions of the films.

[22] See Arkadiusz Jaeckel, "Kameraleute: Handwerker oder Mitautoren?", *Kameramann* January 1995: 48-52. Idziak vehemently defends the view that in Polish cinema the director and cameraman are co-authors.

[23] Ibid: 51.

[24] Stok (ed): 170.

[25] Ibid: 154-156.

[26] Ibid: 169.

[27] Ibid: 154.

[28] Miramax Films pressbook for *Blue*.

The curse of the law: *The Decalogue*

Paul Coates

Dekalog (*The Decalogue*, 1988) may well mark the degree zero of literary adaptation. Each episode in the ten-film sequence correlates – more or less – with one of the Ten Commandments. Laconic single sentences, one no more than four words (less in Polish), surely represent the threshold of the adaptable, a blank cheque to the imagination. Some theologians, meanwhile, read the Ten Commandments themselves as an expansion of a series of short, simple prohibitions, such as the one against killing. Kieślowski himself may have felt similarly impelled to expand, fearing that cleaving exclusively to the line of a single commandment might seem intolerably bare, however much he prized short-story terseness and clinical cutting. It is thus hardly surprising that several episodes seem swung in a cat's cradle of more than one commandment, although the multiplication of reference beyond the declared one-to-one format may also indicate (as St James' Epistle would suggest) that rupturing one injunction breaks the whole law. The multiple reference is enhanced by the disparity between the Catholic system for the commandments' subdivision, as employed by Kieślowski, and many Protestant ones (Catholic and Lutheran numberings, for instance, postulate two commandments against covetousness – nine and ten – where others see only one).[1] A sense of possible, only partly pursued, ramification dictates the characters' occasional Balzacian intersections with other episodes' protagonists. The series itself extends doubly beyond itself, two episodes existing in longer versions, and an incident from *Decalogue 9* being fleshed out as *La Double Vie de Véronique* (*The Double Life of Véronique*, 1991). The alternative versions of Kieślowski's series form reflect an acutely modernist sense of the works' variability. This may be read as the arbitrariness that follows the death of the authority incarnated in the father, perhaps the death of patriarchy itself – its meaning summed up in the father's last words to Witek in *Przypadek* (*Blind Chance*, 1981): "nic nie musisz" ("you don't have to do anything"). The state (metaphorically represented perhaps by the tower blocks of the series' housing complex) then becomes the father's ghost, its authority a vague, louring presence limned with continual absence.

This sense of arbitrariness marks the afterlife of Kieślowski the documentarist, for documentarists enjoy a particular freedom in the arrangement and selection of footage. Transferred to feature-making, this documentarist freedom uses omission to generate mystery. The resultant aesthetic is surely "Hebraic" in the sense of Erich Auerbach's famous analysis in *Mimesis*: the biblical text harbours unexplored pockets of shadow and teasing enigma, contrasting with the classical text's bright foregrounding of events.[2] Kieślowski's scepticism of the façades of Socialism in People's Poland surely encompasses doubt of the Enlightenment project in which Marxism originates: his emphasis on the importance of mystery implies more than Hitchcockian MacGuffins, for enigma recurs throughout *The Decalogue*.[3] Causality is often unclear, and *1* and *5* even suspend it: the published screenplay may explain the ice's fatal melting in *Decalogue 1*, but the film does not, and *5* makes no serious effort to motivate Jacek's murder of the taxi-driver. Nevertheless, the mysteries of *The Decalogue* are not necessarily metaphysical: neither myth nor Enlightenment satisfies Kieślowski. His passion for alternative scenarios recognises the limitations of each.

Decalogue 1: between myth and enlightenment

Here the relationship between *Decalogue 1* and its screenplay assumes particular interest. The film's suspension of causality has metaphysical overtones which the screenplay lacks. The opening piercing wind instrument breathes mystery and mortality, later accompanying a shot of a dead, frozen dog, and still later mournfully marking the fishing of Paweł's body from the icy water as the crowd sinks to its knees to acknowledge the *mysterium* of the event. Only Krzysztof, the bereaved father, does not kneel, unlike his believing sister Irena: the rationalist academic had calculated that the ice would support several times Paweł's weight, tested it himself, and allowed him to skate. Its breaking is inexplicable, suggesting malicious intervention by a providence determined to educate the rationalist (at one point, his computer comes on, apparently of its own volition, and the screen says "I'm ready", then a cracking ink bottle intimates disaster, the ink's spread picturing the uncontrollable, and the water below the ice). The tramp-like figure encamped by his lakeside fire at the start – crouched in Afghan coat, medievally meditative and exposed to the elements – is melancholy, impassive.[4] His appearance at the very outset, and subsequent intermittent reappearances in the sequence establish him as a tutelary spirit. It might not be appropriate to term him an "angel", as some critics have done, but his presence in various guises in most of the episodes has a non-realistic, possibly obscurely supernatural aura. Kieślowski may be dealing throughout with characters who have "slipped through God's fingers", as his last interview suggested could occur to human beings.[5] This figure stares at the camera, as if asking the audience the same mute question which his look will address to the series' other protagonists at decisive moments, its later recurrences mere conjugations of this first interrogation of ourselves. After all, may not the auditorium include people in crisis too? We may also participate in what Tadeusz Sobolewski terms "the solidarity of sinners".[6] When he wipes his eyes after Irena has wept for Paweł, the montage suggests both empathy and impassivity, for it may be simply a reaction to smoke. He looks across the ice at Krzysztof walking in the dark, testing the ice; the disaster does not involve experience contradicting reason, but affects all forms of the empirical. The screenplay, however, gives more mundane grounds for the ice snapping, and one character terms it "accidental": an electricity generating plant released warm water into the lake without warning. Where the screenplay's social criticism fits the documentaries' chronicles of officialdom's indifference, the film goes further, much as *Amator* (*Camera Buff*, 1979) had gone beyond its protagonist's documentaries.[7] Does naming the protagonist Krzysztof distance the rationalism of so much of the documentary tradition, part of the double life of the documentarist Kieślowski himself? (Krzysztof is the first to say "I don't know" in this film, using a phrase later repeated both by the computer and Krzysztof's sister – a key phrase for Kieślowski himself, and the title of one of his films.) Kieślowski himself was well-known to friends as an advocate of the virtues of computers.

The miraculous elements that may be deemed to flaw *Decalogue 1* may also be seen as Kieślowski's deliberate cracking of his own artistic bottle, for they identify with the providence that teaches Krzysztof the cruel lesson not to worship the false god of reason. Moreover, their juxtaposition with Irena's religiosity apparently underwrites her orthodox Catholic admiration of the Pope. After Paweł's death, a close-up of Krzysztof bathes him in green light from the computer screen that repeats the earlier, unheeded "I'm ready". Fortunately, Kieślowski's ending, as so often, complicates the matter. Krzysztof enters a church under construction nearby and overturns the candle-laden bench before the altar. The candles above the Madonna tip over, their dripping wax suggesting tears. The miracle of the Weeping Virgin is both bitterly and poignantly ironic: her hot tears are wax, and it is really the father who weeps. The image subtly transposes into another key the question of the relationship between Krzysztof and Paweł's mother, who is mentioned several times but never shown. Is she, like the Virgin, too remote to do anything –

ironically holding (through his death) the child she has, in fact, lost? Piquantly, the motif of remote control, so dear to Kieślowski, is found here too. Paweł shows Irena how the computer opens and closes doors, switches taps off and on... If Krzysztof is right to argue that computers can have personality, has this one exercised remote control over the lake? The questions cannot be answered, or the film itself totalised: a double exposure, it shifts in the light like shot silk. The Virgin's waxen tears show, however, that, although there may be mysteries, signs are not necessarily to be taken for wonders; it is hardly surprising that this film – like *Decalogue 8* – omits the priest of the screenplay's close. The film's latter part centres on Krzysztof; indeed, when Paweł is fished out of the water, there is no identifying close-up of him, only a long shot from Krzysztof's point of view. (Only the screenplay's penultimate scene shows us the dead boy's face.) As Krzysztof presses to his forehead the font's small plug of frozen holy water, its shape renders it a metaphor for the candle he would light upon Paweł's grave. The image is both rich and ironic, for it is also a frozen tear, just another one of the transformations of liquid the film effects – as if Krzysztof and Paweł were simply the hapless, blameless victims of liquid's inherent mutability. Its melting as Krzysztof clasps it to his forehead recalls the tragic melting of the lake.[8]

"What remains after death?", Paweł had asked Krzysztof. Beginning and ending with slow-motion shots of Paweł running at school, the film gives the same answer as *Camera Buff*: the afterlife is the filmed image. It is the same answer Krzysztof had given: what remains is "memory, the memory that someone moved in a certain way". That memory is the province of film. Elsewhere in *The Decalogue*, however, what remains is the name. In *Decalogue 6*, Magda learns Tomek's name only after he has gone to hospital. In *Krótki film o zabijaniu* (*A Short Film About Killing*, 1988), Jacek's name is not given until Beata calls it out halfway through the film, after he has murdered the taxi-driver and obtained his car. Uttering the name seals a fate: a couple of minutes later, the trial is over and Jacek is condemned. As visual contact attenuates, the name that takes its place is the straw at which one grasps – which slips through one's fingers – as the other disappears. For Kieślowski, names are epitaphs and signal the irretrievable. In this context, the answer to the question "what remains?" given in *Decalogue 1* differs from that of the other films only in its deeper helplessness and grief. It is the difference in *Decalogue 7* between Majka's mother crying out her name and Ania's stunned, silent watching (mouth open, unable to speak) as the train carries Majka away. The television image of Paweł is, in fact, a name, uttered with the agonised grief that is silent, for one never saw him go, and cannot comprehend why he had to. Only the mind's eye of the camera holds the forlorn hope of his return.

Decalogue 2: the allegorical world

The motif of a child's life or death recurs, like a musical theme, in *Decalogue 2*, where the tense, compulsively-smoking Dorota presses a doctor to learn whether or not her cancer-stricken husband Andrzej will live: if he will, she feels that she will have to abort the child conceived with another. Her dilemma is protracted and surely meant to become as intolerable for us as for her. The clots of dripping water in Andrzej's hospital room mark time agonisingly. Two sequences of concentrated virtuosity stand out. Each has the lengthy, contrived air of allegory. And for Kieślowski, as for Walter Benjamin, the allegorical world is one of ruin – the disintegration experienced by Dorota's husband – and its basic image is the death's head. The end of allegory is the escape from death. In the first of the two sequences, Dorota peers down through her flat's blinds as the doctor from whom she has sought information walks past; music's entry underlines the scene's significance as she begins to pluck leaves from a plant. Twisting it, unable to snap it, she releases it, and its elasticity permits its slow recoil: somewhere, something seemingly dead is still moving. The other moment begins as a stylistic *tour de force* ending in an allegory whose meaning recalls the plant sequence. It is night and, as so often, Dorota is looking out of a window, this time straight at us; the camera slides down to the doctor at his window, also looking, then swishes rightwards, its blur slowing and clarifying on arrival at Andrzej's hospital bed, where it comes to rest on a wasp busy climbing a spoon to escape the compote which Dorota has brought: allegorically it re-enacts the human escape from "certain" death, and we remember a fellow-patient telling Dorota to leave the jar as she hesitated to do so. Her husband might yet eat its contents.

The allegorical cast of these two moments demonstrates the film's demand that one *infer* connections. Its density can become opaque, however. One moment is so only to the non-Polish viewer, although, since *The Decalogue* was a co-production with Sender Freies Berlin, it indicates Kieślowski's readiness to lose part of his audience. The postman brings Dorota her husband's sick-pay and asks to see her identity card. Her reply, that she only has a passport, has implications probably lost on non-Poles, unaware that the Socialist regime required Poles to apply for passports: Dorota's possession of one indicates very specific travel plans, augmenting the significance of the mountain picture she had sat before in her flat. (That image, nevertheless, is one of Kieślowski's deadpan red herrings: her lover is a musician performing abroad, not the mountaineer who visits her.) Another detail, however, will baffle all viewers: the doctor asks Dorota what she is doing for hot water. The allusion to the incident that made the ice melt in *Decalogue 1* is incomprehensible even to a viewer of *1*, which abandoned its script's reference to the cause.

Thus, causality, so problematic elsewhere in *The Decalogue*, is so here too: when commenting on Andrzej's cancer, the doctor says, "we know nothing about the cause, little of the effects". When he later tells Dorota that death is certain, she is understandably sceptical. She forces him to declare this on oath – and so he takes the name of his God in vain. The doctor has borne false witness, but has he done it "against his neighbour"? It is surely significant that the story of *Decalogue 2* should be summarised in an ethics class in *Decalogue 8*, which also considers the preservation of a child's life, the proscription of false witness, and the role of memories of war (wartime loss of children has made the doctor particularly solicitous of life now). Although one cannot but ask whether the doctor has done the right thing, whether or not there is a right thing at all, and whether Kieślowski himself would endorse the doctor's choice of evils, no clear answer is forthcoming. Although sympathetic to Dorota, the film implies her egotism. Her early appearance before the image of a mountaineer, his eyes obscured by goggles, transforms her lovers into ciphers. But are they so for her, or for the Kieślowski who has only sketched them? Our point of view is so close to hers that it may be impossible to tell. Whether or not she successfully conceals her infidelity, however, is one dilemma accorded little weight.

Decalogue 2 has a stop-start rhythm, alternating between the camera's silent dwelling on Dorota – tense, paralysed, awaiting determination of her fate – and encounters that jerk things forwards marginally like a juddering station clock's hands. Encounter is no relief from solitude, but poses further dilemmas propelling one back into it. The film's mood – Dorota's – is one of inability to live either with people or without them. The rapid camera swish to and past Andrzej's bed near the end is a loosening of tension, of waiting in the shadow of potential death. When, at the very end, Andrzej asks the doctor if he knows what it is to have a child, his happiness is ironised only slightly, for the dripping water and flaking paint of the hospital room have taken us so far into disintegration as to generate relief at his Lazarus-like return, and the existence of the child symbolises the future. The doctor, that stickler for order who made sure it was past 12.00 before he had let Dorota enter, may have breached his code to prevent the abortion ("but you always taught us...", the assistant weakly protests, as the doctor comments on Andrzej's condition), but can he be condemned? Will Dorota do so? If the closing note leaves the question open, the story's reiteration in *Decalogue 8* shows that nothing has become any easier in the meantime, and that true dilemmas never really go away.

Decalogue 3: detectives in the dark

Decalogue 3 dramatises the commandment to keep the sabbath holy by presenting the relationship between a public holy day – Christmas Eve – and a girl's decision to set it aside for a prolonged encounter with her former lover. Thus, on Christmas Eve, Ewa summons Janusz from the bosom of the family where he has just played Santa Claus. Claiming that her husband Edward has vanished, she persuades him to help with her fruitless, night-long search. Only after 7 am does she confess to being still single: when she, Janusz and Edward parted three years ago, Edward married almost immediately. The night with Janusz has walked a knife-edge between indulgence and combating of the suicidal moods that often dog the isolated at Christmas. The ending leaves open the question of their final exorcism.

Decalogue 3 casts us as detectives, furnishing clues (often objects in close-up, weighed in the palm that stands for the pondering mind), but also precluding identification with the people for whom they are significant, and knowledge of quite what they might signify for them. When Janusz tests a razor-blade in the bathroom of Ewa's flat and notes its bluntness, we cannot know whether or not he deduces that it has been planted as unconvincing evidence of the presence of its owner, the Edward whom Ewa claims lives with her. We may even suspect Ewa of purposely planting evidence so feeble as to betray her real solitude. Our suspicions are neither confirmed nor denied, leaving the work in a blank, opaque suspension resolved only with Ewa's confession once she has succeeded in keeping Janusz beside her all night (a limited success, since "spending the night" with him has no amorous outcome: incompetent carollers interrupt an incipient kiss). Paradoxically, by so identifying with her tortuousness as to become tortured itself, the work blocks sympathy with her until the ending. Only then do we grasp how her life has been threatened by the extra weight which loneliness assumes amidst the season's ritually close-knit families. The theme of exclusion is hinted at in the very first moment, as Janusz passes Krzysztof from *Decalogue 1*: Christmas, that time of children, will be especially anguished for him – as it is a time of anguish for so many people. "This will be a Christmas for the children to remember", Janusz's wife comments on seeing him as Santa Claus, and the importance of children is underlined when Janusz's sighting of Ewa at midnight Mass precipitates the camera's slide forward from him and down to them. Our final realisation of Ewa's suicidal condition and the way it has infected Janusz with a self-destructiveness quenched only at the last minute is the traditional detective story coda in which truth emerges retrospectively, but the genre's intellectual bias and Ewa's abrasiveness paralyse the empathy with which Kieślowski so often irradiates the isolated. Our non-empathetic understanding dawns coldly after a night out, when we know what we should feel, but numbness prevents us doing so. Sharing Janusz's ignorance of the true state of affairs, in the end, we – like him – must modify our view of Ewa from exasperation to compassion. But, since our ignorance exceeds even that of Janusz, who at least knows throughout what Ewa once meant to him, we may feel excluded. The prevalence of the detective story form checkmates emotion. Moreover, even that form is undermined: not until the end are we given the problem to be solved. *Decalogue 3* feels laboriously contrived, its ending merely prompting a weary statement: "so that's why she...". The film is less an illumination of Ewa's condition than a lengthy postponement of its revelation. Its greatest interest may lie in the way in which the red, white and blue of the clothes, snow, night and police car lights flashforward to the trilogy, whose concern with liberty, equality and fraternity (and last-minute shifts in perspective) it also displays in capsule form.

Decalogue 4: playing Electra

Subtle contrivance and ambiguity characterise *Decalogue 4* as much as *Decalogue 3*, yet its fusion of calm and suspense (reflected in Zbigniew Preisner's score) is far more haunting and gripping. Indeed, this film begins the work's strongest sequence, the triptych deservedly placed at its heart. What makes it so impressive? Two factors seem paramount: the focus on a single character permits identification with her struggle with enigma, rather than suspending it tantalisingly between two characters (in *Decalogue 3*, Janusz and Ewa have mutual knowledge to which we are not privy, and the degree to which he divines the ground of her actions is never clarified); and that character's status as a daughter taps a theme central to the later films with Irène Jacob, and surely partly autobiographically-motivated, that of father-daughter relations, while the greater role accorded to the look of the witness, whose appearance halts Anka's toying with the letter addressed to her, corresponds to the greater sense of the numinous in Kieślowski's father-daughter films.

In *Decalogue 4*, Anka, an acting student, lives alone with her father Michał, and, although she has a boyfriend, her strongest affection is for her father. When Michał takes a trip, she finds a letter marked "to be opened after my death", toys with it, opens it, and finds another letter inside. We never see her open this second letter, addressed to her in her dead mother's handwriting, but, on Michał's return, she tells him she has read it and now knows him not to be her father. This changed status legitimates her offer of her affections. Since Michał resists seduction, she fears she has alienated him. On waking to find him absent, she panics. Seeing him outside, she rushes to him and says that she never really opened the letter. Together they burn it.

Decalogue 4 grows in cunning and density as it proceeds, ambiguity creeping up on it, its characters and ourselves. Its combination of passion and pure form reflects awareness that filmic passion itself may be purely a matter of form: of the *acting* of which Anka is a student. Where the face reveals nothing essential, one recalls that the actor's face began as a mask. The behaviourism of film, the externalism that can preclude certainty about a character's thoughts, comes consummately into play. The contrast between the two appearances of the "witness" figure illustrates this. As Anka lingers beside the water, musing on whether to open her mother's letter, the boat-bearing witness looks her in the eye. Opened, the letter could be a Pandora's box. So when Anka runs to Michał and says that she lied about having read it and the witness walks away, face unseen, it shows that the knot of conscious and unconscious motive – delusion and perhaps self-delusion – may now be too twisted for any look to cut through it. Anka pretends that nothing is irreversible, and seeks to banish the spectres of incest and memories of her bared torso; her flight from the irrevocable echoes that of many of *The Decalogue*'s characters. We never *see* her read the letter, only recite a text that may or may not be identical with it. As so often in Kieślowski's work, absence may or may not signify, and an ellipsis apparently motivated by laconicism may indicate repression. Does he expect us to remember that the text Anka recited began differently from the letter she burns? If *Decalogue 4* has a fault it may be that too much depends on a detail not all viewers will recall. Since Anka had voiced her dislike of irreversibility, a viewer may legitimately read her final volte-face as perhaps itself another untruth. In recalling the opening with the girl in her nightdress at the balcony, the end suggests the tantalising possibility of the past's undoing. The final pan that passes Anka's stuffed toy and comes to rest on the photograph of her mother and the men in her life asks, nevertheless, whether her daughter's step can ever be undone and full innocence restored; slow music overlays it thoughtfully, even mournfully. The gamble having failed, Anka withdraws her stake; but may not the croupier already have raked it in?

The key motifs of *Decalogue 4* concern ambiguous silence and incestuous fantasy. The majority of the silences feature Anka alone, unable to voice her fantasy, and are interleaved neatly with brief visits to the flat by ineffectual males (her boyfriend Jarek, and Michał's bald friend, Adam – the latter's second visit providing a somewhat forced, if necessary, interlude in Anka's intense duel with Michał). Silence within dialogues signifies too: Michał says nothing as Anka asks him to promise not to drench her (significantly, she opens the bathroom door nevertheless) and is again mute as Anka asks him to replace the other telephone (she tells Jarek he has, although she cannot be sure, and one may wonder retrospectively whether she was). When the oculist tests her sight with the word "father", she guesses the last letters, the motif of guesswork recurring when Michał says that she guessed the letter's contents. The father-daughter relationship is echoed by the one between the Professor and Anka at the theatre school. The exercise between herself as princess in love and her lover is framed to accentuate the presence of the Professor, who shocks her with his final masterful seizure of her chin. The relationship with Michał is summarised pregnantly in the opening images, unlocalisable anywhere in the film, of Anka watching him smoking through darkened blinds, and him then glancing down. Michał may smoke as they seek a bearable accommodation with truth and untruth, but the precise opening image does not recur. It thus acquires symbolic status, the cigarette signifying a sexuality reduced to no more than a sign, the blinds indicating the partiality of knowledge and the obstacles to direct encounter. The sense of coexistent alternatives that fascinates Kieślowski arguably receives its densest embodiment here, where the variants are not successive (as in *Blind Chance* or *The Double Life of Véronique*), but present themselves simultaneously through the work's self-referential meditation on acting. This preoccupation with variants may be most valid when they are logically related as opposites and excluded third, as in *Blind Chance* and here, where the excluded third is the impossible to which Michał refers (the impossible relationship of incest without transgression, or one in which the inequality of youth and age would vanish – the latter an anticipation of *Three Colours: Red* [1994]). *Decalogue 4* was planned initially as three variations, on the model of *Blind Chance*: the father's story; the daughter's; then what really happened. The desire not to repeat the model mechanically generated a different and more difficult formal triumph, in which the stories coexist in a palimpsest.

Theoretical interlude *à propos Decalogue 5* and *6*

Although, at this point, the reader might expect to find a consideration of *Decalogue 5* and *Decalogue 6*, I intend to bypass them, for Charles Eidsvik discusses them earlier in this volume, and my own thoughts about their longer versions can be retrieved elsewhere.[9] Nevertheless, the difference between *Decalogue 5* and the remaining sections can stimulate reflection on what characterises the whole sequence. The degree to which it alone explicitly *proscribes* an action recalls the biblical Ten Commandments, while its stylistic strategies can be juxtaposed suggestively with Kenneth Burke's meditations on negativity and the Decalogue. The Ten Commandments that shape Kieślowski's series comprise predominantly negative injunctions (a negativity that becomes "positive", however, when viewed as bestowing freedom to act by codifying wrong behaviour, rather than issuing prescriptions). Hence, as Burke notes – building on Henri Bergson's theories of negation – "though the injunction, 'Thou shalt not kill' is in essence an *idea*, in its role as *imagery* it can but strike the resonant gong: 'Kill!'".[10] If Burke is correct in arguing that the imagination, "having no negative, induces or deters by changes of intensity",[11] the green filters may represent intensifying deterrents. But, if *Decalogue 5* seeks to deter from killing, paralleling the state-sanctioned killing whose continuance the viewer might conceivably influence with the random private killing which no one can prevent, the effect of its filters also recalls the "dramatism" which Burke deems central to language: "'Dramatism' aims always to make us sensitive to the 'ideas' lurking in 'things,' which might even as social motives seem reducible to their sheerly material nature, unless we can perfect techniques for disclosing their 'enigmatic' or 'emblematic' dimension".[12] By veiling, the filters disclose that dimension of enigma. Kieślowski's dramatisation of negative injunctions surely propels him towards dramatism. The practice of his fiction films thus qualifies his drily objective (documentary?) statement that a filmed object is never more than a thing; it renders us aware that things exist "in the mind's eye", as well as the camera's, and can signify metaphorically. The key elements in this metaphorisation may often stem from collaborators (with Sławomir Idziak suggesting the filters of *Decalogue 5*, and Grażyna Szapołowska the imagined postscript to *Krótki film o miłości* [*A Short Film About Love*, 1988]), but they are far from completely foreign to Kieślowski himself, who has spoken of his wish to present a non-physical world usually resistant to filmic appropriation. For Kant, meanwhile, whose philosophy Burke also addresses, "the supernatural realm" is that in which humans act. Jacek's incarceration in the purely sensory shows his unfreedom and inhumanity even before formal placement behind bars. His identity is expunged definitively as he drives towards the murder and pulls his head up into the darkness to avoid the gaze of the young man – the "angel" figure – who witnesses key moments in the characters' lives. More than anyone else in the sequence, Jacek inhabits a Spinozan world characterised by negation: "For the world of our positive, natural sensations is determined; and in Spinoza's central formula all determination is negation. Such a determined world is, by the same token, inevitably, a realm of 'necessity'".[13] But, even as the leaden necessity bears down through the filters, Kieślowski counterbalances the determinism by problematising causality, suggesting the possibility of freedom, even if Jacek cannot find it. And, if Burke is right to discern the genius of the negative in all surprise,[14] one can begin to understand how Kieślowski's narratives can combine the openness of suspense with a profoundly sober negativity.

The negativity racking so much of *The Decalogue* is that of condemnatory law. The problematic nature of that law is apparent in the opening voice-over, stressing law's failure to prevent murder. Kieślowski's work may not be Christian, but its dramatisation of a law more honoured in the breach than in the observance, which therefore only administers death, may be deemed "negatively Christian", echoing the lament of Romans 7 or Paul's reference in Galatians 3: 13 to "the curse of the law". The concrete blocks of flats are as forbidding as the Mosaic tablets Paul describes as – for all their glory – "the dispensation of death, carved in letters on stone" (II Corinthians 3: 7). Documenting a perversely tortured, darkly unredeemed world may be only "negatively Christian", but it may become more positively so in the last three episodes, which deal with forgiveness and the dawning of unambiguous relationships. The sequence seems to follow a trajectory of descent and ascent, with *Decalogue 5* the nadir from which one cannot but rise. Kieślowski himself might not endorse this view, for he says "when I think of God, it's more often the God of the Old Testament...The God of the Old Testament is a demanding, cruel God."[15] If this is so, *The Decalogue* may benefit from the possible tension between Kieślowski's own Old Testament God and the New Testament one of the Catholic Piesiewicz – the tension between law and love. For the Christian, love finally triumphs over law, mercy over judgment, and the old covenant becomes obsolete (Hebrews 8: 13). *The Decalogue* may be read as depicting deformed life in the old covenant's shadow, recalling the Petrine metaphor of the yoke in Acts 15: 10. The last three episodes may see the beginnings of its replacement.

Decalogue 7: the name of the mother

The least satisfactory episode surely precedes that last triptych, and may well have been cramped by its derivation from an actual incident. In *Decalogue 7*, a daughter steals back the child she bore as a teenager and made over to her mother in a family plot to suppress scandal. The truth of the underlying incident cannot dispel melodrama's ring of falsity. With admirable self-criticism Kieślowski himself has judged it unsatisfyingly over-talky, among other things. There is indeed excessive verbal exposition of preceding events. Although the suspense over why Majka is kidnapping Ania is initially compelling and not prolonged to the point of opacity – as in *Decalogue 3* – the creaky mechanism of retrospective summary in the dialogue between Majka and Wojtek, her former lover, is perilously reminiscent of prime time soaps, as is the superfluous rehearsal of "the family saga" by her mother and father, which ends with the latter saying that they know this story already. Although the female playing is powerful, particularly Maja Barełkowska's evocation of Majka's petulant despair, selfish cunning, hysteria and near-terrorist determination, the men are fatally vague, as benignly anodyne as the teddy bears Wojtek appropriately sews, and the edge of drama is muffled in the cushion of their responses. The verbal allusions to the relevant commandment (Majka's "Can one steal what's already yours?") are over-explicit, even pretentiously paradoxical, and the merely serviceable cinematography becomes heavily predictable during the too-frequent telephone calls. Even Ania's sickliness is a little sickly-sweet. It may well have been impossible to sustain the power of *Decalogue 4, 5* and *6*, but *Decalogue 7* brings the sequence down with a bump from which it arguably never fully recovers, and suggests that Kieślowski's forte is relentless focus on the dynamics of an encounter between only two people. The excess of material and characters here means that too much is treated too sketchily or packed over-neatly into the dialogues' summaries. According to Kieślowski himself, the absence here of the witness figure simply reflects his own failure to film him correctly. It feels fitting for another reason, however: soap opera's permanent crisis prevents any one moment seeming so truly crucial as to warrant marking by his presence. Could his excision even suggest Kieślowski's fantasy of removing his own byline from this work? Only at the level of its names does it intrigue – "Majka" being so near to, yet so far from, the Polish for "mother", "matka", and that itself so fatally far from the intimate "mamo" which Majka cannot make Ania say to her.

Decalogue 8: Gentile as Jew

Decalogue 8 teases out some of the implications of the prohibition of false witness.[16] It begins with the interlocked hands of an adult and child. Darkness is falling, a musical theme invites naming as Yiddish, we are passing from courtyard to courtyard. The relationship between this prologue and the film's remainder will long be unclear: a cut to the morning workout of Zofia, a Warsaw University ethics professor, reveals nothing. Only much later will its haunting of the narrative outside which it hovers – at whose window, as it were, it taps – be understood to represent a wartime trauma's primacy in its protagonists' lives. They are Zofia and Elżbieta, her American Jewish translator. The scene is the only visible trace of Elżbieta's childhood recollection of being led to a potential hiding-place, only to hear Zofia say that she could not accept the child, since to do so would mean lying. Elżbieta cannot comprehend the evolution of the Zofia she knows out of that woman, and this torments and paralyses her.

Elżbieta's earlier efforts to confront Zofia with her deed have been unsuccessful. The way a situation now permits this mirrors Kieślowski's existentialist sense of the forming and deforming impact of situation on choice. While auditing Zofia's class, where a student has just recounted the story of *Decalogue 2*, Elżbieta hears Zofia end its discussion with the words "the important thing is that the child is alive". The comment's implications pull her to the front row, tugging her own story from her. Disruption by a student bursting in almost cuts it short. The interlude with the student both creates suspense and evokes the ease with which the field of events can frustrate individual intention (a frustration which *The Decalogue* records at every level of late-1980s Polish life). Zofia will later mention the need to think things through to the end – perhaps because they so often fail to reach it of their own accord. She listens agonised, and the telling so drains Elżbieta herself that she remains seated when everyone has left, with no natural noise on the soundtrack, only the opening Yiddish theme.

Things might end there, with Zofia seemingly compromised and driven away by shame, but the film thinks them through to the end. Despite the resistance of situations continually threatening to derail the process, the dark matter is worked through. Zofia offers Elżbieta a lift to her hotel but drives her to the primal scene of the courtyard instead. Elżbieta walks around, then hides. Unable to find her, Zofia becomes distraught, and the evocation of her anguish through the Yiddish theme suggests the women's possible meeting in a commonality of suffering. Soon after, in Zofia's flat, an explanation will be furnished: the child's transfer was blocked because the couple due to shelter it were rumoured to be linked to the Gestapo, and might have betrayed the underground organisation to which Zofia and her husband belonged. Before giving the explanation she terms "banal", Zofia tells Elżbieta: "if you crossed the Atlantic expecting a mystery, you'll be disappointed". However, although all is resolved between Elżbieta and Zofia, the conversation shifting to the second person and Zofia's face being shot head-on, intimately, from Elżbieta's viewpoint, on another level there is unfinished business, as the ending shows. On discovering the falsity of the rumour linking the prospective foster couple to the Gestapo, Zofia tried to apologise to the man – "but that is not enough". Elżbieta's efforts to address him are frustrated likewise: a tailor (is it significant for his identification with the Jews that this profession is so often associated with Jewishness?), he will not speak of the past, only of making her a dress. Zofia says that he has perhaps suffered too much, and Elżbieta terms Poland "a strange country". The last image shows him, played by the great Tadeusz Łomnicki, staring through the barred window of his run-down shop at the silent spectacle of the two women beside Zofia's car.

Many critics have noted that several episodes of *The Decalogue* dramatise more than one commandment, or intersect only elliptically with the expected one. The arbitrariness of the illustration may correspond to the disparities both between the protagonists' codes and those of the commandments, and between the Polish *Lebenswelt* and that of the Jews. Zofia may seem to be in the dock at first, but Catholicism is not. After Elżbieta's story, a student condemns the factitious reasoning of the couple who refused the child: they could hardly have been Catholic, for the commandment's intent is to forbid false witness to one's neighbour's harm. In the published screenplay – although not in the film – Elżbieta says that after many years she became interested in Catholicism. The screenplay also includes a priest's provision of a false identity card for the Jewish child, ending with Zofia telling a priest – one presumes the same one – that the child is alive. Since Kieślowski discards anything that has not registered well on celluloid, the motive for omitting these details is probably aesthetic, although is it possible that a tension exists here between the work of the Catholic Piesiewicz and Kieślowski himself?

In *Decalogue 8*, Jewish and Catholic experiences mingle, as well as diverge. I have already mentioned the use of the Yiddish theme to evoke Zofia's consternation at Elżbieta's disappearance. Equally importantly, her unwillingness to use the word "God" in her work echoes Judaic proscriptions. "Można nie wątpić nie używając słów", she remarks, almost untranslatably. ("One can be without doubt without using the words" perhaps.) The witness figure (the camera slides sideways to find him during Elżbieta's telling of her story) resembles the invariably winged messengers of Christian iconography less than the young men who visit Abraham in the Old Testament. (His description as "young man" in the screenplays neatly avoids the taint of late-1980s angelology, while also sanctioning it by recalling those angels' manifestation to Abraham.)[17] I have mentioned already how Kieślowski's aesthetic of gaps echoes the biblical one described by Auerbach. *Decalogue 8* shows both possible reconciliation and the enormous odds against it. The final isolation of the tailor, trapped still in his traumas, reminds us that it could easily not have happened. A sort of reprise, it recalls others in need of liberation still. Meanwhile, the Praga district in which the film ends becomes another version of the uncanny place represented by the opening's courtyard. In 1986, just before the shooting of Kieślowski's film, German poet and essayist Hans Magnus Enzensberger travelled to Poland – historically a place of "the Other" for many Germans – and visited Praga. Opposite the main body of Warsaw, on the far side of the Vistula, it alone was untouched by the Warsaw Uprising and the city's wholesale devastation in its aftermath. Enzensberger recalls Alfred Döblin's description of it, almost 60 years earlier, as a place whose "vendors are almost all Jews", and adds "[o]nly the Jews are no longer there. Kreuzberg, Prenzlauer Berg, Wedding, and Lichtenberg – what are these Berlin remnants compared to Praga, the only quarter of Warsaw dominated not by postwar but by prewar times? Faces here are marked by an older vitality, indissolubly mixed with an older misery."[18] Perhaps he stood before the shop Kieślowski gives his tailor? "The tiny shop window of the hatmaker: dust on pastel-colored creations, melancholy reminiscence of the time when Warsaw was known as the Paris of the East".[19] In *Decalogue 8*, abandonment is an historical experience that links Poles and Jews.

Decalogue 9: "A Short Film About Telephones"

One of the sequence's richest works, *Decalogue 9* may be read as asking how much a person needs to live. We begin with Roman (Romek) learning of his impotence. When he then almost crashes his car, the proximity of the witness suggests it was a suicide attempt. How to live with self-image impaired, expectations horribly reduced? Can Romek live without sexuality? Can his wife Hanka? Casting the theme in another key, can the gifted, hospitalised singer really survive on the very little she says that she needs, foregoing singing? (*The Double Life of Véronique* will reiterate this question.)

Romek's impairment makes him feel only half a man – whence the proliferating mirror images and Hanka's splitting of her needs between him and a lover who gives physical release. (Does the lover's *youth* indicate that he, too, is not fully a man, and hence no real rival to Romek, only his detached other half?) Gazing firmly into the camera at the outset, Romek may seem able to "look the facts in the face", but when Hanka asks "do you love me?" and he silently turns away (she has to turn his face to her), one may suspect that, just as she does not want to talk everything out (a motif from *Decalogue 8*), so there are things he cannot face up to. This shared incapacity renders them deeply akin, and the crosscutting, compositions and racked focus repeatedly suggest simultaneous separation and co-presence. Hanka and Romek may be apart as she lies in bed and he pushes his bike in the river, but she starts as if woken by the splash. Walls and doors across the screen divide them, but the way in which separation graduates into unity can be seen at work paradigmatically as Romek asks Hanka a physics question when she enters the bathroom: he may seem to look one way and she another, but, as she moves forward, her reflection's appearance shows that she has been facing him all the time. This movement arguably is that of the film as a whole.

Many of the images of *Decalogue 9* are partly occluded, betraying the partial nature of the characters' mutual knowledge, holding always before us Romek's sense that he is not whole. The image is equally impaired. If, for Freud, blinding means castration, may not restricted vision correspond to impotence? And lest we feel superior, our knowledge is often equally limited. It is guillotined when Romek picks up the telephone and passes it over to Hanka, the call being for her: the soundtrack that began by carrying both the voices on the line now carries only Hanka's, and, as the camera focuses on Romek, we are forced into his position of distant, jealous surmise. The blue colour scheme and the melancholy of the "Van den Budenmayer" song playing at this moment push us further into Romek's corner of depressed exclusion. (Indeed, blue dominates throughout, appearing on Hanka's ski-boots and KLM uniform, Mariusz's anorak, Romek's hospital shift, the train Hanka takes to Zakopane, and in the many night scenes.) Frequent shots through doors cramp characters, restricting their space and options. Sitting in the car – watching as others act – Romek is constricted, and the imagery of cars ironically taps their association with sexuality, power and release. When he holds a filter for a man filling his tank, one cannot ignore the ironic phallic overtones, and wonders whether Romek himself can do so. The effect of Romek's predicament on his status is dramatised in the plethora of high- and low-angle shots, with him often seated or crouching, enjoying prestige only at the hospital, where his first dialogue with the singer is shot to emphasise his greater height (and stress perhaps that only *vis-à-vis* a female patient is his status still intact). Near the end, however, the usually fraught visual vocabulary of high and low angles and restricted vision conjugates happily into Romek's look down through a window at a child playing. It represents the child that will make all the difference to the marriage, the child Romek and Hanka never wanted but are now preparing to adopt.

Decalogue 9 resembles a composite image of Kieślowski's last four films, the chrysalis from which they emerged. The girl with a heart ailment is a sketch for Weronika and Véronique; the blue colour scheme anticipates *Trois couleurs: bleu* (*Three Colours: Blue*, 1993) (and shows the colouristic mastery that surely caused Sobociński's selection for *Three Colours: Red*); Romek's impotence anticipates *Trois couleurs: blanc* (*Three Colours: White*, 1994); and phone-tapping after rejection foreshadows *Red*, as does Sobociński's pertinaciously racking focus. As *The Decalogue* approaches its end, it seems to become aware of having an history itself, perhaps responding to the changing mood in its last three parts. Where *Decalogue 8* quoted the story of *Decalogue 2*, following the "asymmetrical composition" which Tadeusz Szyma discerns in the sequence,[20] *Decalogue 9* sends out feelers to *Decalogue 6*. There is a moment in that film when Tomek, the young postal official about to insert a forged summons in Magda's letter-box, passes a man wheeling his bike out of the stairwell. *Decalogue 9* identifies that man as Romek. His earlier appearance was surely no accident. The two episodes become variants, each centred on a teenage love of an older woman, the interconnection underlined by each girl's frizzy blondeness. *Decalogue 9* consigns this love to a sub-theme: Mariusz may seem truly to love Hanka (his hope of retaining her love even without sex echoes her earlier avowal to Romek), but we do not see his reaction to losing her. Indeed, like Magda, Hanka may not love him – she looks sideways during intercourse, as if, for her, unlike Magda, love's physicality is its nether side, not "all there is to it". Tomek's slashed wrists recall Jiří Menzel's *Ostře sledované vlaky* (*Closely Observed Trains*, 1966), ironically demonstrating that, even when the lovelorn teenager takes the advice Menzel's doctor offers and finds an older woman to help overcome *ejaculatio præcox*, the result is no happier. *Decalogue 9* may revise Kieślowski's own revision of Menzel.

In asking how much a person needs to live, *Decalogue 9* asks how much isolation anyone can stand. Much of it unfolds in the gripping, silent solitude typical of Kieślowski. The witness' presence, as it were, personifies the camera's. For, even when most isolated, neither Romek nor Hanka is so entirely; as in *Decalogue 6* – which only ends when surveillance does – there are hidden monitors. But, if Romek survives his second suicide attempt and Hanka's fruitless long-distance efforts to avert it (her call to Warsaw being thrice frustrated: by a garrulous local hogging the pay-phone; by the engaged signal; and by Romek's position in the door, unwilling to pick up the phone, his mind already made up), a providence seems to be at work all the same, over and above the Pope who is a man in a funny postcard and whose mock-binoculars wittily recall *Decalogue 6*. When Romek rings Hanka from the hospital, having failed to kill himself, her words (almost the film's last ones, and its first mention of God) are "God, you're there". Relieved casual profanity, or implicit admission that God is there too? One way or another – whichever variant one picks – it is a happy end, before the alternative happy end of the satyr play of *Decalogue 10*.

Decalogue 10: exchange and robbery

That satyr play is self-reflexive, satirising the moralist's seduction by what he condemns. It is also about brotherhood, the first panel in a diptych on brotherhood completed by *Three Colours: White*, which again pairs the marvellous Jerzy Stuhr with Zbigniew Zamachowski. Although Artur, dishevelled lead singer of the fictive City Death, gives the episode an unusually raucous beginning – Kieślowski letting *his* hair down? – and belts out "Kill, commit adultery, covet things every day of the week", the director knows the advocacy to be ironic, and is far from blaming rock music for society's systematic transgression of the Commandments. "I don't want a thing from you and I won't give you a thing" runs a later lyric: Artur appears commendably free of covetousness: "Where does it come from, this urge to have something?", he later asks brother Jerzy. Jerzy should know: besuited, bourgeois, married, with a permanently offended, toadlike grimace, he is the reverse of his footloose younger brother. Events' conspiracy gives Artur an answer to his question. For when the brothers inherit their father's stamp collection and their jaws drop on discovering its fabulous worth, Artur – the artist and, to some extent, the double of Kieślowski himself – finds the itch to own creeping up on him too. He it is who first worries about security arrangements, and when only Jerzy's kidney can obtain the Austrian rose mercury and complete a priceless set, he urges the sacrifice, even resorting to the moral blackmail of terming it a humane gesture towards the daughter of the dealer who offered the exchange. Not that Jerzy licks his lips any less over the hoard. When the philatelic society's chairman reveals its value, dramatic drums roll; epiphanic music sounds as the album-filled cabinet opens. Jerzy goes through with the operation, but, while he is under the knife, and Artur – in hospital to visit him – is busy with an adoring nurse, thieves clean them out: a sardonic montage shows the nurse's hat cast aside, Artur's bag landing on it, surgical gloves sucked onto hands – and a blowlamp at work on a bar. The crisply disdainful cutting between metonymic objects displays the world-rulership of things. Left only with the Austrian rose mercury, the brothers may seem at rock-bottom, but worse is to come: each informs a detective that he suspects the other. But, although the crime has the hallmarks of an inside job, when they see the bent dealer meet another one, each accompanied by a guard dog remarkably like the one they had been persuaded to buy, they realise why Lokis was so docile when the intruders came. The negative doubling of mutual denunciation, their low-point, becomes positive instead. Each has bought the same set of new issues – inheriting the father's passion – and each confesses to shopping the other. Laughing, facing each other like mirrors bookending the screen, they recover the childhood camaraderie that first resurfaced when planning how to guard the hoard. For all their differences, they are brothers, and laughter has the last laugh over the dead body of covetousness. "If you don't want it, it ceases to exist", Artur had said earlier. Perhaps they did not sufficiently want the treasure to keep it in existence. Perhaps what they really wanted was their once-lost friendship. Satire does not have the last word, for *Decalogue 10* knows satirists, too, are open to seduction by the fatal strategies of things. This satirist does not deem himself superior, and invites others to shed their sense of mutual superiority too, as do Artur and Jerzy. For, if and when we do, we, too, become brothers.

Notes

[1]   Thus, Véronique Campan's view that the excision from Kieślowski's *Decalogue* of "the second commandment" forbidding graven images is a significant, and perhaps even "structuring" absence, overlooks the commandment's absorption into the first in the Catholic numbering system employed in Kieślowski's native Poland. The numbering that offers two commandments against covetousness, meanwhile, owes more to Deuteronomy than Exodus, since only in Deuteronomy is the neighbour's wife mentioned first. (Incidentally, Deuteronomy prefaces Moses' reiteration of the Law with a particular insistence on the proscription of graven images – 4: 12, 15-19 and 23 – which surely decreases the likelihood of a division of the commandments based upon Deuteronomy being deaf to that prohibition.) The numbering controversy dates back to Augustine and Philo, and resurfaces in the theological debates of the 16th century. But, although Campan's premise is shaky, her reading of the functions of absence in *The Decalogue* is often sensitive and fruitful. See Véronique Campan, *Dix brèves histoires d'image* (Paris: Presses de la Sorbonne Nouvelle, 1993).

[2]   Erich Auerbach, *Mimesis: The Representation of Reality in Western Literature*, translated by Willard R Trask (Princeton: Princeton University Press, 1953): 3-23.

[3]   See his interview with Michel Ciment for *Le Monde*, "'Ce qui m'intéresse c'est l'homme'", 16 September 1989: 19, stating that "[e]n accordant trop d'importance à la raison, nos contemporains ont perdu une dimension de la vie" ("in attributing too much importance to reason, our contemporaries have lost one of life's dimensions"), or his stated interest in rendering on film the "realm of superstitions, fortune-telling, presentiments, intuition, dreams". See Danusia Stok (ed), *Kieślowski on Kieślowski* (London; Boston: Faber and Faber, 1993): 194.

[4]   Various critics have described this figure as an "angel" (for example, Georgia Brown, "Angels Passing", *The Village Voice* 6 November 1990: 69), although Kieślowski himself notes that the taxi-drivers bringing Artur Barciś to the set termed him "the devil" (Stok [ed]: 159). For more remarks on this figure, see note 17 below.

[5]   Interview with Jacek Błach and Agata Otrębska, "Ponieważ są ciągle ci ludzie..." ["Since there are always these people..."], *Incipit* 2 (April 1996), reprinted in Tadeusz Lubelski (ed), *Kino Krzysztofa Kieślowskiego* (Kraków: Universitas, 1997): 296: "Myślę, że jeżeli jest ktoś taki jak Pan Bóg, który stworzył to wszystko, co nas otacza i nas także, to my mu się bardzo wymykamy z ręki" ("I think that if someone like a God above exists, someone who made everything around us, and made us too, then we very much slip out of his grasp").

[6]   Krzysztof Kieślowski and Krzysztof Piesiewicz, *Decalogue: The Ten Commandments*, translated by Phil Cavendish and Suzannah Bluh (London; Boston: Faber and Faber, 1991): 1-30. Although, for some, the film's omission of the tragedy's everyday cause might lay it open to charges of mystery-mongering, it also omits the screenplay's somewhat supernatural scene 26, with its lengthy dialogue between Krzysztof and his computer, and removes the final scene's priest. It is preferable to the screenplay in many respects. Its treatment of Krzysztof's reactions to Paweł's enquiry about death, for instance, is more fine-grained, sensitive and generous to Krzysztof, who no longer responds by despatching Paweł to the dictionary for a definition, but speaks it himself. The face-to-face reply enhances his intimacy with his wide-eyed, inquisitive son, showing them sharing life as a scientific adventure. Similarly, the film has Krzysztof pitch the opening poser to Paweł at his level, using Miss Piggy as one of its imaginary protagonists. The film surely also benefits from the omission of the screenplay's final, halting but over-explicit "who to talk to?". Ironically and sadly, the censoriousness towards Krzysztof manifested by certain overtly religious commentators is, I think, less genuinely Christian than the position of Kieślowski himself. (*Decalogue 5*, for instance, preserves the Christian distinction between the sin and the sinner, alluded to by Piotr in his cell dialogue with Jacek.)

[7]   Tadeusz Sobolewski, "Solidarność grzesznych. O *Dekalogu* Krzysztofa Kieślowskiego", *NaGłos* 1: 1 (1990): 91-101.

[8]   See Joël Magny, "*Decalogue*, I; le feu et la glace", in Michel Estève (ed), *Études cinématographiques 203-210: Krzysztof Kieślowski* (Paris: Lettres Modernes, 1994): 91: "les images constituent une série d'échos, d'associations de formes ou de matières – eau, lait, glace, encre, larmes, cire de bougie – et surtout de transformations: le lait en glace blanche puis, réchauffé, en une bouillie infâme" ("the images comprise a series of echoes, associations of forms or substances – water, milk, ice, tears, candle-wax – and, above all, of transformations: milk into white ice and then, warmed-up, into a foul pap").

[9]   See my *The Gorgon's Gaze: German Cinema, Expressionism, and the Image of Horror* (Cambridge: Cambridge University Press, 1991): 188-192, for

A Short Film About Killing; and *Film at the Intersection of High and Mass Culture* (New York: Cambridge University Press, 1994): 28-32, for *A Short Film About Love*.

[10] Kenneth Burke, "A Dramatistic View of the Origins of Language", in his *Language As Symbolic Action: Essays on Life, Literature, and Method* (Berkeley; Los Angeles: University of California Press, 1966): 431. Emphases in original.

[11] Ibid. Emphases in original.

[12] Ibid: 429.

[13] Ibid: 430.

[14] Ibid: 433.

[15] Stok (ed): 149.

[16] A slightly longer version of this analysis of *Decalogue 8* forms part of my "Walls and Frontiers: Polish Cinema's Imagination of Polish-Jewish Relations", in *POLIN: Studies in Polish Jewry* 10 (1997): 221-246.

[17] Campan's description of his role is particularly useful: "il offre la paradoxale caractéristique d'être aisément reconnaissable sans être pourtant identifiable. On ne le connaîtra jamais, on ne pourra pas lui attribuer de nom, de rôle, de parcours narratif, de vie. Il restera jusqu'au bout un être inassignable, pure surface sans consistance, image" ("he has the paradoxical characteristic of being easily recognisable and yet not, for all that, identifiable. One would never know him or be able to assign him a name, a role, a narrative line, a life. He will remain to the last an unassignable being, a pure surface without consistency, an image") (54-55). Somewhat more controversially, she also likens the "young man" to the Eternal Jew, whose failure to discern the divinity in Christ she links to the dark visibility of the transcendent in general in the film (51). Such invisibility can be characteristic of "sacred" cultures as well as profane ones, however, and is not necessarily a sign of modernity: St Paul can speak of people "entertaining angels *unawares*" (Hebrews 13: 2. Emphasis added.) Sight without insight is blind to the numinous.

[18] Hans Magnus Enzensberger, *Europe, Europe: Forays into a Continent*, translated by Martin Chalmers (London: Hutchinson Radius, 1989): 183.

[19] Ibid.

[20] Translated from the Polish: "kompozycja 'Dekalogu' jest w pewnym sensie asymetryczna" ("the composition of the 'Decalogue' is in a sense asymmetrical"). Tadeusz Szyma, "Dekalog osiem", *Tygodnik powszechny* 11 February 1990.

Women in Kieślowski's late films

Alicja Helman

TRANSLATED FROM THE POLISH BY PAUL COATES

The role which women play in several of the last films of Krzysztof Kieślowski is one of the essential features that allow one to analyse the transformation in his artistic position. Of course, his work has evolved continually, from the very first documentaries to the *Trois couleurs* trilogy (*Three Colours*, 1993-94), but that "evolution" was of the kind that is typical and normal for all developing, maturing talents. The transformation dates from *La Double Vie de Véronique* (*The Double Life of Véronique*, 1991), although several films from the *Dekalog* (*Decalogue*, 1988) foreshadow it. And it occurs through women, or rather in the way in which they are treated: in the functions they fulfil in the narratives, and in their significance for the formulation of the author's message.

It is therefore hardly surprising that there came a time when Kieślowski's work attracted the attention of a wing of feminist criticism, which X-rayed it thoroughly, although without the expected results. Kieślowski had changed his attitude towards women, but had not gone from being a "male chauvinist" to being a "feminist", and this lent a tone of disappointment to these feminist analyses and their conclusions, demonstrating the traditionalism of the director's position in this respect. The instruments of feminist analysis were simply unable to penetrate the specific nature of this transformation, or to define its characteristic features.[1] Kieślowski did not suddenly become a spokesman for "women's issues", but subjected the feminine element in culture and the modern world to subtle analysis – while also becoming, in a sense, its advocate. The female characters of his last films may be regarded as *portes paroles* of the author himself, which must seem surprising in the context of the whole of his previous work, which is masculine *tout court*.

The most traditional treatment of female protagonists can be found in Kieślowski's films such as *Amator* (*Camera Buff*, 1979), *Przypadek* (*Blind Chance*, 1981) and *Bez końca* (*No End*, 1984), although, of course, this does not apply to all their female figures, most of whom are secondary ones. Irena, the wife of Filip Mosz in *Camera Buff*; the doctor who is married to Witek (the hero of *Blind Chance*) in one of its three versions; and Urszula, the main female protagonist of *No End*

116

– these are all what might be called "homebodies", women whose feelings, actions and desires revolve around family life. Where their husbands share these desires and ascribe permanent value to the peace and quiet of the family hearth, everything goes well. We first see Filip at the moment of his child's birth, when he is a happy man, and the life of Witek – who is genuinely devoted to his wife – unfolds smoothly and successfully, but the elements that will ruffle this harmony soon manifest themselves. They stem from a particular conservatism and narrowness in the women, who do not want to see any changes, and fear anything that might divert their husbands' attention from them and the "nest" they have built. *Blind Chance* gives a first tremor of such a possibility: Witek's wife is apprehensive of his trip to Libya, and would prefer him to remain at home. Admittedly, there are mitigating factors: she is pregnant, and perhaps even has a foreboding of Witek's death during the trip. In *Camera Buff*, however, the meek and gentle Irena reacts to her husband's interest in amateur filmmaking by metamorphosing into an hysterical hag. His attention is devoted to his hobby; it soaks up his time; he begins to have some modest success; and, in the end, the prospect of collaboration with television opens up before him. At that point, Irena decides to leave him, convinced that her husband's activity is against the interests of her home and family. Irena is a classic representative of a certain complex of male experiences on the subject of women who want to hold the whip hand at home, keep their men on a tight leash, and subordinate them to a narrow conception of "family interests", with recompense in the form of the virtues of domesticity.

Urszula only appears to be the protagonist of *No End*. Although events revolve around her fortunes, by remaining passive she "hands over" the film to the male figures, who act, experience conflicts and undergo changes – the old lawyer, his trainee and the detained Solidarity activist. We first encounter Urszula immediately after the death of her husband, suffering profoundly, unable to return to normal life. She is a beautiful woman, good translator and tender mother, but none of these roles is capable of reconnecting her to life. She does not seize the possible opportunity to participate in the affairs of her husband, a lawyer who defended Solidarity activists charged under martial law. Urszula decides to commit suicide. She did not realise it, but she was first and foremost a wife, the companion of her husband, his proverbial "other half". Her life was thus merely supplementary to his, not a self-sufficient whole.

In writing of a "masculine" and a "feminine" Kieślowski, however, I do not wish to resort to psychoanalytic categories, even though a psychoanalytically-oriented anthropology maintains that every person's psyche is a bisexual entity comprising features which culture deems fundamentally "masculine" and others fundamentally "feminine", although the proportions between them and the extent to which one predominates perhaps vary at different periods in life. I do not intend to view Kieślowski the artist and man from this angle, but rather as the authorial image that can be read from the works alone, without any other form of verification.

If we set *The Decalogue* against his four last films (or rather three, for *Trois couleurs: blanc* [*Three Colours: White*, 1994] does not fit the model I aim to present) – *The Double Life of Véronique*, *Trois couleurs: bleu* (*Three Colours: Blue*, 1993) and *Trois couleurs: rouge* (*Three Colours: Red*, 1994) – we immediately note a fundamental change. For all their differences, the films' individual figures clearly form two constellations. One contains the Polish actresses of *The Decalogue*, while the other – considerably smaller – one comprises Irène Jacob and Juliette Binoche. This does not mean that there is a total absence of intermediaries between the two groups. Adrianna Biedrzyńska (Anka in *Decalogue 4*) and the heroine of *Decalogue 8* are closer to the French heroines, while Julie Delpy in *White* is the close sister of the figures in the Polish films. This doubtless spoils the symmetry, but I do not think it undermines the thesis that Kieślowski's position underwent a deep-seated transformation.

Kieślowski as an author of "masculine" films – the Kieślowski of *The Decalogue* – constructs his representational world from a strictly male viewpoint. This world has been summoned into being by, and is exceptionally well-designed for, men: it is the world of male law, and its contradictions, conflicts and dramas are male affairs. It is the men who struggle with this world, are allotted the function of active subjects, and experience its fundamental dramas of mind and conscience. There are sections of *The Decalogue* in which women have no real function (*Decalogue 1*, *5* and *10*), while in the overwhelming majority of its parts their roles exist *vis-à-vis* and for the sake of men. Only parts 7 and 8 speak of purely female conflicts and issues, although one could add that the story told by *Decalogue 8* has universal resonance, and could equally well have played itself out between men.

Numerical considerations are secondary, however. Superficially, one could speak of there being "partnerly" arrangements in *Decalogue 2*, *3*, *4*, *6* and *9*, with the conflict unfolding between a woman and a man in *3*, *4* and *6*, and between a woman and more than one man in *2* and *9*. The essential matter, however, is the conception of woman and femininity. Femininity is a foreign element, fundamentally hostile and threatening to the man, essentially incomprehensible, while a woman is by definition irresponsible, unbalanced, freakish, indifferent to logic and common sense, and subject to uncontrollable emotions.

One could simplify and describe Kieślowski's women as "bad" were it not that their creator placed them "beyond good and evil", because they lack a moral dimension – and this lack seems to be their paramount feature. The effect each exerts on the lives of their men (husbands, lovers, fathers and even strangers) is destructive and dangerous, like a catastrophe to be mastered, an influence to be neutralised as far as possible. In *The Decalogue*, Kieślowski almost invariably presents femininity in a phase of transgression, always, as it were, "excessive", exaggerated, a danger to itself and others, with a strong admixture of the hysterical and even psychopathic. As wife (*Decalogue 2* and *9*), she is faithless, her treachery threatening the man at the very moment of his vulnerability and dependence on her goodwill and generosity (the impotent husband of *9*; the husband with cancer in *2*). As lover, she is vengeful or plays the part of the *femme fatale*, crippling the personality of the weaker partner (*6*). As daughter, she is dangerous and disloyal (the heroine's incestuous attraction to her own father in *4*), and can even cause problems to men who have no link whatsoever with her.

The women in Kieślowski's films seem to exist exclusively in terms of their biological role. They are wives, lovers, mothers or daughters: what they are as human beings seems of little significance. It might be possible to name their professions or social status, but in most cases it would be difficult to argue that they identify with them. Whenever these come into play, the specifically "female" vanishes, and the issue simply becomes a universal human one, as in *Decalogue 8*, whose two heroines are scholars. Their meeting after many years sets up a moral confrontation between the two women, an older professor and a far-younger woman, whose fates once crossed dramatically. One of them had the chance to help save a Jewish child during the Occupation, but rescinded her earlier decision to do so. One can assume that her motives were religious in nature (it was a question of a birth certificate), although essentially they were actually very different and far more complex, which casts an entirely new light on the whole affair. As the professor is conducting her ethics seminar, the mysterious stranger places this problem before her students for discussion. The film's discourse concerns moral, ethical and religious correctness, and poses questions of responsibility for the fate of one's neighbour, of guilt and shared guilt, and the assignment of the interlocutors' roles to women is incidental to these issues. What *is* essential is the question of professional identity – the fact that the protagonists deal with ethical problems, live a professorial life, and, moreover, are indubitably lonely (the older woman) or presumptively so (the younger one).

There is no significance, however, to the fact that Dorota is a musician (*Decalogue 2*), Majka a student (*Decalogue 7*), and Hanka an airline employee (*Decalogue 9*). On the other hand, we do not know the professions of Ewa (*Decalogue 3*) or Magda in *Decalogue 6*, although the latter doubtless pursues one. Perhaps only the fact that the heroine of *Decalogue 4* is a future actress is significant, for Anka really does play a series of grand scenes, albeit in life, rather than in the theatre. All the same, she plans to solve her problem through marriage, not by devoting herself to art.

It is a biologically-conceived gender that determines both the heroines' conditions as filmic figures and their roles within the narratives. The viewer sees them first and foremost as the "eternal Eve", not as historically-conditioned women inhabiting a contemporary Poland, who could – and do – do a thousand things over and above contracting associations with men. These other things, however, do not matter to the director.

Moreover, the heroines of *The Decalogue* lack even the beauty or attractiveness that would explain such ability to harm men. Kieślowski either selects unattractive or physically uninteresting (albeit talented) actresses, or directs and photographs the beautiful ones in a manner suggesting a desire to destroy and devalue them in the viewer's eyes. Grażyna Szapołowska, Krystyna Janda and Adrianna Biedrzyńska are badly dressed, unkempt, made up terribly and shot under a hard, harsh lighting that ruthlessly accentuates all the flaws and imperfections in their good looks. They have nothing beautiful either within, or in their connections with men. And lest this opinion seems exaggerated, one need only compare the heroines of *The Decalogue* with Irène Jacob, Juliette Binoche and Julie Delpy to see for oneself how women can look when they are not only intrinsically beautiful, but also treated as such by the director and his camera.

A multiplicity of possible negative roles can be found concentrated in Dorota, the heroine of *Decalogue 2*, who is played by Krystyna Janda, and who typifies the women of Kieślowski's films in the problems she causes men. The film's moral drama is only apparently shared by the heroine, all of whose actions are aimed at avoiding choice and shifting the entire burden of responsibility onto men, or at going further still and punishing them for what has befallen her. Dorota plays the violin in an orchestra; this is how she came to meet the famous pianist with whom she is having an affair. She learns that she is carrying his child while her husband is hospitalised, undergoing an operation for cancer and fighting for his life. Dorota's problem is that she has only one chance to bear a child. Should she have an abortion, she will no longer be able to have the children she so desires. But she is convinced that she can only have her lover's child if her husband dies, and she learns of this in time to make the right decision. She exerts intense moral pressure on the old hospital consultant from whom she wants an unequivocal answer. In other words, the consultant has the role of a god whose judgment determines life and death, although he does not grant himself the right to do so. The prognosis is bad, but medicine is no exact science and forbids mathematical certainty. We can add that, for all the authenticity of the consultant's dilemma, the one attributed to Dorota is artificial and contrived. A woman truly desirous of having a child would put its life before everything else, and never reason or act as the film's heroine does. If the character is believable, nevertheless, it is because her behaviour is susceptible of a different interpretation.

Dorota has found herself in an awkward situation whose weight she tries to shift onto men. She displays the extremism of hysterics, who relish playing up the drama of their situations and strive continually to be centre-stage. She does not accept the consultant's refusal of a verdict, and, notwithstanding, compels him to bear the responsibility by announcing her decision to have an abortion. She comes to announce this to him with the clearly-stated aim of disturbing his conscience, and fully succeeds in doing so. The consultant will either pronounce on her husband's life or death, or shoulder the blame for the non-birth of her child. The consultant finds a solution predicated upon the primacy of the child's life. Dorota behaves exceptionally cruelly towards all three men, not just towards the old man whose conscience she violates. She may take no measures against her husband but she treats him as an obstacle to the realisation of her plans, her basic wish to be with her lover and have his child (she is about to travel abroad to see him). When her husband's fatal illness frustrates these plans, she tries to punish her lover for this, drily informing him of her planned abortion and announcing that this decision cancels their future together, regardless of what happens to her husband.

Dorota is a model of the cycle's heroines, and sets the pattern for the behaviour of its other female figures, who will be governed by an equally strong urge to self-dramatisation, although their situations are less extreme. All, or almost all, resemble Dorota in wishing to exist more intensely, more evidently, by attracting the attention of "the world" – which means men – and taking centre-stage. They want to provoke an event that will brightly spotlight something hidden, overlooked, and hence, of necessity, apparently commonplace. This is particularly evident in the spectacles stage-managed by the hysterical heroines of *Decalogue 3* and *4*. In the former, the true situation of Ewa, its heroine, reveals itself only gradually. On Christmas Eve, she vehemently pesters her former lover – now a staid family man – to help her find her husband, who has surely had an accident. The man cannot remain deaf to her appeal, particularly as the situation becomes ever more dramatic as the hunt for the husband proceeds. We witness shocking scenes at a hospital, an emergency ward, and a detoxification cell. When the couple reach the station at daybreak, Ewa decides to unveil the machinery of her drama. Her husband abandoned her long ago to start a new family, and her loneliness is boundless. She had contemplated suicide but, unable to come to a decision, instead chose a strange wager with fate. She believes that, should she succeed in keeping another person beside her for the whole of Christmas Eve, her life will continue somehow and not be at the mercy of sleeping tablets. Ewa is less tragic than pathetic, and only she is to blame for her loneliness – least of all the man she has compelled to witness her spectacle. He may find it in his heart to sympathise with and understand her, but that merely devalues her further in the viewer's eyes.

In *Decalogue 4*, the motive-force behind the action is also a woman, or rather a young girl. Anka, an acting-school student, and her father, an architect, are linked by deep, incestuously-tinged feelings of which neither is fully aware. The girl decides to challenge the father, and, true to the spirit of her profession – which, one may assume, matches her true nature – arranges a kind of spectacle, a psychodrama aimed at disclosing the real character of the feelings between them. With this in mind, she exploits a letter written to her by her mother, who died shortly after giving birth to her. The letter may contain some mystery or reveal something unexpected. Anka does not read it, however, but rewrites it, imitating her mother's handwriting. She presents her father with her own version, which states that he is not her father. This justifies her feelings, and allows her to expect that they will be reciprocated. Anka's dramatic account, set at the highest emotional pitch, is essentially a sexual provocation to which her father does not respond, although he does reveal his own feelings and the drama of a man who would like his daughter always to remain a child, since then he would not have to give her away to anyone. The crisis occurs over a single night, and the conflict's complete revelation and dramatic unfolding seem to lift an evil spell from the protagonists. In the morning, Anka confesses her deed, burns the mother's real letter, and unconditionally accepts her role as daughter. Her spontaneous cry of "Daddy!" appears sincere. Earlier still, she had decided to marry a colleague, a decision made on behalf of them both.

The heroine of *Decalogue 6* – whose longer version is *Krótki film o miłości* (*A Short Film About Love*, 1988) – learns that a young boy is spying on her. She is less outraged than amused and intrigued, for the boy is far from the classic voyeur, his motive being deep fascination by, and love for, the "object". We might think that she would either permit him to continue his game, and join in herself, or end it by lowering the blinds or switching off the light. But this is a classic Kieślowski heroine, who cannot resist the temptation of a significant dramatic part. Szapołowska plays a woman whose contacts with men are strictly instrumental. Doubtless she neither has a very high opinion of them, nor attaches much importance to affairs with them. Her past experiences must have been bitter and painful, for she is convinced of the non-existence of what young people term "love", and that the sexual act never exceeds its purely physiological dimension.

What motivates this heroine's behaviour towards the boy? A wish to punish him? A desire to give him a lesson in "what life is like"? Or perhaps a purely abstract desire to pay back a helpless boy who, at a given moment, simply represents the male? The erotic "spectacle" as performed by Szapołowska is deliberately brief and brutal, essentially provisional or incomplete: purely mechanical, it elicits a merely mechanical reaction. The boy is not only disappointed, but also humiliated. Deeply hurt, his psyche damaged by a kind of mocking rape, he attempts suicide.

The punishment which the heroine metes out to the boy ultimately strikes her. The deed is no sooner done than repented of – all the more deeply when she learns of the boy's suicide attempt. Although it would be hard to credit any change in the heroine and her feelings towards him, she succumbs to the feelings which youthful innocence arouses even in the most hardened. She might now be able to accept the proffered gift, but it is too late. The boy closes things down with his brief "I've stopped spying on you".

Even when the type of relationship between the heroine and her opposite number changes – when it ceases to involve an antagonistic partner – the function, role and nature of the female protagonist of *The Decalogue* do not. In *Decalogue 7*, the fundamental conflict unfolds between a student, Majka, and her mother. The male figures – Majka's father and her former lover – are little more than passive witnesses, the former subject to his wife, the latter to the girl. Majka fights her mother for possession of the infant daughter she bore while still a schoolgirl. To hush up the scandal, the mother had formally acknowledged the girl's child as her own, with its parents' half-willing, half-enforced consent. Whereas the older woman acts out the maternal role to the hilt and with deep satisfaction, after six years Majka realises that she has been robbed of everything, both of her child and its love, and of her own mother whose affections are entirely bound up in the child. Majka wants to win back her daughter, emigrate to Canada and sever all family ties, but she needs her mother's consent to do so. In an effort to gain – or rather compel – it, she abducts the daughter and plays upon her mother with a blackmailer's cold-bloodedness. Kieślowski again shows a heroine acting hysterically, out of extreme emotional tension, motivated less by love of her child than by hatred of the mother she wishes to punish as painfully as possible.

Once again, femininity and the passions that move it are excessive, overwrought and convulsive. Majka's mother is equally violent, unrestrained and bent on victory. The two men try, and fail, to moderate the passions of the women. The child's father, with whom Majka briefly takes refuge, explains that she will damage her child, whom she can offer only anger and immaturity in exchange for loss of home and the person she knew as her mother. All the same, Majka fights desperately to the end, when her parents discover her hiding-place. Thus, even where femininity appears most authentic and complete, finding fulfilment in its maternal calling, Kieślowski discerns nothing more than the unrelenting clash of two egotisms, as Majka and her mother battle like tigresses. What prevails here is less high emotions than unadorned, naked animal instinct. The director seems to suggest that woman's every face is terrifying after a fashion. Woman in love, woman as mother, disappointed woman, woman alone: each is a dangerous entity, following an incomprehensible "female" logic, governed by an unfettered element that overwhelms and flabbergasts the men.

A further extension of this perspective is found in *White*, a film with little in common with the remaining parts of the trilogy. The view of women here is absolutely traditional and of the kind that provokes the most determined feminist attacks. Dominique (Julie Delpy) is the French wife of a Polish emigré, a beautiful, sensual blonde whom the authors and camera treat as a sexual object, the goal of male desire. Sexuality completely determines Dominique's existence, and sex alone motivates her behaviour. Dominique looks and behaves like the embodiment of male dreams. For a second time in Kieślowski (see *Decalogue 9*), impotence is the leitmotif of a situation where the man fails the woman in the area which the author deems most important to her. Symbolically – as feminists would say – he has lost the means of exerting power over women, and is helpless and defenceless. Such is the case with the hapless Karol, the husband of Dominique, for whom he has become both risible and repulsive. The motif's recurrence and treatment (one recalls that the hero of *Decalogue 9* thinks he should either give his wife a divorce or attempt suicide, which he, in fact, does attempt) clearly indicate that, for Kieślowski, sexual dominance is the decisive factor in male-female relationships. It is less a case of the natural character of the physical link between the members of a heterosexual couple than of sex as a means of exerting power over – of subjugating – the woman. The man who lacks such a power (and it need not be through impotence, as *A Short Film About Love* reminds us) becomes the woman's victim. Consequently, in this respect, *White* presents itself as the story of the fall and rise of Karol, who – having suffered painful humiliation by his wife – eventually finds a way to subdue her.

Karol's sexual fiasco causes the divorce which Dominique pursues with unheard-of energy. It is exclusively a matter of sexuality, since, when the hero attempts a reconciliation, Dominique accedes most eagerly. But when he fails physically yet again, her reaction is unrestrained and entirely cruel. She torments her victim by telling Karol to listen through the phone as she makes love to someone else. But, since sex alone motivates her behaviour towards men, once again Dominique submits to Karol unhesitatingly when, having lured her to Poland, he regains his masculine status. Kieślowski's film shows woman's function as sexual object point-blank and without mincing matters. The fact of the "object's" surpassing beauty sufficiently justifies Karol's insistence on its possession.

The plot, whereby Karol both revenges himself and regains Dominique, is very intricate. The conclusion, however, has a metaphorical resonance that is clearly and blatantly open to a feminist reading. Feminist theory postulates that patriarchal culture "imprisons" women by denying them the status of subjects, and reducing them to their allotted roles of mother, sexual object and sign of social exchange among men. Erased from history and culture, woman appears "eternal" and unchanging, constructed by the discourses that imprison her. In *White*, Dominique is simply locked up in prison, thanks to which Karol will be able to regain both her and her affections. The starkness of this solution suggests a metaphor for patriarchal culture, which tells us that only a woman in chains can be possessed. Thus, *White* yields an extremely clear and unambiguous summary of the entire discourse on women conducted in Kieślowski's previous work. Just why he should have reverted to this discourse in the wake of *The Double Life of Véronique* and *Blue* is not fully clear, especially since the fact that *Red* followed *White* makes it impossible to speak of a regression to an old position. Perhaps Kieślowski felt that *The Decalogue* lacked the very summing-up he formulated in *White*, and so succumbed to the temptation to round matters off unambiguously. In imprisoning woman, Kieślowski "settled his accounts" with an image of femininity that had long haunted him, thereby becoming capable of returning to his study of a new and infinitely more fascinating, subtle and complex one: reduced to the terms of a univocal opposition whose filmic realisation is obviously less simple, the image of a woman who is beautiful, wise and good, as opposed to the earlier image of woman as ugly, stupid and bad.

The heroine of *Decalogue 4* certainly shares all the characteristic traits of the cycle's women; nevertheless, in certain respects and to some extent, she already prefigures Kieślowski's later work. It is the first time the author stresses so-called "feminine intuition" to such a considerable extent. Anka seems to possess a very high level of self-knowledge and awareness. For all her youth and inexperience, she outstrips her father in her ability to grasp and analyse the subtlest shades of emotion. What she knows about herself, about him and about the two of them is a matter not of knowledge and experience of life, but of a particular kind of intuition which, for the woman, takes the place of intellectual knowledge based on reason alone. Like her father, the viewer would like to know how she knows so much, for she patently knows more than she "has a right to". She "knows" because she is endowed with a female talent which men completely lack, an extra-rational insight below the surface of things, a gift of illumination that permits an instantaneous penetration of the heart of a matter which men would require a long and complex investigation to reach.

This view of woman as specially gifted dominates *The Double Life of Véronique* and, subsequently, *Blue* and *Red*. However, Kieślowski continues to view women as first and foremost other than men, something for which feminists strongly reproach him. But, in contradistinction to *The Decalogue*, this perspective does not belittle and downgrade, but attempts to present female otherness as a gift – in particular, one that widens the spectrum of awareness to encompass those areas where intuition, emotional knowledge, special sensitivity and subtlety hold sway. Here Kieślowski appears unwittingly to confirm the observation of certain feminist critics for whom women, ousted from the spheres reserved for and dominated by men – particularly those of language and law – seek other forms of utterance. To use Julia Kristeva's metaphor, they express themselves as shamans and dancers.[2] This is not to be taken literally, but as meaning that the instrument of woman's expression is not the word, or the *logos* her home, but that she expresses herself by means of a different "speech" – music, body language, dance – corresponding to her visionary, "shamanistic" knowledge. (It is worth noting here that Kieślowski's brief and beautiful documentary, *Siedem kobiet w różnym wieku* [*Seven Women of Different Ages*, 1978], gives, in synthetic, compendium form, just such a portrait of woman as dancer, from the first efforts of early childhood to the maturity of an achieved career. Thus, Kieślowski "saw" women this way even at the very outset of his career, but only drew conclusions from his observations much later, in the last phase of his artistic work.)

126

Unlike the heroines of *The Decalogue*, who conduct verbal duels, the ones in Kieślowski's French films do not speak – or rather, to be exact, they say little and do so in a highly characteristic way. The phrase that falls most frequently from the lips of Véronique, Julie and Valentine is "I don't know", a kind of declaration of helplessness with regard to a certain way of knowing or gaining knowledge. Were they consciously to grasp the nature of their contact with the world, perhaps they would use such phrases as "I see" or "I foresee". Interpretations of the female characters of these particular films are dominated by descriptions of their heroines' behaviour, the tiny dumb shows and gestural *études* whereby they (the "dancers") express themselves without resort to speech.

In *The Decalogue*, the heroines' professions were matters of complete indifference. Here they have fundamental significance on several planes: they are essential to the unfolding of the story, determine each character's psychology, and are metaphors for woman's position within culture. Iwona Rammel emphasises the particularly intimate link between *The Double Life of Véronique* and *Blue* in this respect:

> All three heroines are linked somehow to the 'practice' of music: Weronika, by her singing; Véronique, by teaching music; Julie, by composing. Their fortunes present three variations on a single theme, that of breaking with music and returning to it. A contusion of Weronika's hand causes her to give up the piano, while the solo singing career she barely begins is to some extent a matter of chance. Véronique abandons singing due to a vague intuition, a foreboding, rather than knowledge, that music represents a threat to her. There is no longer anything mystical about Julie's decision to renounce music – it is an element in her conscious strategy in life. Her idea of continued life rests on a cancellation and forgetting of the past, on grasping her situation as an opportunity for absolute freedom, freedom from everything, including music, which for Julie is a continuation of memory.[3]

This is the first typical feature of the way in which music is treated in the three films under discussion here. Music represents a certain value that is less aesthetic than existential. It is a form of challenge, to which one has to reply "yes" or "no" with one's life. None of the heroines of Kieślowski's films deems music a superfluous ornament, a merely aesthetic supplement or comment tacked onto life.

It could be that for them music *is* life, its meaning and deepest content, although the case of Weronika-Véronique adumbrates a certain alternative pointed out by Rammel, and the choice opens up a particularly dramatic perspective, for, in essence, it means choosing between life and art.

Although she is not connected with music, I would not hesitate to add Valentine (of *Red*) to this trio of heroines. Valentine is a model – moreover, a photographic model (an enormous close-up of her profiled face appears on street posters) – so she not only practises a profession held to be deeply feminine (and one of the few which have a woman's undisputed success as a woman as an immanent component), but also expresses herself through body-speech. Her role is, as it were, a version of that of the dancer. Artistic activity links the four heroines and each is associated with non-verbal forms of communication and knowledge. They live – or perhaps would *like* to live, since they have differing degrees of success in doing so – for music and love. Weronika dies, but the fortunes of the remaining three are clearly open to future fulfilment through love and art, except where they have chosen between them (Véronique).

There is a certain gradation in the heroines' connections with the artistic sphere. Julie's profession is creative, and she has a composer's talent and training. Weronika is a singer, and hence only a performer. Valentine works in the area of applied art, while Véronique teaches music to children, having renounced the possibility of her Polish namesake's career. The music with which she now deals is always a kind of lesser or distorted version of the Polish section's theme. She either hears it through the telephone, or corrects the false notes and fumblings of a children's group.

In *The Double Life of Véronique*, the two heroines have a special kind of connection. It is not finally clear whether it is essentially a question of two distinct figures or the possible alternative experiences of a single subject which the title suggests. After all, it is a matter of a double life whose essence involves making a choice. Weronika-Véronique has a heart ailment, and to continue her singing career is to risk death at any moment, which is exactly what happens, for in one variant of the heroine's fate – the Polish one – she dies. In the second (French) one, she renounces singing and saves her own life, in which love becomes the overriding value.

Reality itself added a tragic postscript to this film – the death of its author who, with his own serious heart condition, wore himself out through hard creative toil. Kieślowski faced the same necessity of choice as his heroine, and we know how he chose. This gives *The Double Life of Véronique* a particular resonance, and seems to explain the turn towards the quest for mysterious affinities and correspondences between human destinies.

The key to the film's interpretation, which the author himself hands the viewer, is the writer's story of two puppets – identical girls inhabiting different countries and towns. Only one appears in the puppet theatre. The writer explains to Véronique that he made two identical dolls in case one was broken. During the puppet show, the dancer breaks a leg, and is transformed into a butterfly. Almost every single twist of the story suggests an opposition between unity and duality. One puppet can replace another, but what is at stake is the ability of two girls to exchange experiences mysteriously. Once one has been burned, the other pulls back from the fire just in time.

Exactly the same thing befalls the film's heroines. At its beginning, Weronika says that she feels she is not alone – and she is not referring to her family or the boy she loves. She seems to have a sense of double existence, although, of course, she knows nothing of Véronique. However, this may equally well be an awareness of the possibility of choice: the girl can fulfil her destiny according to two variants. Once the choice has been made, "doubling" disappears and only unity remains.

Yet, their "meeting", of which they were not conscious and which was no meeting at all (albeit recorded on a photograph), may indicate that we are dealing here with *two* heroines. During her trip to Kraków, Véronique photographs a street from the inside of a coach, and happens to capture the image of Weronika passing by. When Véronique's lover discovers the snapshot, he thinks it is her. In the Polish section, Weronika looks at the coach, but her fleeting impression is not reflected in any of her later statements. Véronique also fails to notice that she is photographing a girl identical with herself. The sight of the photograph causes Véronique tears of despair. Here she finds confirmation of her earlier, intuitive sense of having lost somebody and now being alone. Like Weronika, she is referring not to any concrete figure in her environment, but to a mysterious awareness of affinity with somebody who is herself.

As in the writer's story, there is a transfer of a particular experience, as if, in dying, Weronika had imparted to Véronique an awareness of the clear and certain consequences of the choice she faces. Thanks to Weronika, Véronique "knows" that she will die if she carries on singing. As in the story, when she chooses, she takes the place of the "worn-out" puppet, and only one of the two remains.

The double figure of Weronika-Véronique was embodied marvellously by Irène Jacob, who endowed her heroine/heroines with the full range of female subtlety, delicacy and possible feeling and behaviour. Jacob acts out a particular fulfilment of the feminine mode of being, which finds its fullest expression in music and love. Iwona Rammel lays particular stress on the fact that these heroines live "the aesthetic life...the difference being that Weronika does so of her own free will, whereas the life of Véronique is subject to aestheticisation from without: she is assigned the role of being the prototype of a literary figure. She carries the role off to a tee, albeit unconsciously".[4]

Rammel also points out that the recurrence in the film's finale of the vocal part cut short by Weronika's death establishes the deepest connection between the protagonists' fates:

> Véronique's story is situated in the time of the reverberation of that haunting chord, every note of which cries out for resolution, for some kind of continuation. In classical harmony this kind of chord (the diminished seventh) cannot represent a conclusion; it imparts something of this incompleteness to Weronika's death. Her life echoes – and re-echoes – in the life of Véronique, and that shared resonance questions the proud isolation and uniqueness of human destinies.[5]

Blue, in which the main female role of Julie was played by Juliette Binoche, can be seen as connected in a certain way with *The Double Life of Véronique*. Where the earlier film formulates a particular conception of "the female mode of being", the heroine of *Blue*, a woman who also dwells in the world of feeling and music, attempts to challenge her fate. She does so in a special way, in special circumstances. Julie, once a happy wife and mother, and collaborator with her husband, a famous composer, suddenly loses husband and child in a road accident. She experiences this as the loss of everything, all her past life and self. Binoche renders the boundlessness of the heroine's tragedy through intense concentration and taciturnity. Her despair is silent; she cannot weep. When Julie returns home and asks the servant why she is crying, the woman replies: "Because you aren't". Only a twitch of the eyelids, a stray tear or a flicker of the muscles about the mouth betrays Julie's tragedy. At the same time, we see from her behaviour that she is literally breaking down physically under the burden of existence. She tries to kill herself, but is unable to go through with it. She puts a fistful of pills in her mouth and – after a long pause – spits them out. Left alone in her flat she cannot remain on her feet, but sways and sits down heavily on the stairs.

Rather than kill herself, Julie tries to devise an alternative way of ceasing to exist, by not acting or forging links with other people and the world. By deliberately creating a vacuum around herself she tries to protect herself from suffering and the renewed loss of anything she might gain or use to find herself or rebuild a sense of security. She instructs her lawyer to sell her old home, destroys her husband's uncompleted score (not knowing that a copy has been preserved), and tries to "scare off" Olivier, her husband's former assistant, who is in love with her. She rents a flat which no one else knows anything about. She cuts herself off from the past and closes off any possible future. "I know what I have to do – absolutely nothing" is her deliberate, considered declaration. She drops all former obligations and friendships, and severs all ties. There is no one anywhere near her. Her absent-minded mother in a nursing home does not even recognise her, but continually confuses her with her sister. Julie's everyday life is taken up with trivial rituals – drinking coffee; eating ice cream in the same café; regular swimming; walks; and sunbathing in complete obliviousness of her surroundings.

Julie defends her solitude against Olivier, who tries to track her down, although he immediately submits to her choice. Above all else, she has to fight against music. She does not wrestle with God, although music itself may symbolise the voice of God speaking from a whirlwind. Every now and then, a musical motif emerges from the dark frames and will not go away. And we recall that one of the two things Julie took from her home was some music paper with the notation of a melody (the other is a hanging glass ornament).

Music's voice penetrates the curtain of isolation which Julie had drawn between herself and the world. The film tells us little of the part composition once played in her life. What does it really mean to say that she collaborated with her husband? What kind of activity was involved? Julie's subsequent work on her husband's concerto, when she makes bold creative decisions (replacing the piano with a flute; deepening the timbre of the violins; muting the brass), leads us to infer that she is a fully competent artist, and reminds us of the journalist's suggestion near the start of the film: "they say you wrote your husband's music". We never discover whether this was really so, but are allowed to presume that what reawakens Julie to life is a creative instinct that cannot be silenced or quenched. Olivier, aware that only in this way can Julie find freedom, makes every effort to persuade her to collaborate in the concerto's completion. Julie wishes to actualise a notion of freedom as "freedom from", and, although such action may have been indispensable to her in her first period of loneliness, in the long run it is destructive, cutting her off from the well-springs of life. In the end, she rediscovers herself in a "freedom to" – the freedom to make choices, to enter the stream of life and other people's affairs.

As the voice of music begins to disturb her, other people enter her solitude unobserved. A quotation from her dead husband tells us that Julie is generous and good. We can also see with our own eyes how concerned she is for the fate of others. Even if Julie imagines that she can cease relying upon others and become emotionally independent, receiving nothing, she cannot cease giving. Her gesture as she bends over the busker and her treatment of her neighbour, a girl of somewhat loose morals, betray a profoundly generous nature which, even while consumed with its own suffering, remains sensitive to others' problems.

Life itself delivers the decisive blow that rouses her from her lethargy. She learns that there had long been another woman in her husband's life, and determines to find and contact her. The woman is expecting the husband's child. Julie makes over her former family home to her. She herself returns less to her old life, for this is no longer possible – it has ceased to exist – than to her old self, a woman for whom life's meaning lay in music and love. Together with Olivier she sets about completing her husband's work, and decides to accept and share Olivier's love. The closing scene – that of the concerto, when the choir sings the Greek text of from St Paul's letter to the Corinthians (I Corinthians 13: 1-13) – synthesises love and music, and translates them to another plane, for "love faileth never" and is the greatest of all things.

Valentine, the heroine of *Red*, says that she wants to live in peace, and is apparently without professional ambitions: she carries out her modelling with calm professionalism. She is attracted to the image of the future dreamt for her by the judge: in his dream he saw a 50-year-old Valentine happy at her husband's side. In the meantime, however, Valentine is still young, and her fragility, delicacy and innocence seem to embody youth itself. A special sensitivity to the fortunes of others links her to the heroines of *The Double Life of Véronique* and *Blue*. She perhaps feels even more responsible than they for what befalls the people close to her, and even chance acquaintances. At one point, she says, "I feel that something important is happening around me", but in essence what occurs receives its meaning from her, for she is never indifferent.

She chances upon a retired judge who relishes eavesdropping on his neighbours' conversations, assuming a right to enter their intimate worlds. The girl uncovers his immoral hobby and, although she finds his behaviour repugnant, she maintains her contact with him and allows it to develop into a kind of friendship in which her emotional wisdom and his bitter experience enrich one another. In the end, the judge is the one astonished by Valentine's perceptiveness, intuition and surprising sensitivity. It is he who asks her "how do you know so much?" – not the other way around. The judge also displays profound perceptiveness in matters relating to Valentine, but it is a different kind of understanding, stemming from ratiocination and deduction, his knowledge of the patterns which human fates assume. Valentine's "knowledge" flows from her belief in human goodness, and also from her own, which gives her a compassionate empathy with others' emotions. She reacts with extraordinary subtlety to the situation of one of the victims of the eavesdropping, whom she wants to warn that a stranger is privy to his intimate conversations, but refrains from interfering lest it disturb the fragile balance of the relationships within the man's family.

The girl's life is pervaded by a deep concern for the fate of her younger brother (a drug addict) and efforts to establish contact with their mother, and she reacts patiently and with understanding to the boy's aggressive words on the telephone. It is not hard to see that the feelings and bonds between them are neither happy nor satisfying. Valentine adopts the dog that has been knocked down, lavishing loving care upon it, and helps an old lady in the street. Her every gesture towards others is, in a sense, one of giving and understanding by someone specially endowed by fate.

Valentine's life, like that of Kieślowski's other heroines, is inscribed into a certain *a priori* and apparently somewhat artificial structure of mysterious correspondences and affinities between human destinies, which play themselves out through symmetrical reflections and repetitions. The fates of Valentine and Auguste parallel one another, without intersecting, until they meet after the ferry disaster. And yet, the protagonists continually brush past one another unaware. They drink coffee in the same café, walk their dogs on identical red leads, and seem ineluctably "condemned" to meet. It later emerges that Auguste's experiences have already happened: his fate repeats the judge's in an ideal parallel. The judge never met his Valentine, but Auguste does, and this moment will doubtless change his life – or rather both their lives. Perhaps he is the man in the judge's dream? Not chance but an inevitable determinism seems to govern the world represented in Kieślowski's films. But it is less God or fate than the will of the artist that watches over this world, and, in the last instance, it is responsible for our impression that we are dealing with a created, constructed world which cannot be free or independent, for the trajectories of its heroes' fates are predetermined to assume precisely correct and contrived patterns.

But, irrespective of the fact that the protagonists' fates constitute arguments in Kieślowski's discourse on the world, they themselves – or rather, in our case, the females – are real, credible, flesh-and-blood figures. Irène Jacob's playing of Valentine turns a figure conceived as embodying ideal femininity into a person we, too, could meet. And, at the same time, she is the end-point of the long road Kieślowski and his heroines have travelled, from a world of "male" conflicts, disputes and arguments to one that discloses itself to a "feminine" way of knowing – by intuition and feeling.

Without ever abandoning his conviction of women's fundamental "otherness", in the course of his striving to transmit that conviction to his audience Kieślowski continually raises his estimate of the feminine dimension in nature and culture. The feminine is not viewed as a necessary or even valuable supplement to the masculine, but as an alternative to it. The world as women see and feel it is a different one, with values that can also reveal themselves to a man, if only he divest himself of prejudices and admit new perceptions. In his last films, Kieślowski unequivocally shows women as those who "see" better, feel more deeply, and understand more fully, because they are better "equipped" to do so. They have a greater range of sensitivity, capacity for compassion and ability to open themselves to others.

In the lives of the young, the male and female elements function, above all else, as oppositions, but in maturity we integrate them. Each of us discovers the "woman" or "man" within, and harmoniously incorporates that image into his or her psyche. *The Double Life of Véronique, Blue* and *Red* show how Krzysztof Kieślowski did just that.

Notes

[1]   This information is based on various feminist texts sent to me for a reader's report. However, Polish film journals were not interested in publishing them.

[2]   See Julia Kristeva, *Powers of Horror: An Essay on Abjection*, translated by Leon S Roudiez (New York: Columbia University Press, 1982).

[3]   Translated from the Polish: "Wszystkie trzy bohaterki są jakoś związane z 'uprawianiem' muzyki: Weronika – śpiewając, Véronique – ucząc muzyki, Julie – komponując. Ich losy to trzy wariacje na wspólny temat, którym jest zerwanie z muzyką i powrót do niej. Weronika na skutek kontuzji ręki rezygnuje z pianistyki, zaś jej ledwo rozpoczęta solistyczna kariera, jako śpiewaczki jest po trosze dziełem przypadku. Véronique porzuca śpiew pod wpływem niejasnego impulsu, przeczuwając raczej niż wiedząc, że muzyka jest dla niej zagrożeniem. W zerwaniu z muzyką, na które decyduje się Julie, nie ma już niczego mistycznego – jest ono elementem świadomej strategii wobec życia. Jej pomysł na dalsze życie polega na przekreśleniu przeszłości i zapomnieniu o niej, na postrzeżeniu własnej sytuacji jako szansy na absolutną wolność, wolność od wszystkiego. Także od muzyki, która jest dla Julie trwaniem i pamięcią." Iwona Rammel, "Van Den Budenmeyer i jemu podobni. O muzyce w ostatnich filmach Kieślowskiego", *Kwartalnik filmowy* 6 (1994): 134.

[4]   Translated from the Polish: "Obie żyją życiem estetycznym. Tyle że Weronika z własnej woli, natomiast życie Véronique zostaje poddane estetyzacji z zewnątrz: powierzono jej rolę 'bycia pierwowzorem' postaci literackiej. Véronique wywiązuje się z tego zadania doskonale, acz bezwiednie". Ibid: 135.

5   Translated from the Polish: "Historia Véronique zostaje ulokowana w czasie wybrzmiewania owego pamiętnego akordu, w którym każdy dźwięk woła o rozwiązanie, o jakikolwiek ciąg dalszy. W myśl reguł harmonii klasycznej – tego typu akord (tj. septymowy akord zmniejszony) nie może stanowić zakończenia – i coś z jego 'nieostateczności' udziela się śmierci Weroniki. Jej życie wybrzmiewa i pobrzmiewa – w życiu Véronique, a to współbrzmienie kwestionuje dumną izolację i jednostkowość ludzkiego losu". Ibid: 135-136.

The Double Life of Véronique **and** Three Colours: an escape from politics?

Janina Falkowska

Krzysztof Kieślowski repeatedly stated in many interviews that politics never interested him much, and that he was mostly interested in reality, the here and now. Although most of his films produced prior to the *Dekalog* (*The Decalogue*, 1988) series were read as profoundly political in content, he claimed that in all these films his interest was of general nature – to present human beings in all their beauty and ugliness, and stress their helplessness in the face of fate. This aspect of Kieślowski's films points to their documentary origin, a passionate attempt by the filmmaker to capture the essence of life in its entirety. The director stated in the last interview before his death:

> In the beginning I thought that I had to describe the world. I think it has not yet been described. When I finished doing this, the camera appeared to be a perfect tool for describing the world.[1]

His earlier documentary films attest to this credo. His feature films, however, present the social in the context of the political, an approach inevitably taken in most films by other Polish film directors. For instance, Kieślowski's *Przypadek* (*Blind Chance*, 1981) and *Bez końca* (*No End*, 1984), present, respectively, the growth of the opposition movement in Poland in the 1970s, and the suppression of the Solidarity movement during martial law in the 1980s. Nevertheless, unlike in the films of such politically-engaged filmmakers as Andrzej Wajda and Kazimierz Kutz, in Kieślowski's films a direct involvement in political issues gives way to a type of emotional dissociation, and an intellectual distance from both the presented events and the protagonists involved in them. Although these films clearly refer to political events, the latter function only as building-blocks for the films' plots and character developments. As the protagonists die at the end of both films, however, these works turn into a commentary on the sense of overall political effort. In their senselessness and hopelessness, the deaths of the protagonists signify more important matters than any political developments. The films direct the attention of viewers to spiritual and philosophical issues, rather than to down-to-earth matters of political reality.

This concentration on general questions is explicit in Kieślowski's next series of films, *The Decalogue*, in which political events in Poland are treated anecdotally, and appear as a remote cause. In fact, the social reality presented with documentary accuracy in all the films of the series tells more about the political situation of Poles than about a straight presentation of political phenomena. In his last films, *La Double Vie de Véronique* (*The Double Life of Véronique*, 1991) and the trilogy *Trois couleurs* (*Three Colours*, 1993-94), the shift from the social and the political towards the spiritual and the philosophical is especially pronounced.

In *The Double Life of Véronique* and *Three Colours*, the main films discussed in this essay, rigorous ideological questions give way to moral dilemmas and religious incertitude as the films progress. Like Zanussi in *Iluminacja* (*Illumination*, 1973), Kieślowski positions his films in the context of existential and ethical universalism. In this sense, the director's reflections on fate and on man's moral and ethical responses to it problematise the political conflicts of opposing factions – as presented in orthodox political films – and point to their absurdity in the face of fate and blind chance.

Aesthetically, the last four films constitute a testament to Kieślowski's successful employment of various film techniques. Among them are an enigmatic delineation of narrative; a sensitivity to colour and light; a careful composition of sequences; and an excellent arrangement of sound and music. In creating his films, Kieślowski relied heavily on collaboration with his screenwriter Krzysztof Piesiewicz, the film music composer Zbigniew Preisner, and his excellent cinematographers Sławomir Idziak, Edward Kłosiński and Piotr Sobociński. Nevertheless, the final shape of the films belongs to Kieślowski himself, who spent long hours at the editing table, polishing and mastering the ideal version of the films.

All Kieślowski's films reveal strong emotions that seem about to burst through the surface of the elegantly composed images. In every film the director seems to open a Pandora's box of feelings, and he does not close the box's lid at the end of the film. *The Double Life of Véronique*, *Trois couleurs: bleu* (*Three Colours: Blue*, 1993), *Trois couleurs: blanc* (*Three Colours: White*, 1994) and *Trois couleurs: rouge* (*Three Colours: Red*, 1994) demonstrate this emotional undercurrent in a powerful manner.

The Double Life of Véronique

The Double Life of Véronique is a film about two identical women born on the same day, both raised primarily by their fathers, who lead parallel lives in Poland and France. The first half-hour of the film depicts the life of Weronika (Irène Jacob), a young aspiring choir singer with a beautiful voice. She moves to Kraków from a small town where she lived alone with her widowed father (Władysław Kowalski). During an orchestra rehearsal in Kraków, the choir trainer (Kalina Jędrusik) overhears her clear and strong voice. Weronika is asked to participate in a singing competition, which she wins, and thus is invited to sing at a concert.

This is a volatile time in Poland, a time of political uncertainty, strikes and demonstrations. During one political demonstration at the market-place in Kraków, Weronika catches a glimpse of, and is photographed by, a French tourist who resembles her in an uncanny manner. Weronika subsequently rehearses for a concert in Kraków. After one such rehearsal, she suffers a mild heart attack in the park, and later, during the concert, she dies while finishing a song on a high note.

Véronique (Irène Jacob), a young music teacher in France, becomes aware of the presence of the dead Weronika. This is the same young woman whom Weronika saw in Kraków and who unwittingly photographed her double. The second, longer part of the film concentrates on Véronique and her feelings. At the primary school where she teaches, Véronique meets Aleksandre Fabbri (Philippe Volter) the puppeteer. It is after this meeting that Véronique begins to receive mysterious messages and gifts that at first allude to the dead Weronika, and eventually lead to her meeting with Alexandre in a café. During this encounter, Véronique realises that Alexandre has used her as a part of his psychological experiment for a book. Hurt, Véronique runs away, only to be followed by Alexandre. Back in Alexandre's flat, after the two reconverge in a small hotel, Véronique sees herself in a puppet that Alexandre has produced. Suddenly frightened by the sight of two puppets (Alexandre explains that he always makes two puppets "because they damage easily"), Véronique leaves Alexandre and returns to her father (Claude Duneton).

This short synopsis merely provides the structural framework to a highly reflexive film, in which an interplay of philosophical and artistic motives leads the viewer into the world of the inexplicable. In a conversation with Danusia Stok, Kieślowski stated that "the inner life of a human being...is the hardest thing to film".[2] He analysed his role as film director as that of one who has "to capture what lies within us, but there's no way of filming it. You can only get nearer to it. It's a great subject for literature. It's probably the only subject in the world."[3]

With this subject in mind, Kieślowski creates an emotional parable with a complex narrative and elaborate aesthetic. Already in the beginning of the film, Weronika is introduced as a slanted image, as if seen through a glass ball. The elegance of this elongated image is later repeated in the inverted image of the church that Weronika sees in a glass ball on her trip to Kraków. These images seem to question the "realness" of the world that Weronika inhabits, and subvert "reality"'s tangibility.

The part of the film devoted to the life of Weronika continues in a series of painstakingly composed tableaux, among which the most memorable are the conversation with her father about premonitions concerning the presence of another person in Weronika's life; the sequence on the train to Kraków; and a sequence in her aunt's (Halina Gryglaszewska) flat in the city. All these sequences are carefully constructed with a fractured composition of interiors (similar to those projected in the judge's house in *Three Colours: Red*). In the context of these serene scenes, the political demonstration at the Kraków market-place, with the riot police unit (ZOMO) in the background, is a surprising disruption to both the film's thematic and aesthetic consistencies. The running people, the shouts and the confusion not only startle Weronika, who crosses the market on her way to the rehearsal, but also introduce a moment of uncertainty and instability into the serene beauty of the film.

This political scene is a reminder of the times in which the action of the film takes place. The late-1980s is the time of abrupt democratisation in Poland. This is a time of many strikes and demonstrations, and Poles' persistent fight for a complete freedom of speech. However, in *The Double Life of Véronique*, this politically important scene is pivotal not for its revolutionary meaning, but for the development of the spiritual elements in the narrative. The demonstration is significant because it brings together two women who will unwittingly remember the event as the trigger to the uncanny presence of "the Other".[4] In this remarkable treatment of the political as a stimulus for the spiritual, as in *No End*, Kieślowski seems to question the revolutionary moments as the ones leading to social change. Instead, he treats them as life events that cause other, more universal developments.

In addition to exquisite imagery, music is an important aesthetic element of the film. The music, composed by Zbigniew Preisner, later resounds in the film in the form of a persistent musical motif accompanying the life of Véronique in France. Music, youth and its joys and sorrows dominate the first part of the film. The social situation of the country is subordinated and never discussed among the protagonists. Nevertheless, it is shamelessly present in the background: for instance, in the sequences depicting Weronika in a long, ungainly skirt running between the potholes and passing the ugly walls of dilapidated houses. Apart from the political demonstration in Kraków, the only reference to the political situation in the first part of the film appears as a sequence in which a Socialist statue is taken away in a truck. This event is a reference to the disappearing Socialist system – the initial symptom of which was disposing of the hated statues throughout the country. Kieślowski never makes the political importance of this sequence explicit. The dark, brownish filter through which this event has been shot distances the viewer from it, and presents the incident as just another life event, neither more nor less important for the plot development than Weronika's singing or the conversations with her father.

The film continues with a sequence of seemingly unrelated events. An incident demarcating the imminence of Weronika's death – her first heart attack in the park – is immediately followed by the incident in which an exhibitionist approaches her with his penis showing. Life, in its exuberance and joy and its celebration of male virility, intrudes upon the premonitions of death and decay predominant in the images of the falling leaves and the sad autumnal landscapes of Kraków. This subcurrent of sexuality appears later in the image of the white lipstick that Weronika uses to treat her chapped lips. The life motif is continued in the unexpected visit to Kraków by Antek (Jerzy Gudejko), who declares his constant love for Weronika; in the image of an old woman whom the young woman watches from her aunt's window; and in the exuberance and power of the music that Weronika sings. The sudden disruption – by death – of life's richness and power, unusually presented in the middle of the film's diegesis, surprises and saddens the viewer.

The musical motif with which Weronika ends her song and her life mysteriously reappears in the second part of the film, when it accompanies Weronika's double, Véronique, in her life in Paris. This musical motif returns at the marionette's funeral; when Véronique receives a letter from Poland containing a shoelace; and when she observes the light reflected by a mirror on the walls in her room. When the dancing light remains with no mirror in sight, both Véronique and the viewers acknowledge the presence of a deep mystery which permeates every layer of the film.

While the music creates aural parallels between the lives of Weronika and Véronique, the death of Weronika in Kraków acts as a direct stimulus in Véronique's lived experience. Véronique uncannily experiences the moment of Weronika's death when she makes love to her boyfriend. She then stops her singing lessons, becomes interested in the mysterious spectacle in which the dead figurines are brought to life by a commanding puppeteer, and, overall, wakes up to unusual events and inconsistencies in people's behaviour, acknowledging spiritual phenomena of which she was previously only vaguely and depressively aware.

Politics again remain a background presence. The third political incident – an explosion of a car (a possible act of terrorism) parked on the street where Alexandre is waiting for Véronique in the Gare St Lazare – is entirely incidental to the principal action. As in the earlier scenes with political content, the director does not provide a single clue to the nature of this incident. It seems not very important to him, and fades into the background of the crucial phenomena, such as, for instance, the compatibility between the hotel room numbers (287) which were occupied, respectively, by Antek at the Holiday Inn in the first part of the film, and by Véronique in the second one. The reappearance of the musical motif in the same room in the second part of the film provides an artistic and spiritual closure, additionally reinforced by a sudden sadness expressed by Véronique when, among the objects in her handbag, she notices the photograph she has taken of Weronika in Kraków.

The circular structure of the film incorporates the repetition of the motif of a white lipstick, a glass ball and a love scene, all of which appear in the first and second parts of the film. As a final chord and proof of the inevitability of the supernatural presence and the imminence of fate that brought Weronika and Véronique together, Alexandre shows Véronique two identical puppets that make Weronika's and Véronique's premonitions palpable. Probably this presentation leads Véronique back to her down-to-earth father who, nevertheless, takes the presence of the spiritual for granted. Véronique's constant returns to her father, like Weronika's deep relationship with hers, suggest a religious kind of connection that is later articulated in Kieślowski's depiction of the relationship between Valentine (Irène Jacob) and judge Kern (Jean-Louis Trintignant) in *Red*. The preoccupation with death and the mystery of supernatural existence seem to be the main focus of the film. Indeed, both young women die in the film. However, while Weronika's death is clearly depicted, the death of Véronique is implied, rather than shown: when she revisits her father in the last scene, her hand on the bell-push suddenly rigidifies and drops. The director does not explain what has happened. He leaves us with unanswered questions on the mystery of life and death. Similarly, Kieślowski's last creation, *Three Colours*, leaves the viewer pondering the mysteries of the ineffable.

Three Colours trilogy

Kieślowski's sudden death accords his last films the status of an epitaph for his life and creative output. Not prone to loud declarations or political outbursts, the director lived the quiet life of an introvert, contemplating his projects in a thick cloud of cigarette smoke. Sadly, this smoke brought his life to an end. *Blue*, *White* and *Red* function as a grand conclusion to his artistic career, and a deeply philosophical commentary on the essence of life and death.

Three Colours was designed to correspond to the colours of the French flag – blue, white and red – and their accompanying slogans of liberté, égalité and fraternité. However, in its final shape, the trilogy bursts through its initial layout and delves into other areas. The three nouns enter other semantic fields which constitute vast areas of semantic and cultural ambiguity.

Blue

Three Colours: Blue explores the theme of liberty. It tells the story of Julie (Juliette Binoche) who loses her young daughter Anna and her husband Patrice (Claude Duneton), a celebrated composer, in a car accident. The experience is so overwhelming that Julie resolves to withdraw from the world. To make a clean break with the past, she assumes a virtual hermit's life in Paris. In an effort to forget the past and start a new life, she moves to a flat in a working-class neighbourhood, and tries to lose herself in the anonymity of city life. Life goes on, however, and she is slowly being pulled by its currents. Firstly, Julie is approached by Olivier (Benoît Régent), her husband's assistant, who tries to negotiate her help in completing Patrice's final score; next, her assistance is sought by Lucille (Charlotte Véry), a prostitute who risks being expelled from Julie's building; finally, Julie herself confronts Sandrine (Florence Pernel), a lawyer and her husband's lover of many years, who is carrying the dead man's child. All these events shake her from her lethargy. Julie emerges from her isolation, lodges her pregnant rival in her home, finishes her husband's "Song for the Unification of Europe" and begins a new chapter in her life – she re-establishes ties with Olivier, her admirer.

The film's narrative unfolds slowly and hesitantly. Shot from the point of view of Julie, it begins and ends with a close-up of an eye. The eyelashes and the retina provide an aesthetic and ideological framework to the narrative which explores the life fragments created by the filmmaker to illustrate Julie's internal development. Julie's rise from the ashes of her psychological death and her return to the world of the living are painted in masterly strokes, among which the colour blue, the sudden fade-outs and the unexpected musical intrusions are most striking.

The film's overall aesthetic signifier is the colour blue. The film's opening sequence starts with a blue candy paper fluttering in the wind, and ends with a car crash in the bluish fog at dawn. Blue, with its connotations of melancholy, changes into the colour of mourning when we learn from the subsequent sequence that Julie's husband and daughter have died in the accident. Only as an afterthought does the strange image of a boy who appeared at the scene of the accident come back to one's mind. Who is he, and why was he there? Was he there accidentally, or, as in *The Decalogue*, is the boy an angel of death who appears at the scene only because someone is going to die? A coincidence, blind chance or the deep mystery of life – already in the beginning of the film Kieślowski makes us question the logical development of presented events.

The colour blue introduced in this opening sequence appears throughout the film as a link with the past and as a reminder of the tragedy. Its dark, clear hue adorns the glittering lampshade, the object taken by Julie from her house after the accident, and it saturates every inch of the swimming pool in which Julie swims. When she emerges from the water, the deep blue returns her suddenly to the past, a return accompanied by an outburst of the musical motif which Julie remembers from her earlier life. The memory is followed by a short fade to black which conveys the living from the outside world into the world of the dead. The effect is stunning in its spiritual uncertainty, especially given that these fade-outs disrupt mundane scenes with a realistic, documentary touch. As in all Kieślowski's films, the accuracy of documentary sequences fades in the context of the purpose for which they are used. They become significant only as these fragments of reality which lead to the reconsideration of such issues as memory, death, love and compassion.

Julie slowly re-enters the world not because she wants to, but because life's events pull her into it. She must make certain decisions, some of them practical, and others of a moral nature. During one such precipitous moment, Julie watches a brawl outside the window of her flat. On hearing the commotion, she reluctantly leaves her flat in a nightgown to see whether somebody is hiding in the corridor, and she accidentally gets shut out. While she spends the night on the stairs, she becomes an unwitting witness to a clandestine meeting between a prostitute and a lodger. These people are the first ones who will lead Julie out of her psychological, self-imposed exile.

Julie must make a series of decisions: one concerning Lucille, the prostitute living in the same building; another pertaining to the mouse and her new babies in Julie's flat; and, finally, one which involves her own life. The photographs she sees during a television interview rouse Julie from her emotional lethargy; the pain caused by the discovery of her husband's mistress of many years makes her act. Olivier, Julie's long-time admirer, comments on this event with relief, "You finally have to say, 'I want' or 'I don't want'. You act, you do something, you suffer." Julie's decision to meet her husband's pregnant mistress and to give the woman's unborn son Patrice's house and his last name is a splendid act of grace. Julie replaces envy, hatred and grief with generosity and love.

In the process of this emotional awakening, Julie decides to fulfil her husband's and Olivier's dream, and generously finishes work on the "Song for the Unification of Europe". Through this humility and renunciation of her own egoistic right to submerge herself in mourning, Julie reaches a state of spiritual and emotional liberation, a state of grace which puts a faint, almost indiscernible smile on her face. The act of self-renunciation finds its stunning expression in the final sequence of the film, in which all the narrative themes find their conclusion.

The sequence, a long panning movement of the camera from the left to the right and, later, from the right to the left, starts with an image of Julie and Olivier making love; shows the young witness of the car accident; presents Lucille, the prostitute, in a peep show; depicts Julie's mother in the nursing home; cuts to Sandrine, Julie's husband's mistress, on the hospital bed; shows Sandrine's unborn son on the X-ray screen; and ends with a reflection of Julie's smiling face. The prevailing colour of the film, deep clear blue, begins the sequence and ends it. But the most stunning element of the sequence, indicating the ultimate masterly stroke of the filmmaker, is his incorporation of the magnificent musical arrangement of "The Hymn about Love", the Greek hymn written by the Apostle Paul in his letter to Corinthians (I Corinthians 13: 1-13). The predominant theme in the hymn is love: humble, powerful and selfless. This love offered by Julie makes life meaningful to all the film's protagonists. Moreover, her act of generosity towards them brings a final liberation to Julie herself. The powerful music supported by the words of the hymn provides an emotional and spiritual closure to Julie's suffering and to the film itself, which starts to live its own life from this point. The new life of the film emerges in the form of religious and spiritual meanings which the film evokes. *Blue* creates potent spiritual meanings, a fact which has been noted not only by film critics, but also by Catholic priests.[5]

Along these lines, Reverend Paprocki interprets Julie's escape after the death of her husband as a feat of self-renunciation. In his words, Julie's retreat to the thirteenth *arrondissement* of Paris "is not so much an act of ascetic resignation as it is one of despair: an act of conscious elimination of oneself from life".[6] The only element which brings her back to the past is the blue lampshade hanging from the ceiling – proof that to cut oneself off from the past is impossible. For Julie, "self-imposed isolation becomes a burden, especially since memory cannot be erased".[7] The music of her husband suddenly returns in the moments when it is least expected. The recurring motif is not accidental. It is the word "love" transformed into a few musical strains. As a result of the accident, she collides head-on with the brutality of life, and through her suffering she achieves a liberation voiced at the end of the film in the Greek hymn written by the Apostle Paul about love.

In the final sequence of the film, Paprocki proposes, Kieślowski refers to the theory of illumination of Augustine of Hippo, that suggests that a sudden transformation in man's life is possible:

> In this 'suddenness', according to the words of Simon of the New Theology, man experiences enlightenment, illumination. Julie experiences this feeling through the meeting with her husband's mistress and through music. Art shatters the negative intellectual paradigm in which she is locked and calls into question her cloistered world-view. Julie discovers a religious text in the last frames of the film. The discovery of this text opens a new perspective before her: that of love.[8]

This analysis describes the feelings of a person who, a deep believer himself, reacts to the film's spirituality at a personal level, and absorbs its complex philosophical message as his own experience. Reverend Paprocki reacts to the intricate interplay of visual and acoustic effects in the film at a deeply spiritual level, without analysing the complexity of the cinematic means. Reverend Sochoń is more specific in his analysis of the film when he refers to its sophisticated symbolics:

> The sign of a work's greatness, and not only that of a cinematic one, lies in the skill of the presentation of events and in the manipulation of symbols and associations so that the viewer can discover a fragment of his own experience in them. When the language of a film moves the viewer and touches his inner self, it then becomes a mark of reconciliation, a symbol, although I know that Kieślowski does not like this term. But after all, the ability to render events in symbols is one of the hardest to achieve. We aren't dealing with a shallow allegorical view of reality here, but with a difficult process of reconciliation before one can experience the everyday aspects of things. The symbol is a sign referring not only to the world of 'the ineffable', but it is also a marker of the forces connecting various aspects of an individual's life with that of the collectivity. It evokes in viewers an

interpretation which often surpasses the artist's vision.[9]

The opinions of these two Catholic priests clearly indicate that *Blue* provokes an intense debate on those aspects of spirituality in the film which can be interpreted as religious. However, the same elements, including the reference to Corinthians, can also be understood as a general, philosophical question which effects an interpretation of spirituality in a general sense, and not in a particular religious context. In this understanding, Kieślowski's films can be compared with the films of Robert Bresson and Andrej Tarkovskij. As Dan Millar states:

> Krzysztof Kieślowski is not interested in Sin. In fact, he is not a 'theological' director although he is best known for his series *The Ten Commandments*, 1987-88. But who is a theological director? John Ford, with his Irish Catholic sentiments and Protestant hymns? Obviously not. The austere Robert Bresson? Bresson wisely cut out the theological verbiage when filming Bernanos' *Diary of a Country Priest* [novel: 1936; film: 1950], keeping the drama – and the diary itself.[10]

The religious aspect of spirituality is echoed in the two other films of the trilogy, *White* and *Red*. As in *Blue*, biblical allusions are everywhere in these films. While the colour of *Blue* may be linked to the iconography of Mary, the Mater Dolorosa whose iconographic colour is blue in Julie's story, in *White* the mock-resurrections which accompany Karol on his journey associate him with Christ, if in a satirical manner. *Red*, on the other hand, has its roots in the Old Testament's depiction – as Dave Kehr puts it – of a "prickly, cranky, jealous God who keeps close tabs on his creations, judging them harshly and sending down rains and floods when they fail to perform to His expectations".[11]

In fact, *Blue*, *White* and *Red* continue the overall theme of spirituality and religious overtones conveyed in Kieślowski's earlier films, *No End* and *The Decalogue*. However, the three films, with their spiritual longings and philosophical deliberations, move us in other directions than Kieślowski's *Decalogue*. While the earlier series is clearly triggered by the Catholic doctrines of the Ten Commandments, the whole trilogy can be interpreted as a philosophical debate which presents the issues of spirituality in a more general manner than that accepted by one or other religious school of thought in a way specific to its beliefs.

The spirituality which pervades the films submerges them in semantic ambiguities. The blue trinket and the sudden sound of music in *Blue*, the porcelain figure of a woman in *White*, indicating a love which verges on worship for the Madonna-like woman, and the huge advertisement for the chewing-gum in *Red* all introduce moments of supernatural tension, a longing for some solutions in the lives full of despair and loneliness, and a desire to understand the inexplicable spiritual experience.

White

The second film of the trilogy, *White*, introduces the theme of equality. Here Kieślowski returns to the theme of social-orientation, which he so profoundly explored in *Blind Chance* and *Amator (Camera Buff,* 1979). *White* begins in Paris where Karol (Zbigniew Zamachowski), a Polish hairdresser, lives through an ordeal of a divorce and, as a result of his French wife's cruelty, lives on the fringes of society. His wife Dominique (Julie Delpy) humiliates him by citing his sexual impotence as the cause of the divorce, by taking his passport away, and, finally, by denying him access to their joint bank account. In order to survive, Karol is forced to play Polish folk songs on a comb in the subway. Another Pole, Mikołaj (Janusz Gajos), a professional bridge player, takes pity on his compatriot and smuggles him back to Warsaw in a huge suitcase. Karol finds himself back in the modest home he shares with his brother Jurek (Jerzy Stuhr). The second part of the film takes place in Warsaw, where Karol slowly climbs the social and financial ladders. From a hairdresser he turns into a bodyguard, next into a hard currency dealer, and then, by sheer shrewdness, amasses a fortune in a shady deal. However, Dominique is still in his heart and soul; he desires revenge and wants to get even with her. He devises a plan with which he lures Dominique back to Poland. Framed by Karol for his own alleged murder, Dominique is taken to prison and begs a mysteriously resuscitated Karol to marry her again. The film ends on an ambiguous note: although Karol cries when he sees Dominique imprisoned and powerless, Kieślowski leaves the viewer unsure of whether the couple will reunite, or whether Dominique will stay imprisoned forever.

White is clearly embedded in the political and social context of two countries, France and Poland. The theme of equality is not idealistically depicted in the framework of spirituality or brotherhood, but becomes a relative term, a comparative concept which takes these two countries as the platforms for comparison. In Poland, Karol feels superior to his wife both psychologically and sexually. In France, he is humiliated as a husband, as an entrepreneur and as a man. Literally and symbolically castrated by the situation in which he finds himself, he is unable to satisfy his wife sexually, unable to find a job, and unable to function in French society because he cannot speak the language. The Freudian and Lacanian connotations become excruciatingly obvious in this clever narrative.

The feelings of humiliation and helplessness set the tone for the film, with the protagonist appearing in the first sequences in trodden-down shoes, shoddy coat and crooked tie. Shot in a steely and grimy whiteness, the film introduces its colour motif in the form of pigeon excrement falling on Karol's coat when he stands in front of the Palais de Justice in Paris. This humiliating situation is later echoed in the bleakness and cruel indifference of the courtroom in which Karol reluctantly agrees with the judge that his sexual impotence constitutes grounds for divorce.

The colour white constitutes one of the elements of a tripartite motif which appears in almost every sequence of the film. Flashbacks in the form of the repeated scenes from the marriage ceremony shot in white are interspersed with flashforwards showing Dominique in a hotel room in Warsaw, and are followed by shots depicting the suitcase in which Karol will be transported to Poland. These three types of sequences come before and after contemporary sequences showing the present action in a documentary fashion. These diverse types of sequences constitute an interplay of motifs which determine both the narrative and the aesthetic structures of the film.

The huge suitcase which Dominique discards just after the pronouncement of their divorce conceals all Karol's possessions. The suitcase turns into a symbol of survival which refers to the endless emigrations of Poles who were often forced to live out of a suitcase for years. Finally, the suitcase functions as a means of escape from the world of humiliation and inequality. Its pervasive presence and symbolism are matched in the film by another symbolic motif, repeated throughout the whole trilogy. The motif presents old people engaged in similar acts. One such act in *White* involves an old man trying to throw a bottle into a tall recycling container. Karol watches the man doing this on the night he spends in the streets having been thrown out of his house by Dominique. His look is full of sympathy for the man, who slowly and patiently tries to accomplish this task. Kieślowski presents the sadness, but also the optimism of this situation when the man finally attains his goal. Perversely, the theme of attainment is simultaneously questioned when the bottle does not go right through. In this way, Kieślowski questions the happy ending to this event, as if balancing the positive aspects of life with the negative ones, distancing himself from the former in this carefully constructed image.[12]

The scene presenting the old man, one of many marginal personae in Kieślowski's films, parallels the scene involving the old lady in *Blue* whom Julie notices when she patiently attempts to place an empty bottle in a similar recycling container. The repeated motif binds *White* and *Blue* thematically and aesthetically, and provides a philosophical link to *Red* in which a similar event takes place. Such marginal but important personae also appear in other Kieślowski films, a phenomenon commented on by the Italian critic Gina Lagorio:

> Some of the marginal personae in Kieślowski's films are not really of secondary importance because of the meaning attributed to them: the beggar by the riverbank, warming himself, the traveller hauling his bags through the darkness, the pilgrim in rapt attention in the pristine silence – all of these figures could very well be the messengers of a paternal God or of an omniscient witness. Characteristic of Kieślowski is his subtlety of allusion. The consummate skill in presenting ideas, the suggestiveness of a certain shudder – without the trappings, decoration or the dialectics of rhetoric – is his great artistic strength. This subtlety constitutes a profundity of thought and an aesthetic zeal in understanding the dignity of one's work in a courageous search for truth which is more than a realistic stream of thoughts converted into images.[13]

Of all the symbolic representations, however, the colour white in the film functions most powerfully. This colour symbolises not only the starkness of Karol's life, but also the cruelty of Dominique's indifference to her ex-husband's suffering. In all the Paris scenes, Dominique's rejection of her husband's advances is grotesquely insensitive. The white colour, with its connotations of cruelty, is reiterated later in a porcelain bust of a female figure which Karol notices in the shop window. The bust's ironical, cold smile illustrates the insensitivity of a female.

A similar colour palette dominates in the later part of *White*, during the first meeting between Karol and his Polish compatriot Mikołaj. The crucial meeting takes place at a subway station, a dark and grim place, the overall gloomy texture of which seems to have been diffused by a white filter. The meeting between Karol and Mikołaj, two lonely and sad compatriots, offers some hope to the former. The two talk, drink some Polish vodka, and listen to a Polish song, played by Karol on a comb. The gestures, the word exchanges, the rituals of a song and a shot of vodka are painfully familiar, bitter in their literal explicitness, but also jarring in a stereotypical presentation of iconic Poles who are sad and romantic in their yearning for their native country. Mikołaj knows someone who does not want to go on living despite the fact that he has a wife and children who love him dearly. It becomes clear to the viewer (and probably to Karol) that Mikołaj has himself in mind. The conversation soon changes its course when the two men start talking about Karol and his desire to return to Poland. A plan is concocted by the two of them whereby Mikołaj decides to smuggle Karol in his huge suitcase. There is nothing in Paris which holds Karol. During his last attempt to contact Dominique on the phone, he hears her panting heavily on the phone in the throes of a powerful orgasm. The two francs which he saves from this telephone conversation will be a painful reminder of his desire for Dominique when he returns to Poland.

Karol's return to his mother country is both unusual and ironic. The corrupted airport workers, lured by the suitcase's imposing look, steal it and take it with other stolen luggage to the rubbish heap on the outskirts of the city. To their surprise, the huge suitcase contains one piece of luggage, a human being. Enraged by the lack of any financial gratification (after all, Karol has only two francs in his pocket), the workers brutally throw him out and beat him savagely. The only object they leave him with is the porcelain bust which Karol lovingly and smilingly discovers next to him when he wakes up from his stupor. "Jesus, home at last", sighs Karol, while a humorous polonaise underlines the irony of the whole situation. This scene links the film to Andrzej Wajda's *Popiół i diament* (*Ashes and Diamonds*, 1958), in which the last scene takes place on a similar rubbish heap. Maciek in *Ashes and Diamonds*, dying in the liberated Socialist Poland in 1945, is resurrected as Karol of *White* in a capitalist, corrupt country in 1994. The irony of the reference to the famous, iconic sequence is bitter, and the Polish musical element introduces even more powerful connotations. Kieślowski transforms this patriotic iconography into a powerful grotesque reminiscent of the writings of Sławomir Mrożek and Witold Gombrowicz.

The ironical paradigm of the whole sequence is later carried over to Karol's meeting with his brother Jurek, to whose dilapidated house Karol returns. Jurek, played by the excellent Polish comic actor Jerzy Stuhr reinforces the satirical aspect of the scene. Karol returns as the prodigal son to his beloved mother Poland, and is lovingly embraced by the fatherly figure of Jurek. The same comedy convention is repeated in all the scenes of Karol's "success" in the shady world of Polish business. Firstly, Karol works as a security man for a small businessman; then he outbids his employer in a questionable financial deal; and finally he becomes a successful businessman himself. Karol's financial success is bolstered by a deal with Mikołaj, who finds him after the return to Poland and again repeats his request for merciful killing. This time, Karol agrees and comes to the scene of the killing fully equipped. The surreal scene, filmed in slow-motion at the dark and gloomy Warsaw subway station, shows Karol shooting Mikołaj with a blank. The scene ends with both the killer and the victim running happily in the snow on the banks of the Vistula. This comic release is accompanied by the musical motif of a tango, providing all the connotations of the Poles' love for the grandiose and the emotional excess that this music evokes.

All these amusing scenes are interspersed with romantic interludes showing Karol at night drenched in sweat and dreaming about Dominique. The film seems to tell the tale of an unfulfilled love, of a perverse devotion to a woman which issues in spiritual and materialistic sacrifice. This presentation of sacrificial love binds the film with, on the one hand, the Polish tradition of romantic love, and, on the other, with the religious devotion to the Madonna figure in the Catholic religion. As in the other films in the trilogy, *White* makes the viewer enter the spiritual domain which overshadows the closure to a typical love story.

The film's final part – Karol's staging of his own funeral in order to lure Dominique to Poland and execute his revenge – combines romantic infatuation and paranoid social confusion with elements of the grotesque. The shredding of Karol's personal documents, the arranging for a corpse to be buried instead of Karol at a Warsaw cemetery, and the bribing of the authorities and the police in order to stage the framing of Dominique for Karol's murder merge with the sequences presenting the encounter of the ex-lovers in a Warsaw hotel, depicting their passionate lovemaking, culminating in a shattering orgasm. The colour white, which blinds the viewer in a sudden white-out of the lovemaking scene in the hotel, signifies the climax of the lovemaking, but also, at another level, illustrates the main thesis of the film. Similarity in sexual powers, in social positioning and in the psychological domain finally binds the two protagonists as equal partners, worthy of each other.

However, the scornful Karol desires absolute revenge, which materialises in the prearranged visit of the Polish officials the morning after their tryst, who promptly arrest Dominique for Karol's murder. The film ends with a romantic scene at the Warsaw prison. Dominique behind bars signals to Karol her wish to marry him, while Karol watches this spectacle through binoculars. The ending is inconclusive: Karol's tearful eyes do not tell us whether he will let Dominique go, whether he will marry her, or whether he will keep her behind bars for his own (sadistic or masochistic?) pleasure. Like Tomek in *Krótki film o miłości* (*A Short Film About Love*, 1988), Karol watches his object of love from a distance, carefully contemplating the odds. The cruel and indifferent white gives way to the warm tones of gold and orange which promise the presence of feelings, however unfulfilled they may be.

Three Colours: White is the film in which the social and documentary aspect of Kieślowski's filmography is most clearly demonstrated, but also perversely subverted in the end. *White* takes place in an insider's Warsaw, a city of new capitalist success, abruptly rising fortunes, new luxurious houses and excellent cars. At the same time, this is a city of crime, poverty and striking contrasts. The new, glittering Warsaw Airport contrasted with a rubbish heap at the city outskirts properly symbolises the atmosphere of social and political chaos in Poland. The country which openly turned to capitalism after 1989 is the country of cynicism, betrayal, failure and disillusionment. Only in this political and social atmosphere of moral disintegration could an ingenious plan to lure Dominique to Poland be fabricated and implemented. Thanks to the wheelings and dealings of Karol in the new Poland, a great fortune could be amassed, and the financial means used to devise a plan which involved a whole machinery of corruption and deceit. In this sense, the picture of the corrupt Poland of the 1990s which Kieślowski presents in *White* is as powerful politically as the picture of the authorities' apparatus in the Poland of the 1980s depicted in *Krótki film o zabijaniu* (*A Short Film About Killing*, 1988). In the latter film, the act of killing a taxi-driver by a young man from the provinces is presented in a similarly detached and cruel manner as is the act of hanging the boy by the Polish state at the end of the film. Equality in the aesthetic treatment of the two acts of murder in this film is followed six years later by an equality in the way in which the emotional revenge is executed by the two lovers in *White*. As in *A Short Film About Killing*, the deliberate and clever use of the powers provided by the state in *White* bring about the protagonists' downfall. After all, without a passport, access to money and pursued by police – all misfortunes directly caused by Dominique, but supported by the French state institutions – Karol could only hope that a miracle or blind chance would save his life. Similarly, in the revenge concocted by Karol in Poland, he uses the state institutions – the lawyer's office, the members of the security force, and the prison – to break Dominique down and make her entirely dependent on his decisions. The emotional powers experienced by the two lovers are not dependent on the individuals themselves, the director seems to be saying. The sweet revenge is possible only due to a particular social and historical situation in which France and Poland found themselves in the 1990s. In this Poland, corruption and lawlessness are rampant, and the law can be bent and manipulated depending on the content of the villain's purse. In this France, homophobia, racism and lack of tolerance are in place, as firmly entrenched in the social fabric as are the state institutional powers.

A suicidal attempt to eliminate oneself from life in order to relive the romantic, idealised emotions of *White* is transformed in *Red* into a poem on love in general, whether for a woman, a man or a dog. The film is an account of separate lives bound together by a blind chance, and, like *Blue*, it is a thesis on the nature of moral dilemmas, brotherhood and friendship.

The action of *Red* takes place in Geneva, where Valentine (Irène Jacob), a student and part-time model, accidentally strikes a German shepherd dog with her car, and takes the wounded dog to its owner, Joseph Kern, a retired judge. The judge, a repugnant old man, is engaged in a morally and legally highly questionable pleasure: listening in to the phone conversations of his neighbours. Although initially disgusted with the judge, Valentine slowly becomes obsessed with him, fascinated by his loneliness and life without love. A friendship evolves between these two unlikely companions, a delicately developing network of dependencies, favours granted and invitations reciprocated. The film develops into a miracle fable, a beautiful story of friendship, fate and lives unwinding in a parallel fashion.

The film proceeds in a series of parallel motifs, both narratively and aesthetically. The main narrative is intercut with one subordinate narrative line presenting the young lawyer Auguste (Jean-Pierre Lorit), and another, hinting at the complex relationship Valentine has with her lover Michel (Jean Schiegel). The camera laterally moves between the two main subplots, traversing physical spaces (Valentine and Auguste live on the same street) and symbolically cutting through the emotional layers of all the protagonists, both those visible in the frames and those, like Michel and Marc, Valentine's brother, hidden from the viewer's pondering eye.

This fragmentary nature of lives, emotions and visual fields is reiterated in the ways in which particular shots are built. Vertical and horizontal lines cut the spaces in the judge's house, Valentine's flat and the young lawyer's room, and uncannily divide the landscape of Geneva into fragments of a city. Like these spaces, the protagonists are also cut into fragments – their body parts, especially hands, faces and eyes, given most prominence. Red is ever-present in the background against which these bodies appear. Starting from the opening sequence and ending with the last shot, red defines the intensity of emotions, among which anger, powerlessness, pity and, finally, friendship are the most prominent.

The overall message of the film is epitomised by a huge poster which depicts Valentine's angry and passionate face against a red background. The intense red saturates her image on the poster, signifies the warmth and friendliness of Café Chez Joseph, permeates the interior of the judge's house, and fills the streets of Geneva with a delicate reddish glow. The colour red defines the essence of human lives presented in the film, in which emotions, the circumstances of fate, premonitions and surprising, unexpected meetings have priority over work, study and other activities in life. *Red* centres on the lives of Valentine, who saves the dog she hits with her car; of the young lawyer who is betrayed by his lover; and of the retired judge who overhears the conversations of his neighbours. Kieślowski gives all these situations a realistic, documentary feeling, with the intensity of fear, revulsion, hatred, love and friendship displayed on the protagonists' faces, on their dirty and unkempt bodies, in their messy houses and flats, and in the reactions of their dogs. The conversations between the judge and Valentine, between Valentine and Michel, and between the young lawyer and his lover are as intense and painful as the look on Valentine's face on the huge poster. As if life and death depended on the resolution to these conversations, the locations in which they take place are saturated in a reddish glow which reinforces their intensity.

In the final sequence of the film, the faint smile on the judge's face after he has learned about Valentine's miraculous escape from the drowning ferry is again juxtaposed with the intense red of the huge poster. The red colour, with its many ambiguities, defines the inexpressible feelings evoked by the film. In its ugliness and beauty, with its loneliness and friendship, and with its hatred and love, life goes on, Kieślowski seems to say. Let us quietly celebrate its multitudinous qualities, and let us participate in both its glorious and its horrible aspects.

Liberty, equality and fraternity: these three themes are contextualised by Kieślowski within certain aspects of civilisation. Despite their overall universalism, the films are placed firmly within the context of contemporary times, the times of spectacular technological developments, on the one hand, and of man's alienation and helplessness on the other. By presenting these disparate aspects of contemporary life in a heart-rending manner, Kieślowski makes a powerful statement critical of contemporary times. In this discursive shift from a locally political statement to one on global aspects of civilisation, Kieślowski's films transcend the mundane aspects of local politics, and make the entanglements of everyday life significant and worthy of concentration.

All the films are set firmly in the contemporary reality of France, Switzerland and Poland. They communicate an acute awareness of alienation and helplessness within the context of civilisation's achievements. In *Blue*, the tragic events are presented amidst the circumstances characteristic of a highly developed country. The death of Julie's family is caused by a car accident; Julie's life is saved by the medical technology; her return to real life is triggered by other technical devices – television and photography. These last mechanisms reveal to Julie her husband's lover. They are cruelly efficient in these revelations. The photographs showing the two lovers are clear and unambiguous in their perfect technical presentation.

Similarly, in *White*, Karol's rescue is made possible thanks to another 20th-century invention, the aeroplane. Karol is rescued by a Polish comrade who sends him to Poland in a huge suitcase. Later, in Poland, Karol's revenge on Dominique is rendered possible due to a specifically Polish form of capitalism, which, in the beginning of the 1990s, produced huge fortunes in a matter of months. Again, the universal themes of betrayal, love and forgiveness are firmly grounded in the context of contemporary times.

Red begins with an image of telephone wires carrying conversations in all geographical directions to many people at the same time. This flashy, exciting, colourful and rapidly moving sequence properly defines the quality of contemporary life in which a telephone conversation (now a conversation on the Internet, which is void of the human voice, with all its nuances and cultural and geographical markers) often replaces real human contact. The image also introduces the key element of the narrative, the main carrier of which is a telephone wire. The telephone line shapes human behaviour, and "monitors" fate itself. The retired judge overhears conversations on the phone. He has the power to disrupt the life of a family (for instance, to inform the wife about her husband's homosexual infidelities) or to decide the fate of a drug dealer. He causes real fear in people who do not suspect him of invading probably the last bastion of privacy and safety, a telephone communication at home. At the same time, it is through a telephone weather report that the judge learns about the weather before Valentine crosses the channel in a ferry. Again, the technological invention, so intimately related to contemporary times, plays an important part in the dealings of fate.

In the introduction of the theme of surveillance in *Red*, with its questioning of the territory of privacy, Kieślowski poses issues that are politically volatile as they concern the surveillance problems present in every country. The film action is situated in Switzerland, the country of the highest standard of living in Europe, making this message doubly ironic. The country of affluence and political stability emerges from this film as a country of alienation and helplessness, a much more realistic picture than exotic, fascinating Paris, pulsating with life and full of congenial people in *Blue*. The depiction of human life in Geneva is more in tune with what we know about life in highly developed countries, in which human contact is often limited to technological connections.

In *Red*, the protagonists mainly converse on the phone; the relationships break down on the phone (Valentine and her absent lover express their concerns about their love affair on the phone; Auguste cannot get hold of his lover when he calls her at home); and the main emotional exchanges are carried out on the phone (they are overheard by the retired judge). The film's overall "deep red" colour palette looks quite sad in the beginning of the film. Red, the colour of love and friendship, brightens up when the protagonists engage in a normal, hesitant conversation without any technological mediators involved. In this sense, the film expresses a desperate longing for a human, face-to-face contact, a real brotherhood based on the feelings of trust and respect. In this age of rapid technological development, in which humans are replaced by machines, this message is especially powerful.

In his turning to global life issues, Kieślowski manages to create an important statement on the essence of life in contemporary times, in the Europe of the 1990s. In this Europe, as elsewhere in highly-developed Western countries, technology mixes with spiritual longings, morality and ethical considerations. This fusion of the contemporary and the spiritual is effectively demonstrated in the ways in which Kieślowski aesthetically and ideologically constructs his films.

For instance, the contrasting sequences beginning and ending each film in the trilogy illustrate an ideological tension, a shift from the presentation of signifiers characteristic of contemporary times – the car's hydraulic pipe; the transmission belt and the telephone wires – to phenomena belonging to a different realm: spirituality, romantic love, and friendship or brotherhood understood in a deeply philosophical and spiritual sense.

This profound understanding of the social and cultural reality of contemporary times includes the spiritual uncertainty of blind chance as its inherent component. Kieślowski has always ascribed great importance to fate and blind chance as phenomena which control the lives of human beings:

I was always fascinated by blind chance. Our life depends on blind chance very often. I know what part blind chance played in my life, so when I am writing scripts I have to think about it as well. When we ask ourselves a question why someone met with this particular fate, we are looking for reasons, and we discover the meaning of blind chance.[14]

Thus, a theme present in Kieślowski's earlier films, such as *The Decalogue* and *The Double Life of Véronique*, aptly illustrates the narrative developments in *Three Colours*. It is by blind chance that Julie survives the accident and has to live through the process of spiritual reincarnation. Blind chance is responsible for Véronique's meeting with her double in Kraków, and blind chance brings Karol and Mikołaj together in *White*. It is also blind chance which leads Valentine to make friends with the retired judge in *Red*, thus repeating the motif of Kieślowski's whole artistic production. As in *Blind Chance* itself, all Kieślowski's protagonists seem to be at fate's mercy, their will-power and intentions of action being suspended or rendered irrelevant. The human being is not a willing subject in his films, but rather a loosely floating object on political and social waters. In its description of man's helplessness in view of history and fate, Kieślowski's cinema becomes a powerful political statement.

Paradoxically, by turning to more general issues in his last four films, Kieślowski makes a politically powerful statement in a broader sense than merely local politics. Instead of questioning a particular social or political system, the director seems to challenge the whole civilisation with its technological progress, mercantile interests, selfishness and narrow-mindedness. Unwittingly, the films reveal "the truth" about the political time in which they appear. They do not exhibit isomorphic correspondence and temporal direction with the politics of an era, but offer us clues about "the political ethos" or "character"[15] of a period. In this sense, Kieślowski's films are

[A] part of history as valid evidence of the developing sensibilities of people, and may be studied as observable aesthetic artifacts of the unobservable processes of attitude formation and change among populations, constituting the 'climate of opinion' or 'structure of feeling' characteristic of an age.[16]

Notes

[1] Translated from the Polish: "Na początku wydawało mi się, że trzeba opisać świat. Brało się to z tego, że świat nie był w ogóle opisany. I kiedy skończyłem, to wydawało mi się, że kamera jest takim świetnym narzędziem, żeby opisać świat". Marek Henrykowski and Mikołaj Jazdon (eds), "Fragmenty spotkania z Krzysztofem Kieślowskim (24.11.1996) Teatr Ósmego Dnia, Poznań" ["Excerpt from a Meeting with Krzysztof Kieślowski (24.II.1996) The Eighth Day Theatre, Poznań"], *Kino* 29: 5 (May 1996): 9-12, especially 12.

[2] Danusia Stok (ed), *Kieślowski on Kieślowski* (London; Boston: Faber and

Faber, 1993): 194.

3 Ibid.

4 Ellie Ragland and Elizabeth Wright ("*The Double Life of Véronique*. An Inquiry into the Existence of Woman", *Psychoanalytic Psychology* 10: 3 [1993]: 481-486) suggest that the moment "out of joint" experienced by the two Véroniques are "effective metaphors for the uncanny disturbance of the gaze of the Other" (484).

5 Two articles, "Niebieski jak niebo" ("Blue Like the Sky") and "Pokonać śmierć" ("To Defeat Death"), published by Catholic priests, Reverends Henryk Paprocki and Jan Sochoń, respectively, in *Kwartalnik filmowy* 4 (1993-94): 79-112, serve as examples of this spiritual interpretation.

6 Translated from the Polish: "jest nie tyle aktem ascetycznej rezygnacji czy też rozpaczy, ile raczej aktem świadomego wyeliminowania siebie samej z życia". Paprocki: 79.

7 Translated from the Polish: "Pustelnia dobrowolnie zaakceptowana staje się ciężarem, zwłaszcza że nie można zabić pamięci". Ibid.

8 Translated from the Polish: "'Nagle', zgodnie ze słowami Symeona Nowego Teologa, człowiek doświadcza objawienia olśnienia. Julia doznaje tego właśnie uczucia w chwili spotkania z kochanką swego męża, i poprzez muzykę. Sztuka rozbija negatywny schemat myślowy Julie i kwestionuje jej pustelniczy światopogląd. Julie poznaje tekst biblijny w ostatnich kadrach filmu. Poznanie tego tekstu otwiera przed nią inną perspektywę – miłość". Ibid: 80.

9 Translated from the Polish: "Znakiem wielkości dzieła, nie tylko filmowego, jest umiejętność takiego przedstawienia zdarzeń i takiego operowania symbolami i skojarzeniami, aby odbiorca mógł w nich odnaleźć cząstkę własnych doświadczeń. Kiedy język filmu porusza widza, dotyka jego wewnętrznych stanów, wtedy staje się znakiem jednoczącym, symbolem, choć wiem, że Kieślowski nie lubi tego określenia. Ale przecież umiejętność symbolizacji bywa jedną z najtrudniejszych do osiągnięcia. Nie chodzi tutaj o jakąś płytką alegoryzację rzeczywistości, ale o trudny proces jednoczenia ukrytych przed potocznym doświadczeniem aspektów rzeczy. Symbol jest znakiem odsyłającym nie tylko do świata 'niewypowiedzianego', ale jest też znakiem mocy łączącej różne aspekty życia jednostkowego i społecznego. Wyzwala w odbiorcach interpretacje często wykraczające poza zakres kreślony wizją artysty". Sochoń: 84.

10 Dan Millar, "A Great Polish Film-Maker: Krzysztof Kieślowski", *Durham University Journal* 85: 54 (1993): 131.

11 Dave Kehr, "To Save the World: Kieślowski's *Three Colors* Trilogy", *Film Comment* 30: 6 (November/December 1994): 18.

12 I owe this suggestion to Paul Coates, who has always been sceptical of romanticising and idealising Kieślowski's narratives.

[13] Translated from the Italian: "Per questo certe figure marginali nel cinema di Kieślowski non lo sono poi tanto: almeno per il significato che rivestono – un barbone che si scalda in riva al lago, un viaggiatore che sposta le sue valigie nel buio, un infermiere che ascolta tacito e imperscrutabile – sono tutti, o possono esserlo, i messaggeri di un Dio paterno, o testimoni imparziali di un destino. È questa leggerezza di accenni, questa suprema capacità di fare affiorare un'idea, di suggerire un trasalimento, senza appesantirli in compiacimenti di alcuna retorica, né decorativa né dialettica, la grande forza creatrice di Kieślowski. Una leggerezza pari alla gravità di pensiero, di impegno etico, di consapevolezza responsabile anche nella dignità del proprio lavoro, di coraggio nella ricerca di una verità che è ben altro che realistica sequenza di dati trasferiti in immagini." Gina Lagorio, "Il Decalogo di Kieślowski: Ricreazione narrativa", translated by Barbara Stelmaszczyk-Swiontek in *Film na świecie* 3/4 (388/389): 47. Translated from Polish to English by Christopher Johnston.

[14] Translated from the Polish: "Przypadek mnie zawsze frapował. Nasze życie zależy często od przypadku. Obserwuję to przy wielu okazjach. Wiem, jaką rolę pełni w moim własnym życiu, zatem pisząc scenariusze, muszę o nim myśleć. Gdy zadajemy sobie pytanie, dlaczego kogoś spotkał taki lub inny los, szukamy przyczyn i odkrywamy znaczenie przypadku." See "Pańskie filmy sa rentgenogramami duszy... Z Krzysztofem Kieślowskim rozmawiają Michel Ciment et Hubert Niogret" ["Your films are X-rays of the soul... Michel Ciment and Hubert Niogret talk to Krzysztof Kieślowski"], in *Film na świecie* 3/4 (388/389): 31. (Translated from *Positif* [October 1989] by Józef Podgórski; translated into English from the Polish version published in *Film na świecie* by Christopher Johnson.)

[15] James Combs, *Movies and Politics: The Dynamic Relationship* (New York; London: Garland Publishing, 1993): 4.

[16] Ibid.

"The inner life is the only thing that interests me": a conversation with Krzysztof Kieślowski

Paul Coates

[Interview conducted in Warsaw, October 1995; translated from the Polish by Paul Coates. Polish transcript approved by Krzysztof Kieślowski.]

Paul Coates: *I would like to begin with a question that concerns your position in the cinematic tradition. You were once described as continuing the line of Munk in Polish cinema. Do you consider this an appropriate, or the best, way of describing your work, or are there other possible models you would prefer?*

Krzysztof Kieślowski: I do not engage in classifications of this kind, particularly not theoretical classifications, for an objective view is impossible. Everyone who does so has a more objective view than I do, and regardless of whether he does so badly or well, from his own point of view he is right. If there is a tradition that could be subdivided, in the most crass and idiotic manner, into, let us say, the romantic tradition of Wajda and the more rational one of Munk –

As has been done traditionally –

– then I suppose that obviously I stand more in the rational than the romantic one. But I don't think that my films are devoid of romanticism, perhaps not in the sense that is traditional in Polish Romanticism, which is more historical and more closely linked to social movements. My own romanticism is probably more human and personal, more concerned with the fate of the individual, but I think there is a considerable amount of it in these films. So I don't think one can clearly say "I am closest to *this* one". At least I can't personally.

Moving on to a different context, that of world and auteur cinema. There is a scene in Trois couleurs: blanc *[Three Colours: White, 1994] in which a poster for* Le Mépris *[Contempt, 1963] is shown next to Dominique's window, recalling the practices of the Nouvelle Vague of which* Contempt *itself was an expression – the use of posters to pay homage or signal thematic links. Does this mean that you situate yourself in a Nouvelle Vague tradition, and perhaps even render homage to Godard, a director who is not much liked in Poland?*

The answer to that happens to be very simple. I very much like and value Godard's early films and would gladly pay them some kind of homage. Not the later ones, for they are alien to me and I think that unfortunately they are to the public as well. And it isn't a question of whether or not he's liked in Poland – I think he's hardly known. Very few of his films have been screened in Poland, which is the main reason for saying he's little known. Of course, I know the early films and would gladly pay homage to them. The poster from *Contempt* found its way there completely accidentally. I had absolutely no intention of putting up a poster from Godard or *Contempt* or anything that would make any kind of allusion. I wanted to put up a contemporary poster with an actress considered beautiful and sexy – someone like Kim Basinger – and it was a matter of complete indifference to me who it was. But that turned out to be tremendously expensive. So the producer suggested putting up one of his own posters, and since he'd distributed *Contempt* it didn't cost a thing. So we used that. The reasons were purely financial and had nothing to do with homage or love, and absolutely nothing to do with any distaste for anything either.

Would you consider that accidental solution perhaps a better one?

No, the solution was a worse one, only cheaper. It wasn't a matter of principle, and I gladly oblige the producer where non-essentials are concerned and the result will be that the film is cheaper.

When discussing Byłem żołnierzem */I Was a Soldier, 1970/ – which is the first of your documentaries I saw and, to my mind, a shattering film – you said among other things that what interested you most were the soldiers' dreams. Do you see dream as a leitmotif of your films – in the sense of a utopia, a window onto something else?*

Obviously that has been of interest to me all along. It's less a question of dreams as such than of dreams as one expression of people's inner lives. Dreams are the classic expression of inner life: they belong to a single person and, as you well know, a dream is one of the few things that cannot be narrated. Not even the greatest literature has done them justice – not to mention the cinema, which has never done so.

Not even Surrealism?

Not even Surrealism has done dreams justice – no one has. Not even literature, which is far less literal, less real, and allows a far greater margin of interpretive freedom. So they are typical of something one person is unable to share with another. It often happens that we tell someone a dream, or someone tells us one, out of a desire to share our experience. At the same time, dreams are extraordinary because they cannot be shared, for the feeling of helplessness or fear or happiness within the dream only concerns ourselves and cannot be shared in any way. There is no known way of sharing it with anyone. It is a classic element of inner life. And since the inner life – unlike public life – is the only thing that interests me, dreams obviously continue to do so, and you are doubtless right to say that dreams are reflected in various ways in many, many of the films.

You once remarked in an interview that you prefer not to spell things out in full, and prefer to leave the viewer the option of taking something away from the cinema, so the film is not expended when the lights come up. Does that have any connection with your recent tendency to make films in cycles, and do you now only want to make films in cycles?

No, I think I have long believed that the viewer can become a partner. From the very outset it always seemed to me – and I once said as much to a Polish essay and am reproached for it to this day – that I make films for myself. I meant that I make films for people like me, people who are open to sitting down and having a chat, reflecting together, sharing. In other words, I think that, if I share the film with the viewer, the viewer will share its reception with me – which means that there is a certain balance and justice about the matter. I tell him a story and expect him not only to hear it out, but also to enter into some kind of a relationship with it. And, in order for him to be able to do so, the story I tell him must leave him a certain amount of space and freedom to interpret or take it – or certain parts of it – one way or another. I've always thought this and still do today. It has nothing to do with the cycles, which were simply practical. There came a point at which I found it interesting and practical for production reasons. And obviously it is probably linked to a biological feature or trait of mine, which is that I like and want to do a lot and do it quickly in order to have peace and quiet afterwards. But, although I imagine I'll have peace and quiet afterwards, of course I never do, for there is something else that needs to be done. For instance, when making *Dekalog* [*The Decalogue*, 1988], I thought: I'll make ten films and then I'll have peace and quiet and won't have to do anything for five, six or seven years. Meanwhile, it obviously isn't like that at all. There is certainly a kind of psychic need within me to do as much as possible.

The issue of "pessimism" has often been raised in connection with your films. You remarked once, à propos *the ending of* Trois couleurs:

rouge /Three Colours: Red, *1994], that the fact that you had learned how to make a film with an optimistic ending did not mean you had become an optimist. Would you accept Gramsci's famous formula of optimism of the will, pessimism of the intellect?*

I agree completely with Gramsci. There definitely is something of the sort. One could enlarge upon it and speak not only of pessimism of the intellect, but also regarding the sphere for which feelings are responsible, the domain of sensibility. I would be pessimistic with regard to that too. But I agree completely where optimism of the will is concerned.

The motif of cold has appeared from time to time in your films in connection with art – for instance, in Amator /Camera Buff, *1979], Irenka accuses Filip of having become cold, and in* La Double Vie de Véronique /The Double Life of Véronique, *1991], Alexandre betrays Véronique by using her life as material. The theme also appears in other great artists of this century – Thomas Mann, for instance, or Bergman. Various critiques of your own work, particularly towards the end of the 1980s, even speak of vivisection. Do you think that such a connection necessarily exists? And is that the reason why you do not accept the word "artist" as a description of yourself?*

I do not consider myself to be an artist at all. As you know, I have never said I was an artist, since I think that word has to be reserved for certain special people and events of which – one has to admit – there have been fewer and fewer in recent decades. There are fewer and fewer people worthy of the name. That is also why I do not use the word of myself.

But neither did Bergman – he described himself as an artisan working on a cathedral.

I use the word "artisan" too. I've always viewed film as artisanal, and every film as something produced in a single edition. That is a feature both of artworks and artisanal work. There is only one Notre Dame Cathedral, but every piece of artisanal work is unique too, for that is what underlies the craftsman's feel for it as he produces it. It requires a certain feel for it, for giving something of oneself. An artisan is not just someone who works with his hands but someone who imparts to the work he is producing something of his own heart or intellect, as Gramsci would have it. I has nothing to do with coldness. Coldness or cynicism...

They're not the same thing –

They're not the same at all, but coldness, cynicism, distance – all these things have a common identity somewhere. And this is very characteristic of our era. I have the impression that we are increasingly cold and cynical towards one another and create ever-greater distances. I even have the impression that I can remember a time when it was warmer, and that over the 50 years of my life I have been watching it grow colder around each and every one of us. We treat others more coolly and they do the same to us. I think this is a trend we are witnessing and that everything in the world changes at some point. It can easily be observed and so it obviously finds its way into the films I have made, for I have tried to depict the times in which we live.

I would like to revert to the documentaries and gradually work through various films from your career. Traditionally documentary has been considered an "educational" form. Does the fact that you have ceased making documentaries have something to do with a shift to a more agnostic position?

No. In Poland the documentary does not have an educational tradition – so much so that in Poland there has been a very clear institutional and milieu-based distinction between the educational film and the documentary, which need not have any ambitions to teach. During the period of Communism there were two production studios – the Wytwórnia Filmów Oświatowych [Educational Film Studio] in Łódź and the Documentary Film Studio in Warsaw – so there was an institutional separation. And on top of that there were completely different sections for documentarists and educational film directors within the Association of Polish Filmmakers. Thus, postwar Poland saw the creation of a tradition in which the documentary did not have to educate at all, but concerned itself rather with description. That is, it was concerned to answer the question "what is the world like?", rather than "what ought it to look like, or how good it would be if it looked this way?". No one imposed an educational function upon documentarists. The public made no such demand nor, in fact, did the authorities, who provided the money. Obviously, the authorities wanted one to describe the world as better than it was, and that was why they had censorship and various other instruments. But that doesn't mean they required any educational function of us.

Documentaries mostly tend to be short, although perhaps that tradition has altered somewhat in recent years, with the films of Lanzmann, Ophüls and so on. Did you ever consider this a fundamental problem with the way in which this form is used and did you ever aspire to making longer documentaries, even especially long ones, in the manner of Lanzmann?

Of course, I did have ambitions of that kind and even made some long films and wanted to make some – as you put it – exceptionally long ones. That wasn't possible, but I did want to do that, and I made several documentaries of over an hour and fifteen minutes. That possibility existed. Of course, there was always the problem of how to distribute them, except that – unlike today, when the costs have to be met – at that time they didn't, so one could go ahead and freely make films which didn't have to cover their costs. It was a completely different way of thinking, and Western viewers or readers find it terribly hard to understand that there was a time in Poland, under Communism, when film – which is now a product, and also an element in an economic game – was not and did not have to be a product. I could make a documentary that lasted an hour and twenty minutes and was not screened anywhere, and this was not held against me at all. Of course, I was criticised on the grounds that these films were not particularly pro-government, and perhaps even opposed to the authorities, but not because they didn't pay their way. Incidentally, despite everything, the films I made *did* make money, for they were sold abroad and shown many times within Poland. I never had the problem of feeling that I owed the state any money. I made a few films like that. One was called *Życiorys* [*Curriculum Vitae*, 1975], another *Pierwsza miłość* [*First Love*, 1974], and yet another *Nie wiem* [*I Don't Know*, 1977]. These films lasted about an hour. I probably even made one that was even longer, I'm not sure which, but I probably did.

I would like to move on to Blizna *[The Scar, 1976], since, in your interview with Danusia Stok, which is well-known to English readers, you described this film as "Socialist realism à rebours". I do not think you have been completely fair to your own film. Would you like to say a bit more about it?*

I simply didn't like this film and never have done – neither when I made it nor today.

Why?

It seems to me – to start with – that it was based on a script with a completely false concept. And it is probably so badly directed that I don't think it could appeal to anyone for any reason. I personally dislike it so it's hard for me to have a better attitude to it. Muddled, messy, badly made, badly acted, badly edited, overlong and, in general, I don't know if it's any good for anything to anyone.

Did you deliberately begin making "short films" – to use a title that was later to have its own career – because of certain criticisms levelled at your earlier films (for instance, Bez końca *[No End, 1984], which immediately preceded the change), charges of incoherence and containing too much material?*

Those criticisms are accurate and correct. These films really are too long and do not cohere; they really do fall apart. Of course, some of them may contain an idea that holds them together, but it is harder to discern one in the others. That is true. In using the title "short", I did not deliberately set out to embark on a new path. To tell the truth, the idea of calling these films "short films" came to me when they were already finished, when the first had already been edited.

Was this a kind of substitute title, like The Double Life of Véronique, *with which you have expressed dissatisfaction?*

No, it wasn't. These films didn't have any titles at all, since we thought we'd call them, for example, *Decalogue 5*, and that would be that. Later, when making the film version I already knew, of course, that I would have to find a title, but I never found one I seriously considered. I remember that we were at the stage of completing the editing of the film about killing. I went to the post office to post a letter somewhere and on my way back, just as I was leaving the post office, the idea "a short film about killing" came to me. I thought it was a good idea, because it was true: it really was about killing, really was short, and was a film. I thought it was a good title because it would then make it possible to call the next film, which we had finished shooting and were starting to edit, *Krótki film o miłości [A Short Film About Love,* 1988]. And this would create a sort of cycle, as you put it. For quite apart from the fact that *The Decalogue* is a television cycle, within it there emerged an additional tiny film cycle made up of two films. At one point, there was even a plan to make a feature out of another one of the films in *The Decalogue*, and to shoot extra material for it.

Which one would that have been?

Zanussi, who heads our production unit, wanted to do this with *Decalogue 9*. One could calmly have added some incidents, shot them and made a feature that would simply have been called *A Short Film About Jealousy*.

Would that have been due to the fact that Decalogue 9 *and* A Short Film About Love *have often been linked, since there are certain obvious connections?*

Yes, there are obvious connections. I don't know whether the film would have been about love or about jealousy – it would have been a film about two sides of the same feeling, the same coin. So they would naturally have to have been connected in some way. For

Zanussi, it was rather a question of it being a story that was very attractive and told briskly, and that it could be turned into a feature with only a small injection of finance. And in connection with that there began to be talk of the money's importance, and that some money could perhaps be made on it. But to tell the truth I didn't have the strength to set about it. I no longer wanted to.

You had no desire to do it?

I did not have any strong desire. This was after producing those ten films, after over a year's shooting with editing at the same time: it was all too much. I suppose that, had I been fresher and more relaxed, I would have decided to do it. But since I was already really all-in I simply felt I didn't want to.

Since The Decalogue, *words such as "mystery" and "mysticism" begin to appear in articles about your films, and you yourself have often used the word "mystery" to designate a certain value. Would you like to define it more precisely? Does it have a certain religious undertone, for instance?*

No, there are no religious undertones. I think it has very clear existential connotations – that it is purely and simply the mystery we actually face every day. The mystery of life, of death, of what follows death, what preceded life: the general mystery of our presence in the world at this particular time, in this particular social, political, personal and familial context, and any other context you might think of. Strictly speaking, every question contains a mystery. And it doesn't seem to me to be an issue whether or not we succeed in deciphering it, since obviously we won't. Since this is how I think about life – both my own, and life in general – this way of thinking obviously must be inherent in my films, since I don't just pursue directing as a profession, but make my own films with my own stories. This is the heart of the matter. Of course, within the framework of the film, the story one tells, what appears on the screen, these mysteries often involve very small things or things that are inexplicable, things the heroes do not want to explain, or things about the heroes I do not want to explain myself. They are often very tiny, insignificant things. But I think that there is a point at which all these trifling matters, all these little mysteries, come together like droplets of mercury to form a larger question about the meaning of life, about our presence here, what in fact went before and what will come after, whether there is someone who controls all this, or whether it all depends on our own reason or on someone or something else. That mystery is there all the time. Of course, it has certain religious connotations, but those connotations fundamentally arise out of the existential questions, rather than the other way around.

Although it is only with The Decalogue *that the word begins to appear in your own interviews and in essays about your films, would you see any continuity with your earlier films here?*

Definitely. You mentioned *I Was a Soldier*: after all, the dreams of people who lost their sight during the war, what they imagine, is, in fact, a mystery. Perhaps – no one can know, but perhaps – it is thanks to their having dreams (and, as some of them said, even in colour) that they are able to live through each successive day. That is a mystery. This mystery has always been a part of my films because I have always tried to get close to people, whether the film is a documentary or fiction – to get close to the heroes. If one is close to the heroes that mystery is bound to come out, for it really does exist.

I would like to take this question a step further. Since this religio-mystical, mysterious element appears most clearly in the films you have co-written with Krzysztof Piesiewicz, although it seems to me less in the films themselves than in the scripts (for instance, in the script for Three Colours: Red, *Valentine crosses herself on entering the church, and this is absent from the film, while the priest who appears at the end of the script to* Decalogue 8 *isn't in the film, and so on), can one say that your contribution to this collaboration is more agnostic than that of Piesiewicz?*

I don't know. I don't think one can say that. I think that the priest, or the need for belief, for example, appears tremendously clearly in *Przypadek* [*Blind Chance*, 1981], if you've seen it.

Yes, I have.

In the second section, the hero has a clear need to discover some sort of meaning in life and belief. I'm not certain whether a priest appears there, and that's not terribly important, but perhaps the most religious scene in all the films I've made occurs in *Blind Chance*, when the hero kneels during baptism and prays "O God, I have been baptised, I ask only one thing of you: be there. I ask only that: be there". This is perhaps the most religious scene in all my films and I wrote its script by myself. So I do not think that there was a difference between Krzysztof Piesiewicz and myself concerning belief, God, and the meaning of belief, which affected my view of these things in any way. Overall, I have done perhaps two religious scenes – that is, two scenes about belief. One, in *Blind Chance*, about the need for belief, and the other, which is also about the need for belief – through negation – when the hero overturns the altar in *Decalogue 1*. In one, it is a matter of a screenplay I wrote myself; in the other, of one I co-wrote with Piesiewicz. Valentine does not cross herself in the church for the simple reason that we thought it took up too much time. That church interior was not so attractive that it was worth saying much about it, although doubtless if I had thought about Valentine's attitude she ought to have crossed herself – except that we did not even shoot this, for it would definitely have gone on too long. In *Decalogue 8*, we cut out an element we had already shot, because it was too obvious.

With regard to Trois couleurs *[Three Colours, 1993-94], did you ever consider giving these films different titles – for instance, "Liberté, égalité and fraternité"?*

No, I never considered titles of that kind, just as I never considered naming the parts of *The Decalogue* after the commandments – particularly since in the case of *The Decalogue*, as you know, there is the problem of the different numbering in the translations into different languages. That would have been meaningless. But it wasn't for that reason that I didn't name the parts of *The Decalogue* after the commandments, or call *Trois couleurs: bleu* [*Three Colours: Blue*, 1993] "Liberty", but because it seems to me to be a question of the partnership with the viewer, the possibility of opening a dialogue. The moment something is named, the possibility of free interpretation is cut off. The moment you leave something unnamed, and leave the place of the name open, that place can be filled by anyone in the cinema, everyone who has bought a ticket. If *I* fill that space, it cannot be filled by the viewer. It's very simple, logical.

So you would consider the name of a colour more open than that of a concept?

Quite definitely, since, although people may know that to some extent I am referring to freedom, if I don't name it outright then everyone can imagine equally well that the question at issue is the negation of whatever is, or could be, contained in the title. Logic dictates that it is definitely more open. It is simple logic, and not my own intentions, that causes this to be more open than naming it outright as "freedom".

But in various cultures, and perhaps even most of them, colours have certain conventional associations – for instance, blue with cold, depression and so on.

You could say so, but it is not necessarily the case – it depends.

At least within our culture...

It depends which cultures. Even within ours – "ours" being the so-called West European culture – there are massive differences.

For instance, "I am blue today", as one could say in English.

Which means "sad", of course. But on the other hand in Spain – or perhaps Portugal, I'm not sure – it's quite the reverse: their age-old traditions identify blue with something vital and full of energy. I can't quite recall the examples, but I've met numerous people from various parts of the world – and even from our cultural sphere – who have explained that there are vastly different relations with these colours. In Greece, too – which unfortunately I won't be visiting in two days' time – the relationship with the colour is completely different. How strange! It is not necessarily the case that our area classifies a single colour unambiguously. But the fact that in English – or, in fact, in American – blue is associated with sadness, as in "the blues", does not mean that it is associated with freedom. Freedom has nothing whatsoever in common with sadness or cold – one could say, quite the reverse. Actually, freedom ought to be in red, since if we really wished to reflect on what is associated with liberty, what colour flag, it would be with revolution, blood, and so on. But I term it "blue" for the simple reason that on the French flag – and the film's finances came from France – blue is the first colour. If a different country had provided the finance – Germany, for instance – and I had made it as a German film, then yellow would have taken the place of blue and one would have had "yellow, red and black". It really is not important. However, the very fact that it has this name means that it is open to possible interpretations, as is shown by our current discussion; that it can be associated with the meanings this colour has in our culture and with other meanings in other cultures; that "blue" need not mean "freedom" at all, but actually be its complete opposite; and that it can be freedom, too – for why shouldn't it? Consequently, as I've said, it is logically far more open. Of course, I considered other titles and, to tell the truth, I even think it would be better if one could find different titles for these films – not "liberty", "equality" and "brotherhood", but completely different ones. I stopped puzzling over this when the producer said he liked it. I told him that I didn't like the fact that, in a certain sense, *Three Colours* falls under a particular Godardian tradition of the title. But he told me that he liked that a lot. And, since he was quite definite, I realised that there could be two opinions on this matter and gave up my search for a title. What is more I knew what terrible problems I have finding titles, and, since he liked it, I left it at that.

Within the first two films at least you allude to their possible titles, since the word "liberté" appears in one shot as Julie climbs the steps of the Palais de Justice, and the next film reveals the next word, "égalité" – but one never sees "fraternité". Is this just because that story is set in

Geneva and does not involve Paris?

Precisely for that reason. If it had had some link with Paris we would definitely have repeated this joke – for it is anecdotal and has nothing to do with the heart of the matter – for a third time, but we didn't succeed. And unfortunately there is no such inscription on Geneva's Palais de Justice.

So although you value surprise very highly – it is a word that appears often in your interviews, and you like the documentary because not everything is predictable, worked out in advance – you did not do this in order to surprise those viewers who expected that word to appear?

No, for you know hardly anyone notices those words. Those sort of things are for very sophisticated and attentive viewers.

But critics kept on writing about the concepts that were linked to the colours.

And they were right to do so. Debates and meditations about what these words actually mean seem appropriate to me, for we often use words whose meanings we have forgotten. They become merely symbols of certain events and so become detached from reality, life, the concrete. They become symbols or metaphors, things that seem self-evident. However, as soon as we cease to consider them self-evident and begin to reflect again on the meanings of these words, and our relationship to those meanings, the word acquires a concrete context, that of a person's life. I think it is time to ponder the actual meaning of everything within our tradition – I mean the Judaeo-Christian, West European tradition that shapes us. We have to reflect not only on where we find ourselves, but also on the meaning of these words that have shaped us throughout history, through eras, years, wars, revolutions and generations. These things are where we come from – the first, second and tenth commandments, but also "liberty, equality and brotherhood" – and we are as we are today because once upon a time somebody gave his head for these three words, allowed himself to be crucified for these ten commandments. All these things have a certain significance for modern life and our relationship with the world and each other. They all build and shape us. So the question arises – where are they located within us, what is our real attitude to them? I think the question is worth revisiting because, if we fail to understand where we came from and what we are made of, we cannot understand who we are, what we are doing on this earth, where we are headed. Of course, I do not advocate any historicist way of thinking or situating the present in the context of history, but I do not think one should overlook where a person is coming from.

Do you have any intention of making historical films?

No, that doesn't interest me at all.

You have often spoken very warmly of actors, and one can see the effect in the strength of the performances in your films. I wonder, did you find any difficulties – or even find it frustrating – working with actors who use languages you do not know and dialogue that lacks colloquial contact with your everyday reality here?

No, overall I did not find that uncomfortable. It was simply unimportant, since I think people make themselves understood independently of language. It really isn't that important. Of course, it is very important to make oneself understood on a basic level, but once you reach a level even a little bit above the basic it is not language that determines whether or not we understand one another.

It has been said on occasions that your films have become increasingly elliptical. One example of this particularly interests me – and how you would read it and react to my own reaction to it. I am thinking of the ending of Three Colours: White, *and how it should be read – for criticism of the film concerned the ending in particular, which, for me, seemed to interweave three of your earlier films: the short films about love and killing, and also* No End, *since Karol is now "dead" and officially a ghost. How do you feel this ending ought to be read?*

For me, it's a very simple ending to the story.

But the story continues in Three Colours: Red.

It simply means that the story ends well. The fact that the hero goes to some prison to get in touch with the heroine, who is up there behind bars at some window, and yet nevertheless they make contact – that simply means that the story ends well, that there is – so to speak – a "happy end". Of course, this "happy end" was incomparably more developed in the script, and was later cut down considerably. A whole block of the story was cut out.

Why?

Mainly because it wasn't done too well and was simply rather messy – we failed to do things precisely and that prolonged the film terribly and added nothing essential, since for me the essential thing was a kind of "happy end", and the fact that between these two people, who hated each other and ought to have hated each other – her hating him and him hating her for humiliating him – love won out over hatred. And I thought that if we succeeded in saying that it would be enough. I agree with those criticisms that say the ending is not clear, but nevertheless I did not think it worthwhile burdening the viewer with a long story – for it went on for at least another ten minutes that in effect said the same thing. It might perhaps have been clearer, but it would have been more of the same. For I am terribly afraid of overextending a film. The viewer has a certain amount of staying power, but, although he is capable of sitting through tremendously attractive chases, escapes and shootouts – particularly when they are expensive and the money can be seen on the screen – he is not able to bear stories that are far subtler, far less dramatic and action-packed. So to save him from leaving the cinema – and myself from having him leave – I prefer to shorten the story.

Yet, it seems to me that the tendency of auteur cinema is rather going in the opposite direction, that we are seeing more and more films that last two and a half hours.

Yes. I very much fear that these films will have fewer and fewer viewers. More money is needed to make a two-and-a-half-hour film than an hour-and-a-half one, so far more viewers are needed to cover its costs. I don't know how things will be in the future. I know that today my colleagues in various countries – Angelopoulos, for instance – are making very protracted stories.

But Angelopoulos has always made very long films.

He always has. But who is going to watch these two-and-a-half-hour films today, with life's current tempo? I am afraid that there won't be enough people to make a second film possible.

But Pulp Fiction *[1994] lasts that long.*

But *Pulp Fiction* is a classic example of the action film. Of course, one can say it is an auteur film by Tarantino, since he wrote it himself, but it is a film that situates itself on the side of commercial films, action films, films of brutality and violence, rather than the side of reflection and certain subtle, dimly-apprehended feelings, the side usually occupied by the auteur film. I am simply afraid of longer films.

Music has been foregrounded increasingly in your recent films, particularly in The Double Life of Véronique *and* Three Colours: White. *Zbigniew Preisner himself has said that his film music is not "serious music". How would you relate this view to the compositions of Julie – or her husband, it is not clear – in* Three Colours: Blue? *How are we to take the symphony – as a masterpiece, or ironically?*

I think that symphony might have sounded worthy, if only... Do not forget that we wrote the script in 1990, when the unification of Europe was planned for the middle of 1992. As you know, every fourth year works are commissioned for the Olympics from the most distinguished composers. Europe would unify for the first time in history, and so it would require exceptional scene-setting. And then one could say that all sorts of elevated tones and exceptionally weighty words – to put it positively – or bombast – to put it negatively – would sound and be in accord with the ceremony of European unification. Since, as we know, Europe did not unite and will not – certainly not in the way some Euro-optimists imagine – it clearly has to be taken ironically as a programme. It is rather as if we had planned to celebrate a name-day or birthday, had ordered an enormous cake with a large number of candles, and had taken exceptional care to make sure that it looked right, tasted right – except that when the birthday came the person celebrating it doesn't, for he has other business elsewhere. At that moment the cake becomes ironic, bitterly ironic in relation to what had been supposed to happen. It is exactly the same with this work, which is just such a cake. Except that the person for whom it was meant did not come.

Does that mean that the words that accompany that music are also to be taken ironically?

No, the words remain relevant anyway, except that they sound differently depending on whether a marriage takes place or not. It is rather as if what you had prepared was not a cake but the music we are discussing for a wedding at which a certain beautiful woman is to marry a handsome and worthy man. To mark the occasion someone composes a song that speaks of the love that binds, and the wedding approaches. So far, so good. But in the meantime either the man or the woman backs out, and the song is left standing. Does it lose its value? No. There is only a certain kind of bitterness over the disappointment, for we had expected more of our marriage candidates – we had expected them to unite. But they do not. Are they unworthy of this love? Perhaps, since they do not unite. Perhaps they do not feel it in a way that would take them to the altar. It's very simple. One does not have to treat this as something that loses its value, for it doesn't in the least. The same words will be just as much to the point for the next couple that comes to the church and unites as they were for the couple that didn't. They remain just as valid. It could be that one day our heroes – the man and the woman – will find their other halves, she her man and he his woman, and the words will again be just as valid and appropriate as they would have been had they been united. But they continue to be valid – for the French, the English, the Germans, the Spanish, the Portuguese. They did not unite but the words retain their validity. These words about love continue to be just as valid.

Krzysztof Kieślowski: filmography

Compiled by Paul Coates

This filmography collates data from the credits of the films themselves, from the production details contained in the films' reviews, and from various published filmographies. Distribution details appear courtesy of TOR, and award details stem from Film Polski, whose help is gratefully acknowledged.

The following abbreviations have been used:

ad	art director	m	minutes
bw	black and white	*m*	music
co-p	co-producer	*p*	producer
col	colour	*pc*	production company
cost	costume designer	*ph*	cinematographer
D	documentary	*sc*	scriptwriter
d	director	*sd*	sound
dist	distributor	*set dec*	set decorator
ed	editor	WFD	Wytwórnia Filmów
ep	executive producer		Dokumentalnych
F	feature		(Documentary
KK	Krzysztof Kieślowski		Production Studios)
KP	Krzysztof Piesiewicz		

[Unless indicated otherwise, all films are directed by Krzysztof Kieślowski and produced in Poland.]

Tramwaj
The Tram
1966 6m bw 35mm short F
pc Łódź Film School *sc* KK *ph* Zdzisław Kaczmarek *main cast* Jerzy Braszka, Maria Janiec.

Urząd
The Office
1966 6m bw 35mm D
pc Łódź Film School *sc* KK *ph* Lechosław Trzęsowski

Koncert życzeń
Concert of Requests
1967 17m bw 35mm short F
pc Łódź Film School *sc* KK *ph* Lechosław Trzęsowski *ed* Janina Grosicka *main cast* Jerzy Fedorowicz, Ewa Konarska.

Zdjęcie
The Photograph
1968 32m bw 16mm D
pc Polish Television *ph* Marek Jóźwiak *ed* Niusia Ciucka

Z miasta Łodzi
From the City of Łódź
1969 17m bw 35mm D
p Stanisław Abrantowicz, Andrzej Cylwik *pc* WFD *ph* Janusz Kreczmański,
Piotr Kwiatkowski, Stanisław Niedbalski *sd* Krystyna Pohorecka, R Sulewski
ed Elżbieta Kurkowska, Lidia Zonn

Byłem żołnierzem
I Was a Soldier
1970 16m bw 35mm D
pc Czołówka *sc* KK, Ryszard Zgórecki *ph* Stanisław Niedbalski
awards "Złoty Kord" ["Golden Cord"] Prize, XI National Short Film Festival,
Kraków, 1971; Ministry of National Defence Prize.

Fabryka
Factory
1970 17m bw 35mm D
p Halina Krawecka *pc* WFD *ph* Stanisław Niedbalski, Jacek Tworek
sd Małgorzata Jaworska *ed* Maria Leszczyńska
award "Głos robotniczy" ["The Worker's Voice"] Prize, XI National Short
Film Festival, Kraków, 1971.

Przed rajdem
Before the Rally
1971 15m bw/col 35mm D
p Waldemar Kowalski *pc* WFD *ph* Piotr Kwiatkowski, Jacek Petrycki
sd Małgorzata Jaworska *ed* Lidia Zonn

Refren
Refrain
1972 10m bw 35mm D
p Waldemar Kowalski *pc* WFD *ph* Witold Stok *sd* Małgorzata Jaworska,
Michał Żarnecki *ed* Maryla Czołnik

Między Wrocławiem a Zieloną Górą
Between Wrocław and Zieloną Górą
1972 10m col 35mm promotional documentary
p Jerzy Herman *pc* WFD, to a commission by Lubin Copper Mine *ph* Jacek
Petrycki *sd* Andrzej Bohdanowicz *ed* Lidia Zonn

Podstawy BHP w kopalnii miedzi
The Principles of Safety and Hygiene in a Copper Mine
1972 21m bw 35mm instructional film
p Jerzy Herman *pc* WFD, to a commission by Lubin Copper Mine *ph* Jacek
Petrycki *sd* Andrzej Bohdanowicz *ed* Lidia Zonn

Robotnicy '71: nic o nas bez nas
Workers '71: Nothing About Us Without Us
1972 46m bw 16mm D
p Tomasz Gołębiewski, Mirosław Podolski, Wojciech Szczęsny pc WFD
d KK, Tomasz Zygadło, Wojciech Wiszniewski, Paweł Kędzierski, Tadeusz
Walendowski ph Witold Stok, Stanisław Mroziuk, Jacek Petrycki sd Jacek
Szymański, Alina Hojnacka ed Lidia Zonn, Maryla Czołnik, Joanna
Dorożyńska, Daniela Cieplińska
award "Człowiek-Praca-Twórczość" ["Man-Work-Creativity"] Prize, Film
Festival, Świdnik, 1981.

Murarz
Bricklayer
1973 17m col 35mm D
p Tomasz Gołębiewski pc WFD ph Witold Stok sd Małgorzata Jaworska
ed Lidia Zonn

Przejście podziemne
Pedestrian Subway
1973 30m bw 35mm TV drama
pc Polish Television p Tadeusz Drewno sc Ireneusz Iredyński, KK
ph Sławomir Idziak, K Pełczyński sd Małgorzata Jaworska ed Elżbieta
Kurkowska, J Wiśniewska set dec Teresa Barska, Teresa Gałkowska
cost Ewa Braun main cast Teresa Budzisz-Krzyżanowska, Andrzej Seweryn,
Anna Jaraczówna, Zygmunt Maciejewski, Jan Orsza-Łukasiewicz, Janusz
Skalski.

Prześwietlenie
X-Ray
1974 13m col 35mm D
p Jerzy Tomaszewicz ph Jacek Petrycki sd Michał Żarnecki ed Lidia Zonn

Pierwsza miłość
First Love
1974 30m col 16mm TV D
pc Polish Television ph Jacek Petrycki sd Małgorzata Jaworska, Michał
Żarnecki ed Lidia Zonn
awards Grand Prix ("Złoty Lajkonik"), 14th National Short Film Festival,
Kraków, 1974; Special Jury Prize, 11th International Short Film Festival,
Kraków, 1974.

Życiorys
Curriculum Vitae
1975 45m bw 35mm drama documentary
p Marek Szopiński pc WFD sc Janusz Fastyn, KK ph Jacek Petrycki,
Tadeusz Rusinek sd Spaś Christow ed Lidia Zonn
awards Prize of the "Syrenka Warszawska" Film Critics' Club, 1975; Prize of
the 5th Review of Socio-Political Films, Łódź, 1975.

Personel
Personnel
1975 67m col 16mm TV drama
p Zbigniew Stanek *pc* Polish Television/TOR production unit *sc* KK
ph Witold Stok *sd* Michał Żarnecki, Jan Franciszek *m excerpt* from "Aida", performed by orchestra and soloists of the Teatr Wielki, Warsaw *ed* Lidia Zonn, Alina Siemińska *ad* Tadeusz Kozarewicz, Krystyna Szczepanek, Jerzy Radziwoń *cost* Izabella Konarzewska *main cast* Juliusz Machulski (Romek Januchta), Michał Tarkowski (Sowa), Irena Lorentowicz, Włodzimierz Boruński, Edward Ciosek, Waldemar Karst, Wilchelm Kłonowski, Tomasz Lengren, Ludwik Mika, Henryk Sawicki, Andrzej Siedlecki, Krzysztof Sitarski, Janusz Skalski, Jan Torończak, Krystyna Wachełko, Jan Zieliński, Tomasz Zygadło.
awards Prize of the Catholic Film Mission, 24th International Film Festival, Mannheim, 1975; "Wielki Jantar" Prize, 4th "Youth and Film" Koszalin Film Meeting, 1976; Grand Prix in the television film category and Journalists' Prize, 2nd Festival of Polish Feature Films, Gdańsk, 1975; Andrzej Munk Prize, 1975; Prize of the *Film* weekly, 1975; "Złote Grono" Prize, Lubuskie Summer of Film, Łagów, 1979.

Szpital
Hospital
1976 21m bw 35mm D
p Ryszard Wrzesiński *pc* WFD *ph* Jacek Petrycki *sd* Michał Żarnecki *ed* Lidia Zonn
awards Prize of the Film Critics' Club "Syrenka Warszawska", 1977; Grand Prix ("Złoty Smok"), 16th International Short Film Festival, Kraków, 1977.

Klaps
Slate
1976 6m col 35mm compilation of out-takes from *Blizna* (see below)
ph Sławomir Idziak *sd* Michał Żarnecki *ed* E Dmitroca *participants* Mariusz Dmochowski, Stanisław Igar, E Kowalska, A Miklaszewska, Joanna Orzeszkowa, Franciszek Pieczka, Marek Pietrzak, A Płocki, Mirosława Sada, Jan Skotnicki, Andrzej Skupień, J Stanek, Jerzy Stuhr, Janusz Szela, K Szopa, Michał Tarkowski, Krzysztof Wierzbicki, H Winiarska, M Woźniakowska.

Blizna
The Scar
1976 104m col 35mm F
p Zbigniew Stanek *deputy p* Janusz Szela, K Szopa, R Rall *pc* TOR *sc* KK, based on a novella by Romuald Karaś *dialogue* Romuald Karaś, KK
ph Sławomir Idziak *sd* Michał Żarnecki, H Sznurkowski *m* Stanisław Radwan *ed* Krystyna Górnicka, E Dmitroca *ad* Andrzej Płocki, Ewa Kowalska *cost* Izabella Konarzewska *main cast* Franciszek Pieczka (Bednarz), Mariusz Dmochowski, Jerzy Stuhr, Jan Skotnicki, Stanisław Igar, Stanisław Michalski, Michał Tarkowski, Andrzej Skupień, Halina Winiarska, Joanna Orzechowska, J Bryniarska, Agnieszka Holland, Małgorzata Leśniewska, Asia Łamtiugina, R Baciarelli, F Barfuss, B Ejmont, H Hunko, J Jeruzal, Z Lesien, K Morawski, J Prażmowski, J Stawarz, W Stockinger, K

Sułkowski.
awards Grand Prix, 3rd Festival of Polish Feature Films, Gdańsk, 1976;
"Złote Grono" Prize of the 10th Lubuskie Summer with Film, Łagów, 1978.

Spokój
The Calm
1976 82m col 16mm F
p Jeremi Maruszewski *pc* Polish Television *sc* KK, based on a story by Lech
Borski *dialogue* KK, Jerzy Stuhr *ph* Jacek Petrycki *sd* Wiesław Jurgala,
Mariusz Gajewski *m excerpt* "Dwadzieścia lat, a może mniej" ("Twenty
Years, or Maybe Less") music by Piotr Figiel, words by J Kondratowicz,
sung by J Lech *ed* Maryla Szymańska, Bogumiła Grzelak *ad* Rafał
Waltenberger, Michał Sulkiewicz *cost* Renata Własow, Ewa Parys-Płowik
film excerpt Araby (Arabians), by Zbigniew Raplewski *main cast* Jerzy
Stuhr (Antek Gralak), Izabella Olszewska, Jerzy Trela, Michał Sulkiewicz,
Danuta Ruksza, Jerzy Fedorowicz, Elżbieta Karkonoszka
supporting roles Jan Adamski, Marian Cebulski, Edward Dobrzański,
Ryszard Dreger, Stanisław Gronkowski, Stanisław Marczewski, Stefan
Mienicki, Jan Niziński, Ryszard Palik, Janusz Sykutera, Feliks Szajnert,
Ferdynand Wójcik, Michał Żarnecki.
awards Special Prize, 8th Festival of Polish Feature Films, Gdańsk, 1981;
"Złoty ekran" ["Golden Screen"] Award, 1981.

Z punktu widzenia nocnego portiera
From the Point of View of the Night Porter
1977 17m col 35mm D
p Wojciech Kapczyński *pc* WFD *ph* Witold Stok *sd* Wiesława Dembińska,
Michał Żarnecki *m* Wojciech Kilar *ed* Lidia Zonn
awards Grand Prix ("Złoty Lajkonik"), 19th National Short Film Festival,
Kraków, 1979 [jointly with *Siedem kobiet w różnym wieku*]; FIPRESCI Prize,
19th International Short Film Festival, Kraków, 1979; Jury Prize,
International Short and Documentary Film Festival, Lille 1979; Special Prize,
International Film Festival, Nyon 1979.

Nie wiem
I Don't Know
1977 46m bw 35mm D
p Ryszard Wrzesiński, Wojciech Kapczyński *pc* WFD *ph* Jacek Petrycki
sd Michał Żarnecki *ed* Lidia Zonn

Siedem kobiet w różnym wieku
Seven Women of Different Ages
1978 16m bw 35mm D
p Leszek Grabiński *pc* WFD *ph* Witold Stok *sd* Michał Żarnecki *ed* Alina
Siemińska, Lidia Zonn
award Grand Prix ("Złoty Lajkonik"), 19th National Film Festival, Kraków,
1979 [jointly with *Z punktu widzenia nocnego portiera*].

Amator
Camera Buff
1979 108m col 35mm F
p Wielisława Piotrowska *pc* TOR *sc* KK *dialogue* KK, Jerzy Stuhr *ph* Jacek Petrycki *sd* Michał Żarnecki, Mirosław Dobek, Marian Redlich, Marek Wojtaszewski *sd effects* Zygmunt Nowak *m* Krzysztof Knittel *m extract* "Valse E-minor", by Frédéric Chopin, performed by Krystian Zimmerman *song* "Staropolskim obyczajem" ("In the Old Polish Manner") by Andrzej Skorupka, Włodzimierz Kruszyński, Janusz Odrowąż, performed by Zbigniew Framer, Zofia Framer *ed* Halina Nawrocka, Teresa Miziołek *ad* Rafał Waltenberger *set dec* Borysława Chmielewska, Barbara Kociuba *cost* Gabriela Star-Tyszkiewicz, Janina Wierzbicka *film extract Barwy ochronne* (*Camouflage*, 1977), by Krzysztof Zanussi *main cast* Jerzy Stuhr (Filip Mosz), Małgorzata Ząbkowska (Irka Mosz), Ewa Pokas (Anna Włodarczyk), Stefan Czyżewski (manager), Jerzy Nowak (Marian Osuch), Tadeusz Bradecki (Witek), Marek Litewka (Piotrek Krawczyk), Bogusław Sobczuk (television editor), Krzysztof Zanussi (himself), Andrzej Jurga (himself), Tadeusz Sobolewski (himself).
awards Gold Medal and FIPRESCI Prize, 11th Moscow International Film Festival, 1979; Grand Prix "Złote lwy Gdańskie" ("Golden Lions of Gdańsk"), 6th Festival of Polish Feature Films, Gdańsk, 1979; "Jantar '79" Prize, 7th Koszalin Film Meeting, 1979; International Evangelical Prize, Berlin International Film Festival, 1980; Grand Prix ("Golden Hugo"), Chicago International Film Festival, 1980.

Dworzec
Station
1980 13m bw 35mm D
p Lech Grabiński *pc* WFD *ph* Witold Stok *sd* Michał Żarnecki *ed* Lidia Zonn

Gadające głowy
Talking Heads
1980 15m bw 35mm D
p Lech Grabiński *pc* WFD *ph* Jacek Petrycki, Piotr Kwiatkowski *sd* Michał Żarnecki *ed* Alina Siemińska

Przypadek
Blind Chance
1981 117m col 35mm F
p Jacek Szeligowski *pc* TOR *sc* KK *ph* Krzysztof Pakulski *sd* Michał Żarnecki, Elżbieta Wolbek, Włodzimierz Wiśniewski, Wojciech Lorek, Stanisław Hojden *m* Wojciech Kilar *m performed by* WOSPRiTV, conducted by Janusz Przybylski *ed* Elżbieta Kurkowska, Dorota Madej *ad* Rafał Waltenberger, Barbara Kociuba, Zbigniew Pakula, Borysława Chmielewska *cost* Agnieszka Domaniewska, Beata Banasik, Grażyna Hałupka *main cast* Bogusław Linda (Witek Długosz), Tadeusz Łomnicki (Werner), Zbigniew Zapasiewicz (Adam), Bogusława Pawelec (Czuszka Olkowska), Marzena Trybała (Werka), Jacek Borkowski (Marek), Jacek Sas-Uchrynowski (Daniel), Adam Ferency (Father Stefan), Monika Goździk (Olga Matwiszyn), Zbigniew Hubner (Dean), Irena Byrska (aunt).

award screenplay award, 12th Festival of Polish Feature Films, Gdańsk, 1987.

Krótki dzień pracy
Short Working Day
1981 79m col 35mm F
p Jacek Szeligowski *pc* Polish Television *sc* Hanna Krall, KK, based on Krall's novella, *Widok z okna na pierwszym piętrze* (*The View from the First-Floor Window*, 1980) *ph* Krzysztof Pakulski *sd* Michał Żarnecki *m* Jan Kanty Pawluśkiewicz *main cast* Wacław Ulewicz

Bez końca
No End
1984 107m col 35mm F
p Ryszard Chutkowski *production team* Paweł Mantorski, Włodzimierz Bendych, Jerzy Janicki, Andrzej Cebula, Anna Kowalska, Bożena Mrówczyńska *pc* TOR *sc* KK, KP *ph* Jacek Petrycki *sd* Michał Żarnecki, Elżbieta Zakrzewska, Kazimierz Kucharski, Stanisław Hojden *m* Zbigniew Preisner *m performed by* Orkiestra Filharmonii Łódzkiej, conducted by Zdzisław Szostak *song* "Dylemat" ("Dilemma") by Przemysław Gintrowski *ed* Krystyna Rutkowska, Beata Cichocka *ad* Allan Starski, Elżbieta Łupińska-Stępniak, Grażyna Tkaczyk, Joanna Lelanow *set dec* Magdalena Dipont, Teresa Gruber, Stefan Witkowski, Antoni Tryanowski *cost* Wiesława Starska, Małgorzata Bursztyńska, Henryka Ciok, Jolanta Włodarczyk *main cast* Grażyna Szapołowska (Urszula Zyro), Jerzy Radziwiłłowicz (Antoni Zyro), Artur Barciś (Darek), Aleksander Bardini (Labrador), Marek Kondrat (Tomek), Maria Pakulnis (Joanna), Michał Bajor (Apprentice lawyer), Tadeusz Bradecki (Hypnotist), Daniel Webb (American), Krzysztof Krzemiński (Jacek Zyro), Adam Ferency, Jerzy Kamas, Elżbieta Kilarska, Jan Tesarz, Marzena Trybała, Andrzej Szalawski.
dist Artificial Eye
award "Don Quixote "85" – Award of the Polish Federation of Film Discussion Clubs.

Siedem dni w tygodniu
Seven Days a Week
(part of compliation film *City Life*)
The Netherlands 1988 18m col 35mm D
p Jacek Petrycki *pc* City Life (Rotterdam) *ph* Jacek Petrycki *sd* Michał Żarnecki *m* Frédéric Chopin *ed* Dorota Warduszkiewicz

Krótki film o zabijaniu
A Short Film About Killing
1988 85m col 35mm F
p Ryszard Chutkowski *pc* TOR and Polish Television *sc* KK, KP *ph* Sławomir Idziak *sd* Małgorzata Jaworska *m* Zbigniew Preisner *m performed by* Katowice Orchestra for Radio and Television (WOSPRiTV), conducted by Zdzisław Szostak *song* "Opowiem ci o lwie" ("I'll Tell You About the Lion"): words by W Chotomska, music by W Korcz, played by Reprezentacyjny Zespół ZHP "Gawęda", directed by A Kieruzalski *ed* Ewa

Smal *ad* Halina Dobrowolska *set dec* Grażyna Tkaczyk, Robert Czesak, Magdalena Dipont *cost* Małgorzata Obłoza, Hanna Ćwikło *main cast* Mirosław Baka (Jacek Lazar), Krzysztof Globisz (Piotr Balicki), Jan Tesarz (Waldemar Rekowski), Zbigniew Zapasiewicz (bar examiner), Barbara Dziekan-Vajda (girl in cinema box office), Aleksander Bednarz (executioner), Jerzy Zass (court official), Zdzisław Tobiasz (judge), Artur Barciś (young man), Krystyna Janda, Olgierd Łukasiewicz, L Andrzejewski, W Bednarz, Z Borek, W Byrdy, W Borsucki, A Gawroński, H Guzek, I Głębicka, E Helman, B Hubicki, H Kowalczykowa, K Luft, H Łapiński, B Niewinowski, B Marynowski, M Manteska, M Maciejewski, A Mastalerz, J Mielich, M Miarczyńska, L Pietrasz, M Pieczyńska, Z Plato, Z Rychter, K Stelmaszyk, K Stępkowski, M Szary, C Świtkowski, A Wolska.
dist Cannon City Production; Film 2000
awards Jury Prize and FIPRESCI Prize, Cannes International Film Festival, 1988; Grand Prix "Złote lwy Gdańskie" ("Golden Lions of Gdańsk"), 13th Festival of Polish Feature Films, Gdańsk, 1988 (jointly with *Krótki film o miłości*); Félix '88 for Best European Film; deemed Film of the Year and Best Non-American Film in Danish Cinemas by the Danish Film Academy and Filmworkers Union.

Krótki film o miłości
A Short Film About Love
1988 87m col 35mm F
p Ryszard Chutkowski *sc* KK, KP *ph* Witold Adamek *sd* Nikodem Wołk-Łaniewski *m* Zbigniew Preisner *m performed by* Kraków Orchestra for Television *song* "Miss Piękności 86", by W Kujibida, A Maliszewski, performed by Alex Band *ed* Ewa Smal *ad* Halina Dobrowolska *set dec* Grażyna Tkaczyk, Robert Czesak *cost* Małgorzata Obłoza, Hanna Ćwikło *title design* Mirosław Mentcel *main cast* Grażyna Szapołowska (Magda), Olaf Lubaszenko (Tomek), Stefania Iwińska (godmother), Artur Barciś (young man), Piotr Machalica (Roman), Stanisław Gawlik (postman), Rafał Imbro (bearded man), Jan Piechociński (blond man).
dist Cannon City Production; Film 2000
awards Grand Prix "Złote lwy Gdańskie" ("Golden Lions of Gdańsk"), 13th Festival of Polish Feature Films, Gdańsk, 1988 (jointly with *Krótki film o zabijaniu*), "Silver Lion" for screenplay (jointly with KP); Prize of the Head of Cinematography for 1988 in the area of the feature film (jointly with KP and Witold Adamek); Special Jury Prize, International Film Festival at San Sebastián, 1988, as well as FIPRESCI and Catholic Jury (OCIC) Prizes at the same festival; Prize of the town of Schiltigheim and Prize of the General Assembly of the Lower Rhine, International Film Festival for Human Rights, Strasbourg, 1989; Best Director, "Stars of Tomorrow" Festival, Geneva, 1989; Public's Prize and Critics' Prize, International Film Festival, São Paolo; Prize of the Independent Filmwriters' Circle of the Polish Filmmakers' Association "Złota Taśma" ("Golden Reel") for best film on Polish screens, 1988; Leon Moussinac Prize and French Film Critics' Prize for best foreign film of 1989.

Dekalog
The Decalogue
awards FIPRESCI Prize, Venice International Film Festival, 1989, as well as

that festival's "Youth and Cinema" Prize; Catholic Jury Prize (OCIC), 37th International Film Festival, San Sebastian, 1989; "Silver European Reel", Prize of the Italian Journalists' Union, 1989.

Dekalog 1
Decalogue 1
1988 53m col 35mm TV drama
p Ryszard Chutkowski *pc* Polish Television/Sender Freies Berlin *sc* KK, KP *pb* Wiesław Zdort *sd* Małgorzata Jaworska *m* Zbigniew Preisner *m performed by* Orkiestra Filharmonii Łódzkiej, conducted by Zdzisław Szostak *ed* Ewa Smal *ad* Halina Dobrowolska *set dec* Grażyna Tkaczyk, Robert Czesak, Magdalena Dipont *cost* Małgorzata Obłoza, Hanna Ćwikło *main cast* Henryk Baranowski (Krzysztof), Wojciech Klata (Paweł), Maja Komorowska (Irena), Artur Barciś (young man), Maria Gładkowska (girl), Ewa Kania (Ewa Jezierska), Aleksanda Kisielewska (woman), Aleksanda Majsiuk (Ola), Magda Sroga-Mikołajczyk (journalist), Anna Smal-Romańska, Maciej Sławiński, Piotr Wyrzykowski, Bożena Wróbel.

Dekalog 2
Decalogue 2
1988 57m col 35mm TV drama
p Ryszard Chutkowski *pc* Polish Television/Sender Freies Berlin *sc* KK, KP *pb* Edward Kłosiński *sd* Małgorzata Jaworska *m* Zbigniew Preisner *m performed by* Orkiestra Filharmonii Łódzkiej, conducted by Zdzisław Szostak *piano* Bożena Banaszkiewicz *ed* Ewa Smal *ad* Halina Dobrowolska *set dec* Grażyna Tkaczyk, Robert Czesak, Magdalena Dipont *cost* Małgorzata Obłoza, Hanna Ćwikło *main cast* Krystyna Janda (Dorota), Aleksander Bardini (consultant), Olgierd Łukasiewicz (Andrzej), Artur Barciś (young man), Krystyna Bigelmajer, Karol Dillenius, Ewa Ekwińska, Jerzy Fedorowicz, Stanisław Gawlik, Krzysztof Kumor, Piotr Siejka, Aleksander Trabczyński.

Dekalog 3
Decalogue 3
1988 56m col 35mm TV drama
p Ryszard Chutkowski *pc* Polish Television/Sender Freies Berlin *sc* KK, KP *pb* Piotr Sobociński *sd* Nikodem Wołk-Łaniewski *m* Zbigniew Preisner *m performed by* Orkiestra Filharmonii Łódzkiej, conducted by Zdzisław Szostak *ed* Ewa Smal *ad* Halina Dobrowolska *set dec* Grażyna Tkaczyk, Robert Czesak, Magdalena Dipont *cost* Małgorzata Obłoza, Hanna Ćwikło *main cast* Daniel Olbrychski (Janusz), Maria Pakulnis (Ewa), Joanna Szczepkowska (Janusz's wife), Artur Barciś (tram-driver), Krystyna Drohocka (aunt), Zygmunt Fok, Jacek Kalucki, Barbara Kołodziejska, Maria Krawczyk, Krzysztof Kumor, Włodzimierz Musiał, Jerzy Zygmunt Nowak, Piotr Rzymszkiewicz, Włodzimierz Rzeczycki, Dorota Stalińska.

Dekalog 4
Decalogue 4
1988 55m col 35mm TV drama
p Ryszard Chutkowski *pc* Polish Television/Sender Freies Berlin *sc* KK, KP

ph Krzysztof Pakulski *sd* Małgorzata Jaworska *m* Zbigniew Preisner *m performed by* Orkiestra Filharmonii Łódzkiej, conducted by Zdzisław Szostak *song* "Był sobie król" ("There Was Once a King"): words by J Porazińska; music: traditional *ed* Ewa Smal *ad* Halina Dobrowolska *set dec* Grażyna Tkaczyk, Robert Czesak, Magdalena Dipont *cost* Małgorzata Obłoza, Hanna Ćwikło *main cast* Adrianna Biedrzyńska (Anka), Janusz Gajos (Michał), Artur Barciś (young man), Adam Hanuszkiewicz (professor), Jan Tesarz (taxi-driver), Andrzej Blumenfeld (Michał's friend), Tomasz Kozłowicz (Jarek), Elżbieta Kilarska (Jarek's mother), Helena Norowicz (optician), Igor Śmiałowski.

Dekalog 5
Decalogue 5
1988 57m col 35mm TV drama
Television version of *A Short Film About Killing* (see above)

Dekalog 6
Decalogue 6
1988 58m col 35mm TV drama
Television version of *A Short Film About Love* (see above)

Dekalog 7
Decalogue 7
1988 55m col 35mm TV drama
p Ryszard Chutkowski *pc* Polish Television/Sender Freies Berlin *sc* KK, KP *ph* Dariusz Kuc *sd* Nikodem Wołk-Łaniewski *m* Zbigniew Preisner *m performed by* Orkiestra Filharmonii Łódzkiej, conducted by Zdzisław Szostak *theatrical excerpt* from "O straszliwym smoku" ("About the Terrible Dragon"): by Maria Kownacka, director and choreography: Edward Dobraczyński, scenographer: Adam Kilian, music by Bogumił Pasternak, performed by Zespół Teatru "Lalka" in Warsaw *ed* Ewa Smal *ad* Halina Dobrowolska *set dec* Grażyna Tkaczyk, Robert Czesak, Magdalena Dipont *cost* Małgorzata Obłoza, Hanna Ćwikło *main cast* Anna Polony (Ewa), Maja Barełkowska (Majka), Władysław Kowalski (Stefan), Bogusław Linda (Wojtek), Bożena Dykiel (ticket woman), Katarzyna Piwowarczyk (Ania), Stefania Błońska, Dariusz Jabłoński, Jan Mayzel, Mirosława Maludzińska, Ewa Radzikowska, Wanda Wróblewska.

Dekalog 8
Decalogue 8
1988 55m col 35mm TV drama
p Ryszard Chutkowski *pc* Polish Television/Sender Freies Berlin *sc* KK, KP *ph* Andrzej Jaroszewicz *sd* Wiesława Dembińska *m* Zbigniew Preisner *m performed by* Orkiestra Filharmonii Łódzkiej, conducted by Zdzisław Szostak *ed* Ewa Smal *ad* Halina Dobrowolska *set dec* Grażyna Tkaczyk, Robert Czesak, Magdalena Dipont *cost* Małgorzata Obłoza, Hanna Ćwikło *main cast* Maria Kościałkowska (Zofia), Teresa Marczewska (Elżbieta), Artur Barciś (young man), Tadeusz Łomnicki (tailor), Wojciech Asiński, Marek Kępiński, Janusz Mond, Marian Opania, Krzysztof Rojek, Bronisław Pawlik, Wiktor Sanejko, J Schejbal, Ewa Skibińska, W Starostecki, J

Strzemżalski, Hanna Szczerkowska, Anna Zagórska.

Dekalog 9
Decalogue 9
1988 58m col 35mm TV drama
p Ryszard Chutkowski *pc* Polish Television/Sender Freies Berlin *sc* KK, KP *ph* Piotr Sobociński *sd* Nikodem Wołk-Łaniewski *m* Zbigniew Preisner *m performed by* Orkiestra Filharmonii Łódzkiej, conducted by Zdzisław Szostak *vocal* Elżbieta Towarnicka *film excerpt* fragment of film *Tort*, scripted by Krzysztof Kowalski and Krzysztof Chromiński, music by Janusz Mentel *ed* Ewa Smal *ad* Halina Dobrowolska *set dec* Grażyna Tkaczyk, Robert Czesak, Magdalena Dipont *cost* Małgorzata Obłoza, Hanna Ćwikło *main cast* Ewa Błaszczyk (Hanka), Piotr Machalica (Roman), Artur Barciś (young man), Jan Jankowski (Mariusz), Jolanta Piętek-Górecka (Ola), Katarzyna Piwowarczyk (Ania), Jerzy Trela (Mikołaj), Renata Berger, Małgorzata Boratyńska, Janusz Cywiński, Joanna Cichoń, Sławomir Kwiatkowski, Dariusz Przychoda.

Dekalog 10
Decalogue 10
1988 57m col 35mm TV drama
p Ryszard Chutkowski *pc* Polish Television/Sender Freies Berlin *sc* KK, KP *ph* Jacek Bławut *sd* Nikodem Wołk-Łaniewski *m* Zbigniew Preisner *m performed by* Orkiestra Filharmonii Łódzkiej, conducted by Zdzisław Szostak *song* "Zabijaj, zabijaj" ("Kill, Kill"): words KK, music by P Klatt, performed by Zbigniew Zamachowski and the "Róże Europy" group *ed* Ewa Smal *ad* Halina Dobrowolska *set dec* Grażyna Tkaczyk, Robert Czesak, Magdalena Dipont *cost* Małgorzata Obłoza, Hanna Ćwikło *main cast* Jerzy Stuhr (Jerzy), Zbigniew Zamachowski (Artur), Henryk Bista (shopkeeper), Olaf Lubaszenko (Tomek), Maciej Stuhr (Piotrek), Anna Gronostaj, Cezary Harasimowicz, Dariusz Kozakiewicz, Henryk Majcherek, Elżbieta Panas, Jerzy Turek, Grzegorz Warchoł.

La Double Vie de Véronique
Podwójne życie Weroniki
The Double Life of Véronique
France/Poland 1991 98m col 35mm F
p Leonardo de la Fuente *ep* Bernard-P Guiremand, Ryszard Chutkowski *co-p* Ryszard Straszewski *pc* Sideral Productions in association with Le Studio Canal Plus/TOR Production/Norsk Film *sc* KK, KP *Polish dialogue adaptation* Marcin Latałło *ph* Sławomir Idziak *sd editors* Edith Vassard, Michèle Catonne *m* Zbigniew Preisner *m extract* Dante – 2nd song, "Verso il cielo" *m performed by* Polish Radio and Television Orchestra of Katowice, Philharmonic Choirs of Silesia, soprano: Elżbieta Towarnicka, flute: Jacek Ostaszewski *ed* Jacques Witta *production design* Patrice Mercier, Halina Dobrowolska *ad* Krzysztof Zanussi *cost* Laurence Brignon, Claudy Fellous, Elżbieta Radke *puppets* Bruce Schwartz *main cast* Irène Jacob [dubbed into Polish by Anna Gronostaj] (Weronika/Véronique), Halina Gryglaszewska (aunt), Kalina Jędrusik (gaudy woman), Aleksander Bardini (orchestra conductor), Władysław Kowalski (Weronika's father),

Jerzy Gudejko (Antek), Jan Sterniński (lawyer), Philippe Volter (Aleksandre Fabbri), Sandrine Dumas (Catherine), Louis Ducreux (teacher), Claude Duneton (Véronique's father), Lorraine Evanoff (Claude), Guillaume de Tonquedec (Serge), Gilles Gaston-Dreyfus (Jean-Pierre), Alain Frérot (postman), Youssef Hamid (railwayman), Thierry de Carbonnières (professor), Chantal Neuwirth (receptionist), Nausicaa Rampony (Nicole), Bogusława Schubert (woman with hat), Jacques Potin (man in grey coat).
dist Artificial Eye; Miramax Films
awards FIPRESCI Prize and Ecumenical Jury Prize, Cannes International Film Festival, 1991; "Złota Taśma" ("Golden Reel") Prize of the Independent Filmwriters' Circle of the Association of Polish Filmmakers.

Trois couleurs: bleu
Three Colours: Blue
France/Poland 1993 100m col 35mm F
p Marin Karmitz *ep* Yvonn Crenn *pc* MK2 SA/CED Productions/France 3 Cinema/CAB Productions/TOR Productions *sc* KK, KP
sc consultants Agnieszka Holland, Sławomir Idziak, Edward Żebrowski *ph* Sławomir Idziak *sd editors* Claire Bez, Bertrand Lanclos, Jean-Claude Laureux *m* Zbigniew Preisner *m performed by* Warsaw Symphony Orchestra conducted by Wojciech Michniewski, with the Philharmonic Choirs of Silesia conducted by Jan Wojtacha, soprano: Elżbieta Towarnicka, flute: Jacek Ostaszewski, Piano: Konrad Mastylo *ed* Jacques Witta *ad* Claude Lenoir *cost* Virginie Viard, Naima Lagrange *main cast* Juliette Binoche (Julie), Benoît Régent (Olivier), Florence Pernel (Sandrine), Charlotte Véry (Lucille), Helen Vincent (journalist), Philippe Volter (estate agent), Claude Duneton (Patrice), Emanuelle Riva (mother), Florence Vignon (copyist), Jacek Ostaszewski (flautist), Yann Regouet (Antoine), Isabelle Sadoyan (servant), Daniel Martin (downstairs neighbour), Catherine Therouenne (neighbour next door), Alain Ollivier (lawyer), Pierre Forget (gardener), Julie Delpy (Dominique), Zbigniew Zamachowski (Karol Karol).
dist Artificial Eye; Miramax Films
awards Golden Lion, Venice International Film Festival, 1993; Méliès Prize, 1995 (trilogy).

Trois couleurs: blanc
Three Colours: White
France/Poland 1994 91m col 35mm F
p Yonn Crenn (executive), Marin Karmitz *pc* France 3 Cinema (FR 3)/MK2 Productions SA/TOR Production/CAB Productions SA/Canal+ Productions *sc* KK, KP *sc consultants* Agnieszka Holland, Edward Żebrowski, Edward Kłosiński *ph* Edward Kłosiński *computer animation* Laco Adamik ("Aram", Warsaw) *sd* Jean-Claude Laureux *sd editors* Piotr Zawadzki, Jean-Claude Laureux, Francine Lemaître *sd effects* Jerome Levy, Pascal Mazière, Eric Ferret, Marc-Antoine Beldent *m* Zbigniew Preisner *song* "To ostatnia niedziela" ("It Is the Last Sunday"): by Jerzy Peterburski, Z Friedwald *m performed by* Sextuor à cordes, Le petit orchestre de Zbigniew Preisner *ed* Urszula Lesiak *ad* Claude Lenoir, Magdalena Dipont, Halina Dobrowolska *set dec* Magdalena Dipont *cost* Elżbieta Radke, Teresa Wardzała, Jolanta Łuczak, Virginie Viard *main cast* Zbigniew Zamachowski

(Karol Karol), Julie Delpy (Dominique), Janusz Gajos (Mikołaj), Aleksander
Bardini (lawyer), Grzegorz Warchoł (elegant man), Cezary Harasimowicz
(inspector), Jerzy Nowak (old farmer), Jerzy Trela (Monsieur Bronek),
Cezary Pazura (Bureau de change proprietor), Michel Lisowski (interpreter),
Philippe Morier-Genoud (judge), Piotr Machalica (tall man), Francis Coffinet
(bank employee), Barbara Dziekan (cashier), Yannick Evely (métro
employee), Marzena Trybała (Marriott employee), Jacques Disses
(Dominique's lawyer), Teresa Budzisz-Krzyżanowska (Madame Jadwiga),
Juliette Binoche (Julie), K Bigelmajer, J Dominik, J Grzegorzyk, M
Kaczmarska, A Kalinowsky, Stan Latek, J Ładyńska, M Marciano, J Mayzel,
M Modet, L Otowity, A Papliński, W Paszkowski, Florence Pernel, M
Prażmowska, J Richter, M Robaszkiewicz, B Szymańska, B Topa, M Verner,
Wanda Wróblewska, P Zelt.
dist Artificial Eye; Miramax Films
awards Silver Bear, Berlin Film Festival, 1994; Méliès Prize, 1995 (trilogy).

Trois couleurs: rouge
Three Colours: Red
France/Switzerland/Poland 1994 99m col 35mm F
p Yonn Crenn (executive), Marin Karmitz *director of production* Gerard
Ruey *pc* France 3 Cinema (FR 3)/MK2 Productions SA/TOR Production/
Canal+ Productions/Television Suisse Romande (TSR) With financial
assistance from Les Fonds Eurimages of the Conseil de l'Europe, L'Office
Fédéral de la Culture Suisse du Département Fédéral de l'Intérieur *sc* KK,
KP *ph* Piotr Sobociński *m* Zbigniew Preisner *m performed by* the Warsaw
Sinfonia conducted by Wojciech Michniewski/the Katowice Symphony
Orchestra conducted by Zdzisław Szostak; soprano: Elżbieta Towarnicka/
The Philharmonic Choir of Silesia, choirmaster: Jan Wojtacha, guitar: Janusz
Strobel, cellist: Jerzy Klocek *additional m* Bertrand Leclos *sd* Jean-Claude
Laureux *sd editors* Piotr Zawadzki, Francine Lemaître, Jean-Claude Laureux,
Nicolas Naegelen *sd effects* Jean-Paul Lelong, Mario Melchiorri, Vincent
Arnadi *ed* Jacques Witta *ad* Claude Lenoir *cost* Corinne Jorry, Nadia
Cuenoid, Véronique Michel *choreography* Brigitte Matteuzzi
main cast Irène Jacob (Valentine Dussaut), Jean-Louis Trintignant (Judge
Joseph Kern), Frédérique Feder (Karin), Jean-Pierre Lorit (Auguste Bruner),
Samuel Lebihan (photographer), Marion Stalens (veterinary surgeon), Teco
Celio (barman), Bernard Escalon (record dealer), Jean Schlegel (neighbour),
Elżbieta Jasińska (woman), Paul Vermeulen (Karin's friend), Jean-Marie
Daunas (theatre manager), Roland Carey (drug dealer), Juliette Binoche
(Julie), Julie Delpy (Dominique), Benoît Régent (Olivier), Zbigniew
Zamachowski (Karol Karol).
dist Artificial Eye; Miramax Films
awards LA and New York Critics' Circle Awards for Best Foreign Film,
1994; Grand Prix, Vancouver International Film Festival; "César" for music;
3 Academy Award® nominations (photography, script, direction), 1995;
four BAFTA nominations (direction, script, actress, category of non-English-
language films); Méliès Prize, 1995 (trilogy).

Krzysztof Kieślowski: selected bibliography

Compiled by Paul Coates

The following bibliography has, as its primary sources, the Filmoteka Narodowa (National Film Archive) in Warsaw and the Library of the British Film Institute. I have also benefitted greatly from the selfless aid of Dr Carmen Hendershott, who supplied a large batch of material of North American origin. Since the above-mentioned archives file newspaper reviews as clippings, often without giving page numbers, and Polish conventions of citation usually omit them, it has generally not been possible to supply details of pagination for these items. Given the length of the bibliography, I have prefaced it with an outline of its overall structure and contents. In a further effort to aid scholars' negotiation of the burgeoning mass of relevant material, references have been arranged according to four language groups, headed by the two of greatest significance for Kieślowski scholarship: Polish; French; English; and other languages. Where there are few sources, I have reduced these four categories to two: Polish; and other languages. Since including all Polish-language newspaper reviews would have lengthened appreciably an already unwieldy bibliography, I have tried to select those of most significance, either on grounds of intrinsic merit or because they document the Polish authorities' view of Kieślowski (for example, reviews from the official organ of the Polska Zjednoczona Partia Robotnicza (Polish United Workers' Party), *Trybuna ludu*). Since Kieślowski's own statements are of primary importance, with the giving of interviews becoming, in the end, arguably his main occupation, I have sought to include all such material I could find, and be selective only in the bibliography of secondary materials. Kieślowski websites exist, but at present none even begins to be an adequate substitute for film libraries and archives. (Perhaps the best way into the websites is to use Netsearch to find Cine-Kieślowski, which features words, pictures, chat and various hyperlinks.) The widest range of material is, of course, located at the Filmoteka Narodowa, despite some gaps due to periods of underfunding. For the sake of consistency, foreign-language accents and diacritical marks have been added where omitted in published sources.

Contents

Primary bibliography

A. Published screenplays

Kieślowski, Krzysztof. "Spokój", in *Dialog* 4 (1977): 34-52.

—————————. "Amator", in *Dialog* 4 (1978): 84-105.

—————————. "Przypadek", in *Dialog* 5 (1981): 7-25.

—————————. *Przypadek i inne teksty*, edited by Hanna Krall (Kraków: Znak, 1998) [screenplays of *Personel*, *Spokój*, *Amator* and *Przypadek*].

Kieślowski, Krzysztof and Hanna Krall. "Widok z okna na pierwszym piętrze", in *Dialog* 7 (1981): 5-21.

Kieślowski, Krzysztof and Krzysztof Piesiewicz. "Chórzystka", in *Dialog* 12 (1990): 5-39.

—————————————————. *Dekalog* (Chotomów: Verba, 1990).

—————————————————. *Decalogue: The Ten Commandments*, translated by Phil Cavendish and Suzannah Bluh (London; Boston: Faber and Faber, 1991).

—————————————————. *Three Colours Trilogy: Blue, White, Red*, translated by Danusia Stok (London: Faber and Faber, 1998).

—————————————————. *Tre colori: Blu, Bianco, Rosso*, translated by Marina Fabbri (Milan: Bompiani, 1994).

—————————————————. Trzy kolory: czerwony", in *Film na świecie* 388/389 (3-4: 1992): 78-118.

—————————————————. *Trzy kolory: Niebieski, Biały, Czerwony: Scenariusze filmowe* (Warsaw: Agencja scenariuszowa, 1997).

—————————————————. "Raj", in *Dialog* 3 (1997): 5-33. [The last two sections of Kieślowski's intended *Raj, Czyściec, Piekło* (*Heaven, Purgatory, Hell*) trilogy were scheduled to be completed by co-scenarist Krzysztof Piesiewicz alone: Krzysztof Piesiewicz, "Piekło", published in *Dialog* 5 (1997), is the only other section of this trilogy to have appeared as yet.]

B. Statements by Kieślowski

(i) Books

Stok, Danusia (ed). *Kieślowski on Kieślowski* (London; Boston: Faber and Faber, 1993).

(ii) Articles, letters and diaries

(a) In Polish

"Czy mam prawo ryzykować", *Polska* 5 (1976).

"Dramaturgia rzeczywistości", *Film na świecie* 388-389 (3-4: 1992): 7-9.

"Dziennik 89-90 (1)", *Kino* 25: 12 (December 1991): 38-39.

"Dziennik 89-90 (2)", *Kino* 26: 1 (January 1992): 36-37.

"Dziennik 89-90 (3)", *Kino* 26: 2 (February 1992): 44.

"Funkcje filmu w telewizji i w kinie", *Kino* 13: 1 (January 1978): 20-21.

"Głęboko, zamiast szeroko", *Dialog* 1 (1981): 109-111.

"Jak zrobić teatr w Berlinie Zachodnim?", *Dialog* 10 (1983): 162-164.

"Milczenie Bergmana", in Janusz Wróblewski (ed), *Magia kina* (Warsaw: Tenten, 1995): 53-57.

"Powinna obowiązywać zasada dobrej woli", *Kino* 10: 3 (March 1975): 19-20.

"Szanowna pani Danuto", *Kino* 14: 12 (December 1980): 13-14.

(b) In other languages

"Budget depends on filmer's character, not nationality", *Variety* 27 July 1992: 78.

"'Die Auseinandersetzung mit der Gegenwart fehlt': Zur Situation des polnischen Films 1984", *Medium* 15: 3 (March 1985): 21-25.

"Eigene Wirklichkeit: Das polnische Autorenkino 1970-81", *Medium* 13: 1 (January 1983): 37-41.

"In Depth Rather than Breadth", *Polish Perspectives* 24: 6-7 (June-July 1981): 67-70 [English version of "Głęboko, zamiast szeroko", *Dialog* 1 (1981): 109-111].

"Introduction", in Krzysztof Kieślowski and Krzysztof Piesiewicz, *Decalogue: The Ten Commandments*, translated by Phil Cavendish and Suzannah Bluh (London; Boston: Faber and Faber, 1991): ix-xv.

"La dramaturgie du réel", *Positif* 409 (March 1995): 56-57 [French version of "Dramaturgia rzeczywistości", *Film na świecie* 388-389 (3-4: 1992): 7-9].

"Les Musiciens du dimanche", *Positif* 400 (June 1994): 63-64.

"Ma vie est tout ce que je possède", *Positif* 423 (May 1996): 75-76.

"Quality Cuts", *Index on Censorship* 24: 6 (1995): 110-111.

"Regie lehren: Bericht aus einer Praxis mit Skrupeln", *Medium* 14: 3 (March 1984): 33-37.

"The Sunday Musicians", in Kevin Macdonald and Mark Cousins, *Imagining Reality: The Faber Book of the Documentary* (London; Boston: Faber and Faber, 1996): 214-217 [English translation of "Les Musiciens du dimanche"].

C. Interviews

(i) In Polish

1.1 In books, booklets and periodicals

Cencor, Arkadiusz and Waldemar Wilk. "Uważam się za rejestratora", *Świadomość społeczna w filmach Krzysztofa Kieślowskiego* (Wrocław: D.K.F. Politechnika, 1986): 3-8.

Hendrykowski, Marek and Mikołaj Jazdon. "Fragmenty spotkania z Krzysztofem Kieślowskim (24.11.1996)", *Kino* 29: 5 (May 1996): 9-12.

Karabasz, Kazimierz. "Rozmowa z Krzysztofem Kieślowskim", in Kazimierz Karabasz, *Bez fikcji – z notatek filmowego dokumentalisty* (Warsaw: Wydawnictwo artystyczne i filmowe, 1985): 82-107.

Kołodyński, Andrzej. "Wywiad nie do druku (14.XII.1973)", *Kino* 29: 5 (May 1996).

Marszałek, Maria. "O mnie, o tobie, o wszystkich", *Kino* 21: 8 (August 1987): 8-10.

Orzechowska, Joanna. "Widownia jest podobna do mnie – mówi Krzysztof Kieślowski", *Kino* 25: 5 (May 1991): 40-41.

Ostria, Vincent. "Krzysztof Kieślowski: Wolności nie ma", *Kino* 26: 8 (August 1992): 10-11.

Sobolewski, Tadeusz. "Rozmowa NaGłosu. Z Krzysztofem Kieślowskim rozmawia Tadeusz Sobolewski", *NaGłos* 1: 1 (1990): 89-90.

——————————. "Normalna chwila", *Kino* 24: 6 (June 1990): 19-22.

——————————. "Pogoń za motylem", *Kino* 26: 1 (January 1992); 10-13.

——————————. "Klucz do wrażliwości", *Kino* 27: 9 (September 1993): 13-14.

——————————. "Za kulisami", *Kino* 27: 9 (September 1993): 14-16.

——————————. "Nie szukam inspiracji w Europie...", *Kino* 28: 4 (April 1994).

——————————. "Żyliśmy tam wszyscy", *Kino* 28: 7-8 (July-August 1994): 22-5.

——————————. "Te same pytania", *Film* 5 May 1995: 68-69.

Stankusz, Wit. "Kręcenie zegara", *Kino* 19: 10 (October 1985): 16.

Szczepański, Tadeusz. "Drzewo, które jest", *Film na świecie* 385 (November-December 1991): 10-17.

Takahashi, Hiroshi. "Piękne hasła i tajemnice", *Kino* 27: 9 (September 1993): 11-13.

Wimphen, Catherine. "O wolności i nowych regułach gry", *Kino* 25: 9 (September 1991): 6-9.

Zawiśliński, Stanisław. "Zbliżenie I: Jeden na jednego", in Stanisław Zawiśliński (ed), *Kieślowski bez końca* (Warsaw: Skorpion, 1994): 11-45.

1.2 In newspapers and weeklies

Bajer, Lesław. "O sobie samych dla współczesności", *Literatura* 5 July 1979.

Banaszkiewicz, Grażyna. "Z rzeczywistości", *Tydzień* 14 October 1979.

Bartowska, Lilliana. "Kończę...", *Głos szczeciński* 2 March 1994.

Biełous, Urszula. "Żyjemy osobno", *Kultura* 21 September 1988.

——————————. "Portret człowieka we wnętrzu", *Ela* 2 (1994).

——————————. "Artysta należący do świata", *Wiadomości kulturalne* 17 September 1995.

Błach, Jacek and Agata Otrębska. "Wymykamy się Bogu z ręki", *Gazeta wyborcza* 23-24 March 1996.

"By zrobić dobry film, trzeba ludzi z energią i talentem", *Tygodnik małopolski* 21 October 1993.

Danilewicz, Blanka. "Chcę robić filmy o tym, jak trudno jest żyć", *Myśl społeczna* 24 May 1987.

Dipont, Małgorzata. "Spokój", *Życie Warszawy* 3 October 1991.

Domagała, Jerzy. "Co to znaczy?", *ITD* 18 December 1977.

Ferney, Frédéric and Marie-Noëlle Tranchant. "Kieślowski z pytaniami, które stawiają wszyscy", *Film* 12 (1992): 16-17 [Polish translation of interview first published in *Le Figaro*].

Gajewski, Marek. "Kieślowski w Bajce", *Sztandar młodych* 1 December 1988.

Garbicz, Adam. "Grymas obrzydzenia", *Gazeta krakowska* 4 October 1993.

——————. "Gra z widzem", *Gazeta krakowska* 10 October 1993.

Goszczurny, Stanisław. "Jestem przeciw zabijaniu", *Rzeczpospolita* 4-5 March 1989.

Gwóźdź, Andrzej. "Zmierzać ku diagnozie", *Trybuna robotnicza* 27-29 June 1980.

Hollender, Barbara. "Obrzydzenie do polityki", *Rzeczpospolita* 4 October 1993.

——————. "Nie zaglądam w obiektyw", *Rzeczpospolita* 2-3 December 1995.

Horoszczak, Adam. "Najważniejsza jest miłość", *Dziennik zachodni* 8 June 1994.

"Interesuje mnie połączenie fabuły z dokumentem", *Gazeta olsztyńska* 21 October 1979.

Janicka, Bożena. "Beze mnie", *Film* 23 October 1988: 3-5.

——————. "Sami rozerwaliśmy łączącą nas kiedyś więź", *Film* 17 November 1991: 4-5.

Jastrzębska, Zuzanna. "Chwila namysłu", *Filipinka* 21 October 1979.

Józefowicz, Katarzyna. "Skończyłem z robieniem filmów", *Express wieczorny* 5 October 1993.

——————. "Kieślowski nie sterowany", *Express wieczorny* 1 March 1994.

——————. "Każde życie warte jest filmu", *Express wieczorny* 6 June 1994.

Kałużyński, Zygmunt and Marian Turski. "Zaglądać ludziom pod czaszkę", *Polityka* 6 March 1976.

Karbowiak, Małgorzata. "Trzy sprzeciwy!", *Głos poranny* 1-2 June 1994.

"Kilka pytań do... Krzysztofa Kieślowskiego", *Przekrój* 21 January 1990.

Kostur, Ewa. "Wolność artysty", *Głos szczeciński* 9 October 1991.

Kozbiel, Janina. "Krótka rozmowa", *Odrodzenie* 15 July 1989.

Kozera, Grzegorz. "Polska leży w Europie", *Słowo ludu* 9 December 1988.

Krall, Hanna. "Zrobiłem i mam", *Polityka* 27 January 1979.

Krzywów, Teresa. "Bliżej tego co dziś", *Czas* 16 September 1979.

Kunach, Bogusław. "Teoria przypadku", *Gazeta regionalna* 9 April 1994.

Lewin, Ludwik. "Idę na emeryturę", *Gazeta wyborcza* 27 January 1994.

Łużyńska, Jadwiga Anna. "Nie mam pociągu do Hollywood", *Przegląd tygodniowy* 14 February 1993.

Łużyńska, Jadwiga Anna. "Zawsze robiłem filmy romantyczne", *Sycyna* 22 (24 September 1995): 3-4.

Malatyńska, Maria. "Twoja wygrana oznacza, że ktoś inny przegrał", *Gazeta wyborcza* 29 October 1990.

Marczyński, Jacek and Bogdan Możdżyński. "Mocne strony, słabe strony", *Literatura* 46 (11 November 1976).

Michalczak, Janusz. "Nie wiemy lepiej", *Dziennik polski* 8 October 1993 [interview with Kieślowski, Piesiewicz and Preisner].

——————————. "Każdy z nas 'kombinuje' podobnie", *Dziennik bałtycki* 22 October 1993.

"Nie robię filmów 'pod festiwale'", *Gazeta olsztyńska* 2 December 1988.

Paprocka, Aleksandra. "Kilka prostych pytań które musimy sobie postawić", *Dziennik bałtycki* 15-16 September 1979.

Pawlas, Jerzy. "Zająć się tym, co się dzieje wokół", *Tygodnik kulturalny* 10 February 1980.

——————————. "Propozycja wspólnego myślenia", *Kurier szczeciński* 5-7 April 1980.

Piątek, Andrzej. "Życiorysy nas wszystkich i każdego z osobna", *Nowiny* 7 February 1977.

Pietrasik, Zdzisław. "Średnia przyjemność", *Polityka* 6 July 1985.

Rój, Urszula. "Nie omijać rzeczywistości", *Trybuna robotnicza* 11-12 June 1977.

Sobolewski, Tadeusz. "Niecierpliwość wyższego rzędu", *Gazeta wyborcza* 9 October 1991.

——————————. "Niebieski lizak", *Tygodnik powszechny* 24 October 1993.

Szarłat, Aleksander. "Dotknąć tajemnicy", *Sztandar młodych* 15-17 October 1993.

Szulc, Anna. "Zajączek dla 'Czerwonego'", *Gazeta krakowska* 21 June 1994.

Szyma, Tadeusz. "Pomóc samemu sobie", *Tygodnik powszechny* 12 November 1989.

——————————. "Wokół 'Dekalogu'", *Tygodnik powszechny* 18 March 1990 [interview with Kieślowski and Piesiewicz].

T.K. "Nie wierzę, że filmem można coś zmienić", *Głos wielkopolski* 28 February 1989.

Tymowski, W. "Robię filmy bardzo rzadko...", *Echo dnia* 13 November 1988.

Umer, Teresa. "Dziesięcioro przykazań", *Tygodnik polski* 10 May 1987.

W.J. "Nasza wina", *Czas krakowski* 8 October 1993.

Wojciechowski, Piotr. "Zedrzeć wszystkie skóry", *Przegląd katolicki* 10 (1990).

Wróblewski, J. "Lwie pazury", *Trybuna* 9-10 October 1993 [interview with Kieślowski and Piesiewicz].

——————————. "Miłość ważniejsza jest od wolności", *Życie Warszawy* 12-13 March 1994.

Wronkowska, Maria. "Kultura nie może być dodatkiem do życia", *Kurier polski* 15 September 1980.

Załuski, Mariusz. "Przechodzę na emeryturę", *Nowości* 4-5 March 1994.

Zaradniak, Marek. "Facet przed emeryturą", *Gazeta poznańska* 4 March 1994.

Zawiśliński, Stanisław. "'Najważniejsze jest samo życie...'", *Trybuna* 19 September 1991.

"Złoty Kord dla Krzysztofa Kieślowskiego", *Żołnierz wolności* 4 July 1971.

(ii) In French

2.1 In periodicals

Amiel, Vincent and Michel Ciment. "Entretien avec Krzysztof Kieślowski: 'La fraternité existe dès que l'on est prêt à écouter l'autre'", *Positif* 403 (September 1994): 26-32.

Bergala, Alain. "Krzysztof Kieślowski. Sławomir Idziak", *Cahiers du Cinéma* 409 (June 1988): 28, 30.

Brisset, Stéphane. "Rendez-vous express avec Kieślowski", *Cinéma 91* 478 (June 1991): 13.

Ciment, Michel and Hubert Niogret. "Le Décalogue: entretien avec Krzysztof Kieślowski", *Positif* 346 (December 1989): 36-43.

——————————————. "De Weronica à Véronique", *Positif* 364 (June 1991): 26-31.

——————————————. "Entretien avec Krzysztof Kieślowski: 'La liberté est impossible'", *Positif* 391 (September 1993): 20-25.

Demeure, Jacques. "Entretien avec Krzysztof Kieślowski", *Positif* 227 (February 1980): 23-28.

Gervais, Ginette. "Entretien avec Krzysztof Kieślowski", *Jeune Cinéma* 123 (December 1979/January 1980): 30-31.

H.N. "Entretien avec Krzysztof Kieślowski", *Positif* 332 (October 1988): 17-22.

Latek, Stanisław and Marie-Claude Loiselle. "Entretien avec Krzysztof Kieślowski: L'arme du désespoir", *24 Images* 42 (spring 1989): 62-64.

Loiselle, Marie-Claire and Claude Racine. "Entretien avec Krzysztof Kieślowski: Convoiter l'impossible", *24 Images* 58 (November-December 1991): 10-13.

Ostria, Vincent. "Le hasard et la nécessité. Krzysztof Kieślowski parle à Vincent Ostria", *Les Inrockuptibles* 36 (June 1992).

Tessier, Max. "Donner un sens à la vie: Propos de Krzysztof Kieślowski", *La Revue du Cinéma* 443 (November 1988): 50-52.

Tixeront, Antoine. "Kieślowski: 'l'essentiel, faire un film crédible'", *Cinéma 88* 452 (December 1988): 11-12.

Wimphen, Catherine. "Krzysztof Kieślowski: J'arrête le cinéma!", *Studio Magazine* 90 (September 1994): 104-107.

2.2 In newspapers and weeklies

Anquetil, Gilles. "Le maître du mystère", *Le nouvel observateur (Special Cannes Issue)* 9 May 1991: 122-123.

B.C. "Nous sommes drôles quand nous sommes tragiques", *Libération* 11 October 1989.

Boujut, Michel. "Krzysztof Kieślowski: 'en Pologne, le désespoir a tout anéanti'", *L'événement du jeudi* 19 October 1989.

Ciment, Michel. "'Ce qui m'intéresse c'est l'homme'", *Le Monde* 16 September 1989: 19.

F.C. "Les commandements de Kieślowski", *Le Progrès* 2 November 1988.

Ferenczi, Aurelia. "La parabole moderne du Décalogue", *Quotidien de Paris* 11 October 1989.

Garnier, Philippe. "Il est de plus en plus difficile de trouver des raisons d'espérer", *Libération* 26 October 1988.

——————. "Le Décalogue, tu regarderas", *Libération* 6 March 1990.

Heymann, Danièle. "Les portes s'ouvrent sur un sourire d'exil", *Le Monde* 16 May 1991: 24.

Jonquet, François. "Kieślowski: ma profession de foi", *Quotidien de Paris* 7 March 1990.

Libiot, Éric. "Kieślowski", *Première (France)* September 1993: 84-87.

Pangon, Gérard. "Les bonnes questions", *Télérama* 2074 (11 October 1989): 60.

Remy, Vincent. "Le maître du hasard", *Les dernières nouvelles d'Alsace* 24 March 1990.

Roy, Jean. "Un pessimiste productif", *L'Humanité* 11 October 1989.

Siclier, Jacques. "Le 'pourquoi?' du hasard", *Le Monde* 28 October 1988.

Tranchant, Marie-Noëlle. "Pas de polka pour l'assassin", *Le Figaro* 26 October 1988.

——————. "Krzysztof Kieślowski: Sauve qui peut l'amour!", *Le Figaro* 15 May 1991.

(iii) In English

3.1 In periodicals

Cargin, Peter. "Kieślowski's commandments", *Film (BFFS)* 3: 35 (May/June 1990): 8-9.

Mensonge, Serge. "Three Colours Blue, White and Red: Krzysztof Kieślowski and Friends", *Cinema Papers* 99 (June 1994): 26-32 [plus comments by Binoche, Idziak, Karmitz, Piesiewicz and Preisner].

Moszcz, Gustaw. "No heroics, please", *Sight and Sound* 50: 2 (spring 1981): 90-91.

van der Meulen, Helen and Mart Dominicus. "Trust is Something You Have to Earn", *Félix* 5 (25 November 1994): 58-63 [also in parallel German text].

3.2 In newspapers and weeklies

Andrew, Geoff. "True Blue", *Time Out* 1207 (6-13 October 1993): 20-21.

——————————. "Giving up the ghost", *Time Out* 26 October 1994-2 November 1994: 22-24.

Andrews, Nigel. "Soul-paring style", *The Financial Times* 10 June 1994: 17.

Boyes, Roger. "From the land of uncertainty", *The Times* 16 May 1990: 16.

Clarke, Jeremy. "True Colours", *What's On in London* 13 October 1993: 20.

Curtis, Quentin. "Tell It Like It Is", *Independent on Sunday* 3 October 1993: 20-22.

Dargas, Manohla. "Maître", *The Village Voice* 14 December 1993: 74.

Goldman, Steve. "Short films about success", *The Guardian* 23 November 1989: 22.

Green, William. "Magnetic Pole", *The Sunday Telegraph (Seven Days Magazine)* 6 May 1990: 21.

Gristwood, Sarah. "The reluctant auteur", *The Guardian* 17 May 1991: 37.

Hattenstone, Simon. "Auteur of his own destruction", *The Guardian* 8 November 1994 G2T: 4.

Kerr, Paul. "A revolution that's turned full circle", *The Observer (Arts Section)* 15 May 1995: 4: 14-15.

Robinson, David. "Polished clues to the colour of liberty", *The Times* 12 October 1993: 39.

Romney, Jonathan. "No end to the enigma", *The Guardian* 15 October 1993 G2T: 6.

4. In other languages

Cholodziński, P. "Menneske i Europa", *Film & Kino* 2 (1990): 36-38.

Cieslar, J. "Rozhovor s Krzysztofem Kieślowski o polském filmu a na téma Amatéra", *Film a doba* 26: 6 (June 1980): 340-341.

Cohen, P. "Nieuwe generatie poolse filmers: Krzysztof Kieślowski: 'Amator'", *Skoop* 16 (March-April 1980): 24-25.

Dominicus, Mart and J de Putter. "We zoeken in iedere scène naar een zeker realisme", *Skrien* 183 (April-May 1992): 36-41.

Donev, Aleksandr. "Preskonferencija na Ksistof Keslovski po povod Tri cvjata: bjalo", *Kino* [Bulgaria] 2 (April 1994): 41.

Egger, Christoph. "Für mich ist das ein Film gegen das Töten", *Neue Zürcher Zeitung* 23 February 1989.

Eichenberger, Ambros. "'Ich habe zehn Filme über unsere Zeit gemacht': Interview mit Krzysztof Kieślowski", *Zoom* 9 (1990): 27-33.

Furdal, Małgorzata. "Perché siamo qui?", in Małgorzata Furdal and Roberto Turigliatto (eds), *Kieślowski* (Turin: Museo Nazionale del Cinema, 1989): 13-35.

Göldenboog, Christian and Sławomir Magala. "Ein Gespräch mit Krzysztof Kieślowski: 'Man kann alle Dinge im Leben wiederholen'", *Filmfaust* 33 (April/May 1983): 42-44.

Komers, Rainer. "Fotogenes Leiden: Der polnische Filmregisseur Kieślowski im Gespräch über Dokumentar- und Spielfilm, Politik, Kunst und Moral", *EDI-Bulletin* 3-4 (1990): 54-58.

Kopanevovà, G and P Zvonicek. "Rozhovor s Krzysztofem Kieślowskim", *Film a doba* 37: 4 (winter 1991): 207-214.

Pap, P. "Az élet sürüjében lenni...", *Filmkultúra* 16: 4 (July-August 1980): 36-44.

Piccino, C. "Conversazione con Krzysztof Kieślowski", *Filmcritica* 40 (396-397) (June-July 1989): 394-99.

Rood, J. "Kieślowski: de dilemma's van het privé-leven en de politiek", *Skoop* 17: 3 (April 1981): 14-17.

Rossi, Umberto. "Ci interessa cogliere la vita com'è", *Cinemasessanta* 139 (May-June 1981): 18-20.

Saeveras, N O. "Tross alt, en optimistisk film!", *Film & Kino* 3 (1989): 36-37.

"...Svoe nepovtorimoe slovo: 'nasha pozitaiia dolzhna byt' aktivnoi'", *Iskusstvo Kino* 1 (1980): 67-74.

Trenczak, Heinz. "Von der Macht der Geduld: Interview mit Krzysztof Kieślowski", *Blimp* 14 (summer 1990): 17-18.

Willemsen, P. "'Ik hou van geen enkele institutie': gesprek met Krzysztof Kieślowski", *Andere Sinema* 90 (March-April 1989): 22-24.

D. Articles based on interviews with Kieślowski

(i) In Polish

Andracki, Krzysztof. "Kieślowski w 'Bajce'", *Fakty* 17 December 1988.

Bleja, Agata. "Czarny po czerwonym", *Express wieczorny* 8 June 1994.

Cieślak, Jacek. "Niebieski kolor wolności", *Rzeczpospolita* 2-3 October 1993.

de Riedel Burczycka, Małgorzata. "Sam zastawiłem na siebie pułapkę", *Przekrój* 48 (27 November 1994).

Gołąb, Grzegorz. "Dlaczego świat jest taki...", *Dziennik ludowy* 47 (21 November 1993).

Hollender, Barbara. "Życie, czyli wszystko", *TeleRzeczpospolita* 45 (27 November-3 December 1993). .

Horst, Matylda van. "Złoty lew dla Kieślowskiego", *Słowo ludu* 219 (19 September 1993).

Krasińska, Małgorzata. "'W smutnym kolorze blue'", *Gazeta pomorska* 28 October 1993.

Lewin, Ludwik. "'Ja nie szukam odpowiedzi, ja stawiam pytania': Krzysztof Kieślowski w trzech kolorach", *Tygodnik powszechny* 6 (7 February 1993).

"Młody – Kieślowski z ziemi włoskiej do Polski", *Gazeta poznańska* 235 (8 October 1993).

Piątek, Andrzej. "Niebieski, Biały, Czerwony", *Nowiny* 200 (13 October 1993).

Sobiecka-Awdziejczyk, Ewa. "Kieślowski przez przypadki", *Film* 8 (1994): 81.

TK. "Nos Kieślowskiego", *Kurier poranny* 91 13-15 May 1994.

"Triumf Kieślowskiego", *Kariera* 12 (1993): 5-6.

(ii) In other languages

Abrahamson, Patrick. "Kieślowski's many colours", *Oxford University Student Newspaper* 2 June 1995.

Ayre, Elisabeth. "Kieślowski: The Cinema of Anxiety", *International Herald Tribune* 11 November 1988.

Boujut, Michel. "Les films électrochocs de Kieślowski", *L'événement du jeudi* 27 October 1988.

Fabre, Maurice. "Kieślowski: quatre films à l'affiche en même temps", *France-Soir* 12 November 1988.

Frodon, Jean-Michel. "L'œuvre au noir", *Le Point* 13 November 1988.

Goldman, Steven. "A short interview about Killing", *City Limits* 423 (9-16 November 1989): 21.

Head, Anna. "Kieślowski: à present pas de futur", *Libération* 6 July 1988.

Hétier, Laurence. "Les réalismes et moralismes de Kieślowski", *L'Express* 28 October 1988.

"Le cas Kieślowski", *Quotidien de Paris* 27 October 1988.

Pulleine, Tim. "On Kieślowski", *Time Out* 1004 (15-22 November 1989): 37.

Tranchant, Marie-Noëlle. "Kieślowski l'inconfortable", *L'Aurore* 11 October 1989.

E. *Comments on, and recollections of, Kieślowski by his collaborators*

Bergala, Alain. "Krzysztof Kieślowski. Sławomir Idziak", *Cahiers du Cinéma* 409 (June 1988): 28, 30.

Biełous, Urszula. "Wystarczy być" [with Irène Jacob]; "Wymówić kropkę" [with Jean-Louis Trintignant]; "Krótki film o telefonach" [with Krzysztof Piesiewicz], *Film* 5 (1994): 20-21.

Bloom, Phillipa. "The double life of Irène", *Premiere (UK)* 2: 10 (November 1994): 42-45 [with Irène Jacob].

Brisset, Stéphane. "Irène Jacob, l'inespérée lumière", *Cinéma 91* 479 (July-August 1991): 34-35.

Ciment, Michel. "Entretien avec Krzysztof Piesiewicz, scénariste et avocat", *Positif* 346 (December 1989): 33-35.

Clarke, Jeremy. "White Angel", *What's On in London* 8 June 1994 [with Julie Delpy].

"Colouring the message", *In Camera* autumn 1994: 3-4 [with Piotr Sobociński].

Darke, Chris. "Working with Kieślowski", *Sight and Sound* 6: 5 (May 1996): 20 [with Zbigniew Preisner].

Desjardins, Denis. "Julie Delpy", *Séquences* 170 (March 1994): 31-33.

Fornara, Bruno. "Intervista a Krzysztof Piesiewicz", *Cineforum* 30: 293 (April 1990): 26-32.

Fuksiewicz, Jacek. "Wierzę w przypadek", *Polityka* 16 October 1993 [with Marin Karmitz].

Jabłońska, Katarzyna. "Jestem sam. Z Krzysztofem Piesiewiczem rozmawia Katarzyna Jabłońska", *Więź* 39: 9 (September 1996): 97-112.

Janicka, Bożena. "Coś nadchodzi", *Film* 11 February 1990: 4-5 [with Krzysztof Piesiewicz].

——————. "Zwykły facet – tak, to do mnie pasuje", *Kino* 28: 2 (February 1994): 4-6 [with Zbigniew Zamachowski].

Johnston, Trevor. [untitled] *Time Out* 8 June 1994: 5 [with Julie Delpy].

"Krzysztof Kieślowski we wspomnieniach", *Cinema (Polish)* 5 (1996): 43-50 [short recollections of Kieślowski by a multitude of collaborators].

Latek, Stanisław. "Marin Karmitz – wydawca filmów", *Kino* 25: 6 (June 1991): 18-21.

——————. "Francuski debiut Kieślowskiego", *Kino* 25: 9 (September 1991): 42 [with Leonardo de la Fuente].

Lubaszenko, Olaf. "Travailler avec Kieślowski", *Positif* 346 (December 1989): 32.

Łużyńska, Jadwiga Anna. "Zabłąkany w zawodzie aktora", *Tygodnik kulturalny verte* 15 August 1995: 6 [with Aleksander Bardini].

Macnab, Geoffrey. "Working with Kieślowski", *Sight and Sound* 6: 5 (May 1996): 16-19 [with Witold Stok (16-18) and Andrzej Krauze (19)].

Menanteau, C. "Irène Jacob: première et dernière muse", *Le Mensuel du Cinéma* 18 (June 1994): 22.

Mucharski, Piotr. "'Do źródeł, pod prąd'", *Tygodnik powszechny* 2 June 1996 [with Zbigniew Preisner].

Murat, Pierre. "'Comédien, un métier de flemmard!'", *Télérama* 2331 (14 September 1994): 36-38 [with Jean-Louis Trintignant].

Piesiewicz, Krzysztof. "Śmierć artysty", *Tygodnik Solidarność* 22 March 1996.

Pizzello, Stephen. "Piotr Sobociński *Red*", *American Cinematographer* 76: 6 (June 1995): 68-74.

Reumont, François. "Sławomir Idziak Révèle sa conception de l'image dans 'Bleu'", *Le Technicien Film & Video* 429 (15 November-15 December 1993): 20.

Reynaud, Bérénice. "Irène Jacob: Duet for One", *Interview* November 1991: 40.

Rouchy, Marie-Elisabeth. "Un Polonais qui décoiffe", *Télérama* 2298 (26 January 1994): 29-30 [with Zbigniew Zamachowski].

Sobolewski, Tadeusz. "Dekalog jako prowokacja", *Odra* 1 (1990): 66-69 [with Krzysztof Piesiewicz].

——————. "Grasz to, co masz w sobie", *Kino* 24: 2 (February 1990): 7-9 [with Artur Barciś].

——————. "Ponad podziałami", *Kino* 28: 6 (June 1994): 10-13 [with Krzysztof Piesiewicz].

Stuhr, Jerzy. "My z Kryzsiem. Jerzy Stuhr o Krzysztofie Kieślowskim", *Polityka* 4 (1979).

Williams, Richard. "The music of friendship", *The Guardian* 9 October 1998: 22-23 [about Zbigniew Preisner].

Wróblewski, Janusz. "Zwyciężyliśmy", *Życie Warszawy* 31 May 1994 [with Marin Karmitz].

Secondary bibliography

A. Books

Aghed, Jan et al. *Dekalogen: tio filmer av Krzysztof Kieślowski* (Malmo: Kulturforen, Kedjan, 1990).

Amiel, Vincent. *Kieślowski* (Paris: Rivages, 1995).

——————— (ed). *Krzysztof Kieślowski* (Paris: Editions Jean-Michèle Place, 1997).

Andrew, Geoff. *The 'Three Colours' Trilogy* (London: British Film Institute, 1998).

Campan, Véronique. *Dix brèves histoires d'image: Le Décalogue de Krzysztof Kieślowski* (Paris: Presses de la Sorbonne Nouvelles, 1993).

Carluccio, Giulia, Sara Cortellazzo and Dario Tomasi (eds). *Krzysztof Kieślowski* (Turin: Scriptorium, 1995).

Coretan, Matthias and Walter Lesch (eds). *Das Gewicht der Gebote und die Möglichkeiten der Kunst: Krzysztof Kieślowskis "Dekalog" – Filme als ethische Modelle* (Etudes d'éthique chrétienne. Freiburg (Schweiz): Universitätsverlag; Freiburg (Breisgau): Herder, 1994.

Estève, Michel (ed). *Krzysztof Kieślowski présenté par Michel Estève avec les textes de Yvette Biro et al* (Études cinématographiques 203-210 [Paris: Lettres modernes, 1994]).

Furdal, Małgorzata and Roberto Turigliatto (eds). *Kieślowski* (Turin: Museo Nazionale del Cinema, 1989).

Garbowski, Christopher. *Kieślowski's Decalogue series: the problem of the protagonists and their self-transcendence* (New York: Columbia University Press East European Monographs [452], 1996).

Granados, Janice. *10 bud pa livet: en psykoanalytisk gennemgan af Kieślowski's "Dekalog"-film* ([Copenhagen?]: Borgen, 1994).

Lagorio, Gina (ed). *"Il Decalogo di Kieślowski". Ricreazione narrativa* Casale Monferrato: Piemme 1992.

Lubelski, Tadeusz (ed). *Kino Krzysztofa Kieślowskiego* (Kraków: Universitas, 1997).

Murri, Serafino. *Krzysztof Kieślowski* (Rome: Il Castoro Cinema Press, 1996).

Zawiśliński, Stanisław (ed). *Kieślowski bez końca* (Warsaw: Skorpion, 1994).

———————————. *Kieślowski* (Warsaw: Skorpion, 1996).

——————— (ed). *Kieślowski. Varia* (Warsaw: Skorpion, 1998).

B. Special journal issues and sections

Kwartalnik filmowy 24 (84) (winter 1998)
Contents: "Status ontologiczny filmu dokumentalnego na przykładzie twórczości Krzysztofa Kieślowskiego" by Anna Kaplińska (6-28); "Przestrzeń, czas i bohater", by Christopher Garbowski (29-54); "Między samoświadomością a tajemnicą", by Magdalena Miszczak (56-65); "Opowieść o artyście, motylu, i lustrze", by Magdalena Łapińska (66-84); "Miłość od pierwszego wejrzenia", by Wisława Szymborska (86); "Intuicje sacrum w wierszu Wisławy Szymborskiej *Miłość od pierwszego wejrzenia* oraz w filmie Krzysztofa Kieślowskiego *Trzy kolory: czerwony*", by Marcin Bortkiewicz (87-93); "Trzy kolory", by Piotr Dziubak (94-97); "Kieślowski, Goethe i kolor, który zmienił świat", by Paul Coates (98-104); "Barwy samotności w tryptychu Krzysztofa Kieślowskiego *Trzy kolory – Niebieski, Biały, Czerwony*", by Agnieszka Kulig (105-110); "Ćwiczenia z perspektywy (Rzecz o Krzysztofie Kieślowskim)", by Maria Malatyńska (112-125); "Przeczucie słowa (notatki rosyjskiego filologa o polskim reżyserze)", by Irina Adelgeim (126-132); "*Krótkie filmy, Dekalog* oraz *Podwójne życie Weroniki* Krzysztofa Kieślowskiego w zwierciadle polskiej krytyki filmowej", by Mirosław Przylipiak (133-168); Wybrana bibliografia Krzysztofa Kieślowskiego (169-172).

Kontrapunkt [four-page cultural magazine of *Tygodnik powszechny*] 29 September 1996
Contents: "Powrót do domu", by Krzysztof Kieślowski [Polish version of opening óf *Kieślowski on Kieślowski*]; "Trzy głosy o Kieślowskim", by Tadeusz Sobolewski; "Bez końca", by Andrzej Titkow; "Dziewczyna z psem", by Iwona Siekierzyńska; "To, co się wymyka", by Michał Klinger; "Canneńskie medytacje", by Krzysztof Piesiewicz; "Potrafił słuchać", by Witold Stok.

Positif 403 (September 1994) [special section on *Trois couleurs*]
Contents: "Entretien avec Jean-Louis Trintignant: 'Je crois avoir gagné en sens moral'", by Michel Ciment (9-19); "Trois Couleurs: Rouge: La naïveté du manipulateur", by Alain Masson (21-23); "Plongées dans la passion: Trois Couleurs: Bleu, Blanc, Rouge", by Vincent Amiel (24-25); "Entretien avec Krzysztof Kieślowski: 'La fraternité existe dès que l'on est prêt à écouter l'autre'", by Vincent Amiel and Michel Ciment] (26-32).

Kwartalnik filmowy 4 (winter 1993/1994)
Contents: "Niebieski jak niebo", by Father Henryk Paprocki (79-81); "Pokonać śmierć", by Father Jan Sochoń (83-87); "Zimny kolor wolności", by Janusz Gazda (89-105); "Długi film o miłości", by Zbigniew Benedyktowicz (107-112).

Télérama: La Passion Kieślowski hors série, September 1993
Contents: "Bleu comme la liberté", by Pierre Murat (6-9); "Pour savoir ce qui est inutile, il faut d'abord le tourner", by Vincent Remy (10-14); "Aujourd'hui, vivre devient un art exigeant" [Juliette Binoche interviewed by Vincent Remy] (16-19); "Je n'ai pas de réponse à tout" [Charlotte Véry interviewed by Claude-Marie Trémois] (20); "Chaque chef opérateur lui apporte son monde" [Sławomir Idziak interviewed by Vincent Remy] (22-23); Arrêt sur images (24-25); "Trois couleurs: blanc", by Jean-Claude Trémois (28-29); "Il sait où sont les confitures!", by Claude-Marie Trémois (30-33); "Je dois avoir un type qui plaît au polonais" [Julie Delpy interviewed by Claude-Marie Trémois] (34-35); "Zamachowski, le 'possédé' du cinéma" [Zbigniew Zamachowski interviewed by Claude-Marie Trémois] (36); "Moi, je vis avec le film que je tourne" [Edward Kłosiński interviewed by Claude-Marie Trémois] (37-39); Arrêt sur images (40-43); "Trois couleurs: rouge", by Pierre Murat (44-45); "Le spectateur ne doit jamais ressentir la préméditation", by Pierre Murat (46-49); "Imagine que c'est l'espérance" [Irène Jacob interviewed by Pierre Murat] (50-52);

"Montrer d'abord, expliquer après" [Piotr Sobociński interviewed by Pierre Murat] (53); "Il veut que j'aille vite, encore plus vite" [Jean-Louis Trintignant interviewed by Pierre Murat] (54-57); Arrêt sur images (58-60); "Les comédiens 'rescapés' de la trilogie Kieślowski", by Vincent Remy (62-63); "La trilogie de Kieślowski", by Claude-Marie Trémois (64); "En traduisant, on ment toujours un peu" [Roman Gren interviewed by Vincent Remy] (66-67); "Ne pas être à côté de la plaque, à côté de la vie" [Krzysztof Piesiewicz interviewed by Claude-Marie Trémois] (68-73); "Le vrai-faux van den Budenmeyer" [Zbigniew Preisner interviewed by Vincent Remy] (74-75); "Je sais ce qu'il cherche, lui, connaît mes réactions" [Jean-Claude Laureux interviewed by Vincent Remy] (76-78); "Casser l'image de l'autre, déceler ce qu'il a de vrai" [Leonardo de la Fuente interviewed by Pierre Murat] (79-81); "La liberté d'être exigeant" [Marin Karmitz interviewed by Pierre Murat] (82-86); "Voici quelques remarques sur *Bleu*..." [correspondence with Marin Karmitz] (88-89); "Je doute, je doute toujours" [Kieślowski interviewed by Claude-Marie Trémois and Vincent Remy] (90-96).

Kino 27: 9 (September 1993): Dlaczego Kieślowski
Contents: "Dlaczego Kieślowski – mówi przewodniczący Komitetu Kinematografii", by Waldemar Dąbrowski (2-3); "Wyznanie wiary producenta", by Marin Karmitz (4-6); "O przechodzeniu kładką we mgle" [interview with Krzysztof Zanussi by Andrzej Kołodziejski] (7-9, 45); "Piękne hasła i tajemnice" [interview with Kieślowski by Hiroshi Takahashi] (11-13); "Klucz do wrażliwości [interview with Kieślowski by Tadeusz Sobolewski] (13-14); "Za kulisami" [interview with Kieślowski by Tadeusz Sobolewski] (14-16); "Film czerwony – notatki z planu", by Tadeusz Sobolewski (19-22); "Sfilmowane déjà vu" [Piotr Sobociński interviewed by Tadeusz Sobolewski] (22-23, 46); "Irène", by Irène Jacob (25-26); "Film biały – epitafium dla kina moralnego niepokoju" [Edward Kłosiński interviewed by Andrzej Kołodziejski] (26-30); "Pejzaż wewnętrzny" [Sławomir Idziak interviewed by Katarzyna Skorupska] (33-34).

Film na świecie 388/389 3/4 (1992)
Contents: "à la carte", by T.S. (3); "Przypadek i konieczność" (z Krzysztofem Kieślowskim rozmawia François Forestier) [interview with François Forestier] (5-6); "Dramaturgia rzeczywistości", by Krzysztof Kieślowski (7-9); "Obrazy świata i obrazy piekła", by Vincent Amiel (10-12); "Pochwała chirurga", by Thierry Jousse (13-15); "Kraj ponury i smutny", by Jean A Gili (16-17); "Przeznaczenie i wariacje", by Alain Masson (18-19); "Duch 'Solidarności'", by Éric Derobert (20-21); "Wyzbyć się polonocentryzmu" (z Krzysztofem Piesiewiczem rozmawia Michel Ciment) [interview with Krzysztof Piesiewicz by Michel Ciment] (22-25); "Pańskie filmy są rentgenogramami duszy..." (Z Krzysztofem Kieślowskim rozmawiają Michel Ciment i Hubert Niogret) [interview with Kieślowski by Michel Ciment and Hubert Niogret] (26-25); "Anatomia morderstwa", by Paul Coates (36-37); "Gry miłości i rozpaczy", by Joël Magny (38-39); "DEKALOG Kieślowskiego", by Phil Cavendish (40-44); "Pytania o winę", by Gina Lagorio (45-47); "Dekalog, jeden: Jeden albo zero", by Yann Tobin (49); "Dekalog, dwa: Skąd spadł martwy zając?", by Jean-Pierre Jeancolas (50); "Dekalog, trzy: Moja noc u Ewy", by Vincent Amiel (51); "Dekalog, cztery: Ani Ewa, ani Adam", by Françoise Audé (52); "Dekalog, pięć: Sztuka, przypadek i mała stabilizacja", by Éric Derobert (53); "Dekalog, sześć: Widzieć i być widzianym", by Philippe Rouyer (54); "Dekalog, siedem: Straceni dla niewinności", by Pascal Pernod (55); "Dekalog, osiem: Cień i światło", by Michel Sineux (56); "Dekalog, dziewięć: Pod prąd", by Olivier Curchod (57); "Dekalog, dziesięć: Pod znakiem Sybilii", by Alain Masson (58); "Przykazania jako gra", by Mikael Timm (59-71); "Jak w zwierciadle", by Jonathan Romney (72-73); "Kieślowski: nowe obszary", by Tony Rayns (74-77); "Trzy kolory: czerwony", by Krzysztof Kieślowski and Krzysztof Piesiewicz (78-118); "Biofilmografia", by Michał Gazda (119-126); "Nie

chcę realizować formy poza świadomością reżysera..." (Z Wiesławem Zdortem rozmawia Grzegorz Gazda) [interview with Wiesław Zdort by Grzegorz Gazda] (127-131); "Ożywić trumienkę..." (Z Edwardem Kłosińskim rozmawia Mateusz Werner) [interview with Edward Kłosiński by Mateusz Werner] (132-135); "Profesjonalizm i poezja (Z Witoldem Adamkiem rozmawia Mateusz Werner)" [interview with Witold Adamek by Mateusz Werner] (136-140); "Wspólny rytm (z Ewą Smal, montażystką DEKALOGU, rozmawia Mateusz Werner" [interview with Ewa Smal, editor on "The Decalogue", by Mateusz Werner] (141-146).

Positif 351 (May 1990): Décalogue: la preuve par dix [special section on *Dekalog*] Contents: "Un ou zéro: (Décalogue, un)", by Yann Tobin (32); "D'où est tombé le lièvre mort? (Décalogue, deux)", by Jean-Pierre Jeancolas (33); "Ma nuit chez Ewa (Décalogue, trois)", by Vincent Amiel (34); "Ni d'Eve ni d'Adam (Décalogue, quatre)", by Françoise Audé (35); "L'art, le hasard et le stabilo (Décalogue, cinq)", by Éric Derobert (36); "Voire et être vu (Décalogue, six)", by Philippe Rouyer (37); "Perdus pour l'innocence (Décalogue, sept)", by Pascal Pernod (38); "L'ombre et la lumière (Décalogue, huit)", by Michel Sineux (39); "A contre-courant (Décalogue, neuf)", by Olivier Curchod (40); "Le sibyllin (Décalogue, dix)", by Alain Masson (41).

Cineforum 30: 293 (April 1990) [special section on *Dekalog*] Contents: "Una fotografia, un martello e una vespa", by Bruno Fornara (6-23); "Il 'Decalogo'; un sguardo che ci forza a compatire", by F Grosoli (24-25); "Intervista a Krzysztof Piesiewicz" (26-32); "Le finestre sul cortile", by M Sesti (33-37); "Una storia immorale?", by A Piccardi (38-39); "Due gesti", by A Signorelli (39-43); "Le tavole infrante", by A Scarpellini (44-46).

Télérama 2095 (7 March 1990) [special section on *Dekalog 6-10*] Contents: "'Tu ne seras pas luxurieux'", by Pierre Murat (27); "'Tu ne voleras pas'", by Fabienne Pascaud (28); "'Tu ne mentiras pas'", by Claude-Marie Trémois (29); "'Tu ne convoiteras pas la femme d'autrui'", by Gérard Pangon (30); "'Tu ne convoiteras pas les biens d'autrui'", by Gérard Pangon (31).

Télérama 2094 (28 February 1990) [special section on *Dekalog 1-6*] Contents: "Le Décalogue", by Claude-Marie Trémois (22-23); "'Un seul dieu tu adoreras'", by Gérard Pangon (24); "'Tu ne commettras point de parjure'", by Claude-Marie Trémois (25); "'Tu respecteras le jour du seigneur'", by Gérard Pangon (26); "'Tu honoreras ton père et ta mère'", by Pierre Murat (27); "'Tu ne tueras point'", by Claude-Marie Trémois (28).

Positif 346 (December 1989) [special section on *Dekalog*] Contents: "L'amour des personnages (Brève Histoire d'amour)", by Pascal Pernod (26-27); "Dix blasons de morale (Le Décalogue)", by Philippe Niel (28-31); "Travailler avec Kieślowski", by Olaf Lubaszenko (32); "Entretien avec Krzysztof Piesiewicz, scénariste et avocat", by Michel Ciment (33-35); "Le Décalogue: entretien avec Krzysztof Kieślowski", by Michel Ciment and Hubert Niogret (36-43).

Positif 332 (October 1988) [special section on *Krótki film o zabijaniu*] Contents: "'Mettre le nez dans son caca'", by Michel Sineux (13-14); "Images du monde et de l'enfer", by Vincent Amiel (15-16); "Entretien avec Krzysztof Kieślowski", by Hubert Niogret (17-22); "Biofilmographie de Krzysztof Kieślowski", by Hubert Niogret (22-23).

C. General articles

(i) In Polish

Bolewski, Jacek. "Odmiana życia przez przypadki. Śladami Krzysztofa

Kieślowskiego", *Więź* 42: 1 (January 1999): 35-52.

Fuksiewicz, Jacek. "Blondynka, ładna, wielbicielka Kieślowskiego...", *Rzeczpospolita* 78 (24 April 1994).

Jopkiewicz, Tomasz. "Świadek klęski, świadek tajemnicy", *Film* 16 September 1990: 5.

Krall, Hanna. "Jakiś czas", *Tygodnik powszechny* 16 March 1997: 1, 8.

Kurz, Iwona. "Chórzyści", *Kino* 32: 3 (March 1998): 6-7.

Lubelski, Tadeusz. "Prawdziwy partner. Francuska krytyka o Kieślowskim", *Kwartalnik filmowy* 4 (winter 1993/94): 114-131.

——————. "Być obrońcą być sędzią", *Kino* 32: 3 (March 1998): 4-5, 56.

Łużyńska, Jadwiga Anna. "Fenomen Krzysztofa Kieślowskiego Cz. I", *Iluzjon: Kwartalnik filmowy* 1/2/3/4 (1995): 3-56

——————. "Muzyczny aspekt twórczości Krzysztofa Kieślowskiego", *Ruch muzyczny* 4 (1996) (25 February 1996): 8-10.

Malatyńska, Maria. "Kieślowski", *Życie literackie* 27 November 1988.

Michałek, Bolesław. "Kieślowski – rysy odrębne", *Kino* 24: 2 (February 1990): 1-3.

Mucharski, Piotr. "Wiara w tajemnicę", *Tygodnik powszechny* 24 March 1996.

Niecikowski, Jerzy. "Polska kwadratura koła", *Film* 11 February 1990: 11.

Pietrasik, Zdzisław. "Kolory ochronne", *Polityka* 16 October 1993.

Przylipiak, Mirosław. "Krzysztof Kieślowski – kontynuator Andrzeja Munka", *Kino* 28: 6 (June 1994): 14-15.

——————. "Monter i studentka, czyli jak to było naprawdę z niszczeniem Krzysztofa Kieślowskiego przez polską krytykę filmową", *Kino* 31: 3 (March 1997): 6-9, 50.

Skwara, Janusz. "Krzysztof Kieślowski", *Argumenty* 6 November 1988.

Sobolewski, Tadeusz. "Brzydkie podwórko", *Film* 29 (September 1980): 3-5.

——————. "Droga Kieślowskiego", *Odra* 10 (1986): 29-32.

——————. "Kieślowski: twarzą w twarz", *Kino* 31: 3 (March 1997): 4-5, 59.

——————. "Kino jako rozmowa", *Gazeta wyborcza* 20 April 1994 [review of *Kieślowski on Kieślowski*].

——————. "Niepokój Kieślowskiego", *Kino* 29: 6 (June 1995): 7-9.

Tomczyk, Paweł. "Felix w piekle", *ITD* 8 January 1989.

Tronowicz, Henryk. "Kieślowskiego polowanie na duchy", *Dziennik bałtycki* 3 June 1994.

Zatorski, Janusz. "Felix Kieślowskiego", *Kierunki* 18 December 1988.

——————. "Kino rzeczy ostatecznych – o twórczości Krzysztofa Kieślowskiego", *Słowo: dziennik katolicki* 26 March 1996.

Zmudziński, Bogusław. "Rezygnacja Krzysztofa Kieślowskiego, czyli życie jest gdzie indziej", *Universitas* 11 (1994): 68-70.

(ii) In French

Amiel, Vincent. "Images du monde et de l'enfer", *Positif* 332 (October 1988): 15-16.

——————. "Kieślowski et la méfiance du visible", *Positif* 423 (May 1996): 73-74.

Bergala, Alain. "Krzysztof Kieślowski. Sławomir Idziak", *Cahiers du Cinéma* 409 (June 1988): 28, 30.

Elia, M. "Krzysztof Kieślowski le (bon) sauvage", *Séquences* 140 (June 1989): 44-46.

Gorin, François. "La nécessité du hasard", *Télérama* 2460 (5 March 1997): 74-75.

Kermabon, Jacques. "La vie multiple de Krzysztof Kieślowski", *24 Images* 82 (summer 1996): 8.

Murat, Pierre. "Le hasard tu rencontreras", *Télérama* 2410 (20 March 1996): 44-47.

——————. "1, 2, 3, Kieślowski", *Télérama* 2475 (18 June 1997): 32-34.

Pangon, Gérard. "Kieślowski: carré d'as", *Télérama* 2024 (19 October 1988): 37-41.

Roy, Jean. "La visionnaire broie du noir", *L'Humanité* 28 October 1988.

Siclier, Jacques. "La Pologne sans soleil: quatre films de Krzysztof Kieślowski", *Le Monde* 28 October 1988: 38 [*Amator, Przypadek, Bez końca* and *Krótki film o zabijaniu*].

Tischner, Józef. "J'ai livré le bon combat", *Ciné & Media* 2 (1996): 28-29 [funeral oration].

Waintrop, Edouard. "Kieślowski révélé", *Libération* 26 October 1988.

(iii) In English

Behr, Edward. "Poland's 'Enfant terrible'", *Newsweek* 23 October 1989: 63.

Bowdler, Neil. "Flashback to times of great expectation", *The Guardian* 21 August 1998: 22.

Falkowska, Janina. "'The Political' in the Films of Andrzej Wajda and Krzysztof Kieślowski", *Cinema Journal* 34: 2 (winter 1995): 37-50.

Garbowski, Christopher. "Kieślowski's Seeing I/Eye", *The Polish Review* 40: 1 (1995): 53-60.

Gilbey, Ryan. "Krzysztof Kieślowski 1941-1996", *Premiere (UK)* 4: 4 (May 1996): 28 [obituary].

Hoberman, Jim. "Epilogue", *The Village Voice* 2 April 1996: 59 [obituary].

Jousse, Thierry. "Éloge d'un vivisecteur", *Cahiers du Cinéma* 413 (November 1988): 10-13.

Karimi, Iraj. "Two or three things about Kieślowski", *Film International* 3: 4 (autumn 1995): 40-42.

Kemp, Philip. "Slightly excited", *Sight and Sound* 4: 5 (May 1994): 35.

Kim, John. "Poles Apart 1", *Columbia Film View* 10: 1 (1992): 2-5, 39.

Malcolm, Derek. "Old King Pole", *The Guardian* 12 March 1989: 9.

——————. "Human touch of a master", *The Guardian* 14 March 1996: 15 [obituary].

Weschler, Lawrence. "Poland's Banned Films", *Cineaste* 13: 3 (1984): 11-12.

(iv) In other languages

Cieslar, J. "Krzysztof Kieślowski aneb mravnost faktů", *Film a doba* 26: 6 (June 1980): 336-340.

Hasenberg, Peter. "Der Mensch auf dem Seziertisch: Krzysztof Kieślowski und seine Filme", *Film-Dienst* 26 (27 December 1989): 826-829.

Płażewski, Jerzy. "Krzysztof Kieślowski of de wegen van de interiorisatie", *Andere Sinema* 90 (March-April 1989): 17-21.

Rood, J. "Kieślowski: de dilemma's van het privé-leven en de politiek", *Skoop* 17: 3 (April 1981): 14-17.

Russo, Eduardo A. "Retrato del artiste reticente", *Amante Cine* 49 (March 1996): 43.

D. Selected reviews and articles

Three Colours: Red

(i) In Polish

Kornatowska, Maria. "Kreacja w czerwieni", *Kino* 28: 7-8 (July-August 1994): 28-29.

Lis, Piotr. "Summa", *Kino* 28: 7-8 (July-August 1994): 26-28.

Lubelski, Tadeusz. "Szwajcarski zegarek z duszą", *Tygodnik powszechny* 5 June 1994.

Malatyńska, Maria. "Trzy kolory: Czerwony", *Echo krakowa* 13 June 1994.

Sobolewski, Tadeusz. "Bajka o ludziach", *Tygodnik powszechny* 12 April 1993.

——————. "Notatki z planu", *Kino* 27: 9 (September 1993): 19-22.

——————. "Mit Kieślowskiego", *Gazeta wyborcza* 30 May 1994.

Tatarkiewicz, Anna. "Pobratać się z Walentynką", *Wiadomości kulturalne* 10 July 1994.

Wojciechowski, Piotr. "Orzeł, reszka, Kieślowski i Pan Bóg", *Film* 7 (1994): 49.

Wójcik, Jerzy. "Kolor miłości i braterstwa", *Rzeczpospolita* 30 May 1994.

(ii) In French

D.D. "Trois couleurs Rouge", *L'Avant-Scène du Cinéma* 434 (July 1994): 68.

Elhem, Philippe. "De la communication", *24 Images* 73-74 (September-October 1994): 42-43.

Elia, Maurice. "Trois couleurs – rouge", *Séquences* 174 (September-October 1994): 37-38.

Masson, Alain. "Trois Couleurs: Rouge: La naïveté du manipulateur", *Positif* 403 (September 1994): 21-23.

Strauss, Frédéric. "Tu ne jouiras point", *Cahiers du Cinéma* 483 (September 1994): 62-63.

Trémois, Claude-Marie. "Le bonheur dans un fauteuil", *Télérama* 2315 (25 May 1994): 32-34.

—————————. "Trois couleurs: Rouge", *Télérama* 2331 (14 September 1994): 32-36.

(iii) In English

Andrew, Geoff. "True colours", *Time Out* 9-16 November 1994: 66.

Andrews, Nigel. "At the end of the rainbow", *The Financial Times* 10 November 1994: 21.

Brown, Colin. "Three Colours: Red", *Screen International* 960 (3-9 June 1994): 20.

Brown, Geoff. "King crimson's greatest hit", *The Times* 10 November 1994: 37.

Brown, Georgia. "Too Beautiful for You", *The Village Voice* 29 November 1994: 64.

Curtis, Quentin. "Goodbye and thank you", *Independent on Sunday* 13 November 1994: 22.

Davenport, Hugo. "Swansong of a philosopher", *The Daily Telegraph* 11 November 1994: 24.

French, Philip. "Red's mixed palette", *The Observer Review* 13 November 1994: 9.

Hinson, Hal. "Red", *The Washington Post* 16 December 1994.

Johnstone, Iain. "Polish polish", *The Sunday Times* 13 November 1994.

Kemp, Philip. "Trois Couleurs: Rouge (Three Colours: Red)", *Sight and Sound* 4: 11 (November 1994): 54-55.

Klawans, Stuart. "Three Colours: Red", *The Nation* 12 December 1994: 738-740.

Malcolm, Derek. "True colours", *The Guardian* 10 November 1994 G2T: 12.

Mars-Jones, Adam. "The judge, the dog and the woman in *Red*", *The Independent* 30 November 1994: 25.

Nesselson, Lisa. "Three colors: red", *Variety* 355: 4 (23 May 1994): 52.

Pawełczak, Andy. "Red", *Films in Review* 46: 3/4 (March/April 1995): 60-61.

Romney, Jonathan. "Cinema fraternité", *New Statesman and Society* 11 November 1994.

Shone, Tom. "The director's final cut", *The Sunday Times* 10 November 1994: 7.

(iv) In other languages

Etten, Manfred. "Drei Farben: Rot", *Film-Dienst* 47: 18 (30 August 1994): 18-19.

Koskinen, Maaret. "Miraklet i vardagen. Den röda filmen", *Chaplin* 36: 5 (254) (1994): 65-6.

Lundström, Henry. "Den röda filmen", *Filmrutan* 37: 4 (1994): 30-31.

Svendsen, Erik. "Kunstneren som voyeur", *Kosmorama* 40: 209 (autumn 1994): 16-19.

Visarius, Karsten. "Drei Farben: Rot", *Epd Film* 11: 9 (September 1994): 39.

Three Colours: White

(i) In Polish

Hollender, Barbara. "Fryzjer i człowiek z tajemnicą", *Rzeczpospolita* 25 February 1994.

Janicka, Bożena. "Kamień czy szkiełko", *Kino* 28: 2 (February 1994): 8-10.

Kajewski, Piotr. "Gra znaczeń, nieoznaczoność postaci", *Odra* 5 (1994): 97-98.

Kłosiński, Jerzy. "'Biały' – à la Charlie Chaplin", *Tygodnik Solidarność* 4 March 1994.

Lis, Piotr. "Chłód", *Kino* 28: 6 (June 1994): 16.

Malatyńska, Maria. "Biały", *Echo krakowa* 17 March 1994.

Mazierska, Ewa. "Polski łącznik", *Film* 4 (1994): 62.

Mucharski, Piotr. "Bez koloru", *Tygodnik powszechny* 27 March 1994: 11.

Sobolewski, Tadeusz. "Krótki film o równości", *Gazeta wyborcza* 27 January 1994.

——————————. "Równanie w dół", *Kino* 28: 2 (February 1994): 10-11.

——————————. "Euforia śmietnika", *Kino* 28: 2 (February 1994): 16-18.

——————————. "Tajemnica Kieślowskiego", *Gazeta wyborcza* 25 February 1994.

(ii) In French

Amiel, Vincent. "Trois Couleurs: Blanc: Le milieu, les origines", *Positif* 396 (February 1994): 16-17.

Girard, Martin. "Trois couleurs – blanc", *Séquences* 170 (March 1994): 38-39.

Jousse, Thierry. "Marché noir", *Cahiers du Cinéma* 476 (February 1994): 71-73.

Kermabon, Jacques. "Et de deux", *24 Images* 71 (February-March 1994): 63.

Remy, Vincent. "Trois Couleurs: Blanc", *Télérama* 2298 (26 January 1994): 26-29.

(iii) In English

Andrews, Nigel. "Controlled spleen", *The Financial Times* 9 June 1994: 21.

Brown, Geoff. "White and black and funny all over", *The Times* 9 June 1994: 37.

Brown, Georgia. "Lost and Found", *The Village Voice* 14 June 1994: 52.

Curtis, Quentin. "'White': a paler shade of 'Blue'", *Independent on Sunday* 12 June 1994: 25.

Insdorf, Annette. "An Affectionate Look at Krzysztof Kieślowski's *Three Colors... White*", *Film Comment* 33: 2 (March-April 1997): 46-49.

Johnston, Sheila. "White with a hint of grey", *The Independent* 10 June 1994: 26.

Malcolm, Derek. "Do the white thing", *The Guardian* 9 June 1994 G2T: 6.

Nesselson, Lisa. "Trois couleurs: blanc", *Variety* 353: 13 (31 January 1994): 68.

Pawełczak, Andy. "White", *Films in Review* 45: 7/8 (July/August 1994): 54-55.

Strick, Philip. "Trois couleurs: Blanc (Three Colours: White)", *Sight and Sound* 4: 6 (June 1994): 63-64.

(iv) In other languages

Bernink, Mieke. "Franser dan de Fransen", *Skrien* 195 (April-May 1994): 17.

Greuner, Suzanne. "Drei Farben. Weiss", *Epd Film* 11: 4 (April 1994): 34-35.

Koskinen, Maaret. "Odysse genom upplost Europa", *Chaplin* 36: 2 (251) (1994): 67-68.

Lux, Stefan. "Drei Farben: Weiss", *Film-Dienst* 47: 5 (1 March 1994): 22-23.

Snée, P. "Fehér", *Filmkultúra* 30: 10 (October 1994): 34.

Svendsen, Erik. "Hvid for lighed", *Kosmorama* 40: 207 (spring 1994): 4-5.

Three Colours: Blue

(i) In Polish

Biedroń, Tomasz. "Na skróty do Europy", *Tygodnik powszechny* 17 October 1993.

Cieślak, Jacek and Barbara Hollender. "Pro/Kontra" Hollender: "Pro: Gdybym miłości nie miał"; Cieślak: "Kontra: W stylu rokoko", *Rzeczpospolita* 6 October 1993.

Furdal, Małgorzata and Bożena Janicka. "Wolność jako nic", *Kino* 27: 11 (November 1993): 34.

Jurkowska, Maja. "Błękit", *Twórczość* 1 (1994): 145-6.

Karoń-Ostrowska, Anna. "Tajemnica niebieskich kryształków", *Więź* 3 (1994): 162-163.

Malatyńska, Maria. "Trzy kolory: Niebieski", *Echo krakowa* 5-7 November 1993.

Paprocki, Father Henryk, Father Jan Sochoń, Janusz Gazda and Zbigniew Benedyktowicz. *Kwartalnik filmowy* 4 (winter 1993/94): 79-112 [**see** B. *Special journal issues and sections*].

Pilch, Jerzy. "Zrobiony na niebiesko", *Tygodnik powszechny* 17 October 1993.

Rammel, Iwona. "Van den Budenmeyer i jemu podobni. O muzyce w ostatnich filmach Kieślowskiego", *Kwartalnik filmowy* 6 (summer 1994): 130-140.

Sobolewski, Tadeusz. "Ze śmiercią w tle", *Gazeta wyborcza* 1 October 1993.

——————————. "Lot na uwięzi", *Kino* 27: 10 (October 1993): 4-5.

Wiścicki, Tomasz. "Pusto w środku", *Więź* 37: 3 (March 1994): 161-2.

Wojciechowski, Piotr. "Wyjście z chaosu", *Przegląd katolicki* 21-28 November 1993.

(ii) In French

Beaulieu, Jean. "La vie en bleu", *Cinébulles* 13: 2 (spring 1994): 40-41.

Elia, Maurice. "Les niveaux de liberté", *Séquences* 166 (September-October 1993): 46-48.

Horguelin, Thierry. "La vie derrière soi", *24 Images* 70 (December 1993-January

1994): 64-65.

Murat, Pierre. "Trois Couleurs: Bleu", *Télérama* 2278 (8 September 1993): 34-37.

Ostria, Vincent. "Le hasard et l'indifférence", *Cahiers du Cinéma* 471 (September 1993): 65-67.

Peck, Agnès. "Bleu: Une autre femme", *Positif* 391 (September 1993): 18-19

Roth-Bettoni, Didier. "Trois couleurs: bleu", *Le Mensuel du Cinéma* 9 (September 1993): 25-26.

(iii) In English

Andrews, Nigel. "Struggles for liberty", *The Financial Times* 14 October 1993: 13.

Canby, Vincent. "'Blue': the first installment of a tricolor trilogy", *The New York Times* 4 December 1993: 16.

Hinson, Hal. "Blue", *The Washington Post* 4 March 1994.

Klawans, Stuart. "Three Colours: Blue", *The Nation* 13 December 1993: 778-780.

Lane, Anthony. "Starting Over", *The New Yorker* 13 December 1993: 122-125.

Macnab, Geoffrey. "Trois Couleurs: Bleu (Three Colours: Blue)", *Sight and Sound* 3: 11 (November 1993): 54-55.

Michalski, Milena. "Three Colours: Blue", *The Slavonic and East European Review* 72: 4 (October 1994): 790-791.

Nesselson, Lisa. "Trois couleurs: bleu", *Variety* 342: 6 (20 September 1993): 28.

Pope, Angela. "In Memory", *Sight and Sound* 6: 8 (August 1996): 69.

Vincendeau, Ginette. "Juliette Binoche: From Gamine to Femme Fatale", *Sight and Sound* 3: 12 (December 1993): 22-24.

Wilson, Emma. "*Three Colours: Blue*: Kieślowski, colour and the postmodern subject", *Screen* 39: 4 (winter 1998): 349-362.

(iv) In other languages

Åhlund, Jannike. "Kieślowski sätter punkt", *Chaplin* 35: 5 (248) (November 1993): 44-48.

Bleekere, S. de. "Kieślowski in stemmig blauw", *Film en Televisie* 435 (October 1993): 26-27.

Comuzio, E. "La musica del film", *Cineforum* 327 (September 1993): 63-64.

Fornara, Bruno. "Film blu. Libertà", *Cineforum* 327 (September 1993): 60-64.

Koskinen, Maaret. "En mojlig varld. Frihet – den blå filmen", *Chaplin* 35: 6 (249) (1993): 67-68.

Medici, Antonio. "Film blu", *Cinema Nuovo* 42: 6 (346) (November-December 1993): 40-41.

Messias, Hans. "Drei Farben: Blau", *Film-Dienst* 46: 22 (26 October 1993): 22-23.

Nagel, Josef. "Der Zufall möglicherweise oder die Macht des Zufalls", *Film-Dienst* 46: 22 (26 October 1993): 36-37.

Pflaum, H G. "Drei Farben. Blau", *Epd Film* 10: 11 (November 1993): 39-40.

Simons, Jan. "Metafysisch blauw", *Skrien* 192 (October-November 1993): 26.

Svendsen, Erik. "Blå og blind kærlighed", *Kosmorama* 39: 206 (winter 1993): 4-6.

Three Colours (general articles)

(i) In Polish

Fuksiewicz, Jacek. "Blondynka, ładna, wielbicielka Kieślowskiego...", *Rzeczpospolita* 2-4 April 1994.

Jankun, Mariola. "Trójkolorowy transparent: Vive le chaos!", *Kino* 29: 6 (June 1995): 4-7.

Stachówna, Grażyna. "'Trzy kolory' – nasze miejsce w Europie", *Dialog* 39: 1 (January 1995): 104-7.

Werner, Mateusz. "Kolorowa pustka", *Film* 8 (1994): 72-73.

Wolicki, Krzysztof. "Raz jeszcze o kolorach", *Dialog* 40: 4 (April 1995): 91-96.

(ii) In French and English

Amiel, Vincent. "Plongées dans la passion: Trois Couleurs: Bleu, Blanc, Rouge", *Positif* 403 (September 1994): 24-25.

Coates, Paul. "The Sense of an Ending: Reflections on Kieślowski's Trilogy", *Film Quarterly* 50: 2 (winter 1996-97): 19-26.

Hoberman, Jim. "Red, White and Blue", *Premiere (USA)* 8: 2 (October 1994): 50, 53.

Jean, Marcel. "Voir rouge", *24 Images* 76 (spring 1995): 44-45.

Kehr, Dave. "To Save the World: Kieślowski's Three Colors Trilogy", *Film Comment* 30: 6 (November-December 1994): 10-13, 15-18, 20.

Rayns, Tony. "Glowing in the Dark", *Sight and Sound* 4: 6 (June 1994): 8-10.

The Double Life of Véronique

(i) In Polish

Gondowicz, Jan. "Weronika – dziewczę z baśni", *Gazeta wyborcza* 18 October 1991.

Janicka, Bożena. "Po projekcji...", *Film* 21 July 1991.

Lubelski, Tadeusz. "Podwójne życie Kieślowskiego", *Kino* 25: 9 (September 1991): 2-5.

Malatyńska, Maria. "Podwójne życie Weroniki", *Echo krakowa* 3 November 1991.

Malkowska, Monika. "Spotkanie ze sobą", *Kino* 26: 1 (January 1992): 38.

Miodek, M. "La Double Vie de Véronique", *Filmowy serwis prasowy* 37: 19-20 (1-31 October 1991): 9-10.

Przylipiak, Mirosław. "Bez słów", *Gazeta gdańska* 3 November 1991.

Rammel, Iwona. "Van den Budenmeyer i jemu podobni. O muzyce w ostatnich filmach Kieślowskiego", *Kwartalnik filmowy* 6 (summer 1994): 130-140.

Sobolewski, Tadeusz. "Ostatnie słowo", *Kino* 25: 9 (September 1991): 9.

Tatarkiewicz, Anna. "Dlaczego Weronika umiera?", *Polityka* 2 November 1991.

Wojciechowski, Piotr. "Czy istnieje drugi Kieślowski", *Film* 10 (8 March 1992): 4-5.

Wołoszańska, Jolanta. "Tajemnice Weroniki", *Rzeczpospolita* 15-16 June 1991.

Wróblewski, Janusz. "Gry Kieślowskiego: operacja kartezjańska, czyli niepewność", *Życie Warszawy* 6 August 1992.

(ii) In French

Aimée, Anne. "La Double vie de Véronique", *Jeune Cinéma* 209 (July-August 1991): 13-14.

Baecque, Antoine de. "Kieślowski, cinéaste inconstant", *Cahiers du Cinéma* 445 (June 1991): 59.

Baron, Anne-Marie. "La double vie de Véronique", *Cinéma 91* 478 (June 1991): 12.

Bourgeois, Daniel. "'La double vie de Véronique': La métaphysique et le féminin: libres réflexions sur le film de Krzysztof Kieślowski", *Communio: Revue Catholique Internationale* 16: 5-6 (September-December 1991): 184-205.

Elhem, Philippe. "Les malheurs de Janus", *24 Images* 56-57 (autumn 1991): 30.

Elia, Maurice. "La double vie de Véronique", *Séquences* 156 (January 1992): 61-62.

Grosoli, F. "La double vie de Véronique", *Cineforum* 305 (June 1992): 12-13.

Heymann, Danièle. "Le chant du hasard", *Le Monde* 17 May 1991.

Loiselle, Marie-Claire and Claude Racine. "Entretien avec Irène Jacob: Le secret derrière la voix", *24 Images* 58 (November-December 1991): 14-16.

Masson, Alain. "Subjectivité et singularité: La Double Vie de Véronique", *Positif* 364 (June 1991): 24-25.

Sauvaget, Daniel. "La double vie de Véronique", *La Revue du Cinéma*, hors série 39 (1991): 38.

——————. "La double vie de Véronique", *La Revue du Cinéma* 473 (July/August 1991): 47.

(iii) In English

Andrews, Nigel. "A glittering enigma with hypnotic appeal", *The Financial Times* 27 February 1992: 21.

Bartholomew, D. "The Double Life of Veronica", *Film Journal* 94 (December 1991): 39-40.

Brown, Georgia. "One Sings", *The Village Voice (Film Special)* December 1991: 26.

Canby, Vincent. "Identical women and multiple portents", *The New York Times* 20 September 1991: C18.

——————. "Metaphysical Equation in 'The Double Life of Veronica'", *The New York Times* 24 November 1991: 69.

Coates, Paul. "Metaphysical Love in Two Films by Krzysztof Kieślowski", *The Polish Review* 37: 3 (1992): 335-336, 340-343.

Davenport, Hugo. "Drawn into a waking dream", *The Daily Telegraph* 27 February 1992: 16.

Glaser, G. "Europe's view of 'Véronique'", *The New York Times* 2 February 1992: 22.

Johnson, R. "Burdens of Identity in 'The Double Life'", *Christian Century* 109 (19 February 1992): 196.

Kilbourn, R J A. "Toward a Non-Euclidean Cinema: Kieślowski and Literature", *Canadian Journal of Film Studies/Revue Canadienne d'Etudes Cinématographiques* 6: 2 (autumn 1997): 34-50.

Kissen, Eva H. "The Double Life of Véronique", *Films in Review* 43: 5/6 (May/June 1992): 195-196.

Lane, Anthony. "Unbearable lightness of desire", *Independent on Sunday* 1 March 1992: 19.

Malcolm, Derek. "A double life in French and Polish", *The Guardian* 27 February 1992: 25.

Mars-Jones, Adam. "You only live twice", *The Independent* 28 February 1992: 18.

Ragland, Ellie and Elizabeth Wright. "*The Double Life of Veronica*: An Inquiry Into the Existence of Woman", *Psychoanalytic Pyschology* 10: 3 (1993): 481-486.

Rayns, Tony. "Kieślowski: Crossing over", *Sight and Sound* 1: 11 (March 1992): 22-23.

Romney, Jonathan. "La Double Vie de Véronique (The Double Life of Véronique)", *Sight and Sound* 1: 11 (March 1992): 43.

Ruppert, Peter. "The Double Life of Véronique", *Cineaste* 19: 2-3 (1992): 63-65.

Taubin, Amy. "Krzysztof Kieślowski doubles up", *The Village Voice* 24 September 1991: 56.

Wojdylo, John. "La double vie de Véronique", *Cinema Papers* 93 (May 1993): 46-47.

Yung. "La double vie de Véronique", *Variety* 343: 6 (20 May 1991): 39.

(iv) In other languages

Aas, N K. "Veronikas to liv", *Film & Kino* 4 (1991): 25.

Åhlund, Jannike. "Kieślowski sätter punkt", *Chaplin* 35: 5 (248) (November 1993): 44-48.

Buccheri. "Della vera immagine (saggio su 'La doppia vita di Veronica')", *Cinema & Cinema* 63 (January-April 1992): 105-110.

Cappabianca, Alessandro. "Frammenti d'essere", *Filmcritica* 42 (417-418) (September-October 1991): 465-466.

Engven, I. "Veronikas dubbelliv", *Filmrutan* 34: 4 (1991): 43-44.

Girlanda, E. "La doppia vita di Veronica", *Film* 4 (March-June 1991): he scene-90.

Goethals, Piet. "La double vie de Véronique", *Film en Televisie* 416 (January 1992): 33.

Heuvel, G van den. "Meester van het onbeheersbare", *Skrien* 183 (April-May 1992): 42-43.

Jorholt, Eva. "Tilværelsens forunderlige dobbelthed", *Kosmorama* 38 (199) (spring 1992): 16-20.

Koskinen, Maaret. "Dubbelgangare i tid och rum. Veronikas dubbelliv", *Chaplin* 33: 5 (236) (1991): 67-68.

Lenz, Eva-Marie. "Dunkel des Unbewussten", *Frankfurter Allgemeine Zeitung* 7 November 1991.

Leuken, Verena. "Marionettenspiel", *Frankfurter Allgemeine Zeitung* 16 May 1991.

Lochen, K. "Tilfeldighetenes spill", *Film & Kino* 6 (1991): 8-9.

Massini, M. "La double vie de Véronique", *Skoop* 27 (October 1991): 42-43.

Płażewski, Jerzy. "La double vie de Véronique", *Andere Sinema* 104 (July-August 1991): 52-53.

Pugliese, R. "La doppia vita di Veronica", *Segnocinema* 50 (July-August 1991): 37.

Putter, J. de. "Mystiek van een menselijke maat", *Skrien* 181 (December-January 1991/92): 17-19.

Signorelli, A. "La doppia vita di Veronica", *Cineforum* 306 (July-August 1991): 84-86.

Simons, J. "De dubbele esthetiek van Krzysztof Kieślowski", *Skrien* 181 (December-January 1991/92): 12-16.

Turco, Daniela. "Rinominazioni", *Filmcritica* 42 (415) (June 1991): 269-271.

Visarius, Karsten. "Die zwei Leben der Veronika", *Epd Film* 8: 11 (November 1991): 32.

Vrdlovec, Z. "Dvojno Veronikino zivljenje", *Ekran* 17: 8/9 (1992): 12-13.

Seven Days a Week

Báron, G. "Bábeli csönd", *Filmkultúra* 27: 2 (1991): 20-24.

Dominicus, Mart. "Wankelende toren van Babel", *Skrien* 171 (April-May 1990): 40-41.

Garcia, Jean-Pierre. "City Life", *Cinéma 90* 465 (March 1990): 23-24.

Neeuwaarden, M van. "City Life", *Skrien* 172 (June-July 1990): 57.

Wall. "City Life", *Variety* 338: 6 (14 February 1990): 39-40.

The Decalogue
(i) In Polish

Buttafava, G. "Zrób co możesz", *Kino* 24: 2 (February 1990): 4-7.

Chudy, Wojciech. "Filmowy *Dekalog*", *Ethos* 2: 4 (1989): 338-342.

Jabłońska, Katarzyna. "Wariacje na temat dziesięciorga przykazań", *Kwartalnik filmowy* 18 (summer 1997): 154-178.

Janicka, Bożena. "Dekalog I, Dekalog II", *Film* 45: 49 (12 December 1989): 11.

Kałużyński, Zygmunt. "Pan z fortepianem", *Polityka* 16 (21 April 1990).

Klinger, Michał. "Strażnik wrót", *Kino* 24: 5 (May 1990): 14-17.

Krzemiński, Ireneusz. "Dekalog, Kieślowski i Bóg", *Dialog* 35: 7 (July 1990): 123-127.

Olszewski, Jan. "Dekalog, pięć; Dekalog, sześć", *Film* 45 (21 January 1990): 11.

Przylipiak, Mirosław. "Kompozycje dwójkowe", *Kino* 24: 6 (June 1990): 23-26.

Sobański, Oskar. "Dekalog, trzy; Dekalog, cztery", *Film* 45 (7 January 1990): 11.

——————. "Dekalog, siedem; Dekalog, osiem", *Film* 45 (28 January 1990): 11.

——————. "Dekalog, dziewięć; Dekalog, dziesięć", *Film* 45 (18 February 1990): 14.

Sobolewski, Tadeusz. "Warto zobaczyć 'Dekalog'", *Gazeta wyborcza* 26 October 1989.

——————. "Solidarność grzesznych. O *Dekalogu* Krzysztofa Kieślowskiego", *NaGłos* 1: 1 (1990): 91-101.

Stopierzyńska, Irena. "Dekalog w dziesięciu odsłonach", *Więź* 34: 5-6 (1990): 197-199.

Szpakowska, Małgorzata. "Kieślowski: Jedenaste jest tajemnicą", *Dialog* 35: 12 (411) (1990): 114-118.

Szyma, Tadeusz. "Dekalog, dziesięć", *Tygodnik powszechny* 9 July 1989.

——————. "Kieślowski w Wenecji", *Tygodnik powszechny* 1 October 1989.

——————. "Dekalog, jeden", *Tygodnik powszechny* 24-31 December 1989.

——————. "Dekalog, siedem", *Tygodnik powszechny* 4 February 1990.

——————. "Dekalog, osiem", *Tygodnik powszechny* 11 February 1990.

——————. "Dekalog, dziewięć", *Tygodnik powszechny* 18 February 1990.

——————. "Dekalog, sześć", *Tygodnik powszechny* 18 February 1990.

Toeplitz, Krzysztof Teodor. "Nie lubimy wyrzutów", *Polityka* 3 March 1990.

Wyszyński, Zbigniew. "Ideologia i moralistyka Krzysztofa Kieślowskiego (na przykładzie filmu *Dekalog*)", *Powiększenie* 11: 3-4 (1991): 22-32.

Zielińska, Magda. "Krótko o 'krótkich filmach' Kieślowskiego", *Twórczość* 5 (1989): 118-121.

(ii) In French

Baecque, Antoine de. "Faut-il entrer dans l'église de Kieślowski?", *Cahiers du Cinéma* 429 (March 1990): 32-33.

Baron, Anne-Marie. "Le décalogue: une œuvre forte et cohérente", *Cinéma 89* 461 (November 1989): 36-37.

Bassan, Raphaël. "Le décalogue", *La Revue du Cinéma*, hors série 37 (1990): 33-35.

Beaulieu, Janick. "Tu ne tueras point", *Séquences* 140 (June 1989): 72-73.

Bénard, Marie-Claude. "'Le Décalogue': le rôle du second plan", *CinémAction* 65 (1992): 152-160.

Charbonneau, Alain. "Le décalogue de Krzysztof Kieślowski: les dix amendements", *24 Images* 55 (summer 1991): 6-9.

Ciment, Michel. "Dix films de moins d'une heure", *Le Monde* 16 September 1989: 19.

Elia, Maurice. "L'art du risque calculé", *Séquences* 153-154 (September 1991): 59-64.

H.N. "Dekalog (Décalogue)", *Positif* 341-342 (July-August 1989): 82-83.

Lavoie, A. "Perspectives: 'Le Décalogue'", *Cinébulles* 11: 1 (1991): 38-41.

Magny, Joël. "Les règles du hasard", *Cahiers du Cinéma* 429 (March 1990): 26-29.

Martin, Marcel. "Krzysztof Kieślowski: un cinéma sans anesthésie", *La Revue du Cinéma* 456 (January 1990): 41-45.

Niel, Philippe. "Dix blasons de morale (Le Décalogue)", *Positif* 346 (December 1989): 28-31.

Pangon, Bernard. "Les commandements de Kieślowski", *Télérama* 2074 (11 October 1989): 61-63.

Pérez, Michel. "La leçon de 'Décalogue'", *Le nouvel observateur* 14 March 1990.

Piquet, Patrick. "L'icône des outrages (Sur *Décalogue I* de Kieślowski)", *Communio: Revue Catholique Internationale* 17: 1 (January-February 1992): 80-87.

(iii) In English

Billen, Andrew. "Thou shalt not show any optimism", *The Observer* 6 May 1990: 72.

Brooks, S. "Kieślowski's love and death", *Film* 35 (May-June 1990): 6-7.

Brown, Georgia. "Angels Passing", *The Village Voice* 6 November 1990: 69.

Cavendish, Phil. "Kieślowski's *Decalogue*", *Sight and Sound* 59: 3 (summer 1990): 162-165.

Dunkley, Christopher. "Rules for life, Polish style", *The Financial Times* 13 June 1990: 17.

Edna. "Dekalog (The Ten Commandments)", *Variety* 336: 11 (27 September 1989): 36.

Garbowski, Christopher. "Krzysztof Kieślowski's *Decalogue*: Presenting Religious Topics on Television", *The Polish Review* 37: 3 (1992): 327-334.

Insdorf, Annette. "'The Decalogue' re-examines God's commands", *The New York Times* 28 October 1990: 28, sec 2.

Malcolm, Derek. "The Pole in pole position", *The Guardian* 29 March 1990: 28.

Millar, Dan. "A Great Polish Film-Maker: Krzysztof Kieślowski", *Durham University Journal* 85: 54 (January 1993): 131-135.

Perlmutter, Ruth. "Testament of the Father: Kieślowski's *The Decalogue*", *Film Criticism* 22: 2 (winter 1997-98): 51-65.

Rigney, Francis J, M.D. "*The Decalogue*: A Psychoanalytic Deadlock", *Film Criticism* 14: 3 (spring 1990): 55-71.

Tarantino, M. "The Cave", *Artforum* 29 (December 1990): 22-23.

(iv) In other languages

Barth, Pia. "Krzysztof Kieślowskies 'Dekalog'", *Blimp* 14 (summer 1990): 15-17.

Bernink, Mieke and G Zuilhof. "Zien en weerzien", *Skrien* 171 (April-May 1990): 22-27.

Bini, Luigi. "Il 'Decalogo' di K. Kieślowski: Dieci storie de vita", *Letture* November 1990: 781-796.

Bogani, Giovanni. "Gli scollamenti di vivere", *Quaderni di Cinema* 10 (46) (March-June 1990): 46-52.

——————. "Le tavole del dubbio", *Segnocinema* 10: 45 (September-October 1990): 15-17.

Casagrande, L. "Onbereikbaar ideaal", *Film en Televisie* 398/399 (July-August 1990): 11-13.

Horstmann, Johannes. "Kieślowskis *Dekalog*", *Medien Praktisch* 2 (1992): 53-56.

Kopanevovà, G and P Zvonicek. "Od moralniho neklidu k desateru", *Film a doba* 37: 4 (winter 1991): 207-214.

Kubitz, Peter-Paul. "Die zehn Gebote im Warschau von heute", *Süddeutsche Zeitung* 10 May 1990.

Maudente, F. "Venezia nell'anno del 'Decalogo'", *Cinema Sud* 30: 104 (April-May 1990): 36-38.

Nagel, Josef. "37 Millionen Individualisten: Über Krzysztof Kieślowski und seinen Zyklus *Dekalog*", *FILM-Korrespondenz* 3 (13 February 1990): 7-11.

——————. "Spiel um Vorsehung und Zufall: Krzysztof Kieślowskis Fernseh-Zyklus der 'Zehn Gebote'", *Frankfurter Allgemeine Zeitung* 9 May 1990.

Pomante, Stefania. "La bianchezza della balena", *Filmcritica* 41 (404) (April 1990): 200-203.

Svendsen, Erik. "Kunstens ti bud", *Kosmorama* 36 (193) (autumn 1990): 16-21.

Timm, Mikael. "Budorden som spelparti", *Chaplin* 32: 5 (230) (1990): 246-52.

Tittelbach, Rainer. "Kieślowskis Meisterwerke", *Die Welt* 4 May 1990.

Vörös, I et al. "Kieślowski, a lengyelek Mózese", *Filmkultúra* 27: 4 (1991): 35-54, 62-71.

Wauters, J.-P. "Korte notities in het kantwit bij een groot werk", *Film en Televisie* 398/399 (July-August 1990): 8-10.

Wickbom, Kaj. "Dekalogen – Guds narvaro", *Filmrutan* 34: 2 (1991): 27-28.

A Short Film About Love

(i) In Polish

Korycka, J. "Krótki film o miłości", *Filmowy serwis prasowy* 34: 18 (652) (16 September 1988): 2-5.

Kos, Alicja. "Refleksja czy moralitet", *Kultura* 46 (16 November 1988).

Malatyńska, Maria. "Smutne krajobrazy", *Kino* 23: 1 (January 1989): 5-7.

Markowska, Bożena. "Bezbronna miłość", *Odrodzenie* 10 September 1988.

Netz, Feliks. "Kieślowski", *Tygodnik Tak i Nie* 7 October 1988.

Niecikowski, Jerzy. "Krótki film o samotności", *Film* 43 (18 December 1988): 5.

Sobański, Oskar. "...A miłości bym nie miał", *Film* 43 (4 December 1988): 8-9.

Sobolewski, Tadeusz. "Krzysztofa Kieślowskiego 'dzieje grzechu'", *Przegląd katolicki* 18-25 December 1988.

Szyma, Tadeusz. "Krótki film o miłości", *Tygodnik powszechny* 11 December 1988.

Tatarkiewicz, Anna. "Podglądanie", *Polityka* 26 November 1988.

Zawiśliński, Stanisław. "Delikatna sfera", *Trybuna ludu* 3 November 1988.

Zielińska, Magda. "Krótko o 'krótkich filmach' Kieślowskiego", *Twórczość* 5 (1989): 118-121.

(ii) In French

Bonneville, Leo. "Film bref sur l'amour", *Séquences* 144 (January 1990): 57-58.

Chevassu, François. "Film virtuel film réel: De l'objet film au film perçu", *La Revue du Cinéma* 457 (February 1990): 53-62.

Garnier, Philippe. "L'amour sur cour", *Libération* 26 October 1988.

Horguelin, Thierry. "La femme d'en face", *24 Images* 46 (November-December 1989): 78-79.

Magny, Joël. "Les jeux de l'amour et du désespoir", *Cahiers du Cinéma* 424 (October 1989): 50.

Martin, Marcel. "Krzysztof Kieślowski: un cinéma sans anesthésie", *La Revue du Cinéma* 456 (January 1990): 41-45.

Maupin, Françoise. "Le mal d'aimer", *Le Figaro* 11 October 1989.

M.P. "Kieślowski contre l'image-pute", *Le nouvel observateur* 12 October 1989: 66.

Murat, Pierre. "Brève histoire d'amour", *Télérama* 2074 (11 October 1989): 63-64.

Pernod, Pascal. "L'amour des personnages (Brève Histoire d'amour)", *Positif* 346 (December 1989): 26-27.

Siclier, Jacques. "La femme et le voyeur", *Le Monde* 13 October 1989: 14.

(iii) In English

Andrews, Nigel. "A weird route to love", *The Financial Times* 29 March 1990: 21.

Coates, Paul. "Metaphysical Love in Two Films by Krzysztof Kieślowski", *The Polish Review* 37: 3 (1992): 335-336, 340-343.

Eidsvik, Charles. "Kieślowski's 'Short Films'", *Film Quarterly* 44: 1 (autumn 1990): 50-55.

French, Philip. "Day of the sad male virgin", *The Observer* 1 April 1990: 62.

Keates, Jonathan. "Heartburn: A Short Film About Love", *Sight and Sound* 59: 2 (spring 1990): 132.

Malcolm, Derek. "Just looking for love", *The Guardian* 29 March 1990: 24.

Mars-Jones, Adam. "Neighbourhood watch schemes", *The Independent* 29 March 1990: 17.

Pulleine, Tim. "Krótki Film o Miłości (A Short Film About Love)", *Monthly Film Bulletin* 57: 676 (May 1990): 131-132.

Robinson, David. "On the complexity of love and desire", *The Times* 29 March 1990: 19.

Walker, Alexander. "Peeping Pole", *Evening Standard* 29 March 1990: 30.

Walters, Margaret. "The spy who loved me", *The Listener* 123: 3158 (29 March 1990): 39.

Yung. "Krótki Film O Miłości" ("A Short Film About Love")", *Variety* 332: 11 (5 October 1988): 15.

(iv) In other languages

Bogani, Giovanni. "Non desiderare la donna d'altri", *Segnocinema* 10: 41 (January 1990): 31-32.

Causo, M. "Non desiderare la donna d'altri", *Film* 3 (January-February 1990): 96-97.

Farran-Lee, S. "En liten film om karlek. Den manskliga naden tar vid", *Chaplin* 32: 2 (227) (1990): 101-102.

Garritano, M. "Non desiderare la donna d'altri", *Quaderni di Cinema* 10 (45) (January-February 1990): 56-59.

Kremski, P. "Ein Mann, eine Frau und ein Fernrohr: Krótki film o miłości (Kurzer Film über die Liebe) von Krzysztof Kieślowski", *Film Bulletin* 31: 3 (166) (August 1989): 50-55.

Lundström, Henry. "En liten film om karlek", *Filmrutan* 33: 2 (1990): 31-32.

Mercuri, Lorenza. "L'aspettativa delusa", *Cinema Nuovo* 38: 6 (322) (November-December 1989): 3.

Meyer, Mark-Paul. "Love and killing", *Skrien* 171 (April-May 1990): 28-31.

Orejel, A. "Breve película sobre el amor", *Dicine* 34 (May 1990): 21.

Poros, G. "Imperativuszok – halkan, tünödve", *Filmkultúra* 27: 4 (1991): 40-47.

Poussu, Tarmo. "Silman ja kaden tarina", *Filmihullu* 6-7 (1989): 38-39.

Prokopova, A. "Kratky film o zabijeni, Kratky film o lasce", *Film a doba* 36: 6 (June 1990): 341-344.

Roek, A. "Visuele ethiek", *Skrien* 169 (December-January 1989/90): 66-67.

Sartor, Freddy. "Liefde is...", *Film en Televisie* 393 (February 1990): 14.

Stam, H. "Somberheid doeltreffend vergroot", *Skoop* 25 (March 1989): 24-26.

Stempel, Hans. "Kurzer Film über die Liebe", *Epd Film* 6: 4 (April 1989): 36.

Wiegand, Wilfried. "So macht die Sehnsucht Voyeure aus uns allen", *Frankfurter Allgemeine Zeitung* 26 April 1989.

A Short Film About Killing

(i) In Polish

Dipont, Małgorzata. "Nie zabijaj", *Życie Warszawy* 31 March 1988.

Hollender, Barbara. "Krótki film o zabijaniu", *Odrodzenie* 2 April 1988.

Janicka, Bożena. "K.s.", *Kino* 22: 6 (June 1988): 13-15.

Kałużyński, Zygmunt. "Bankiet w domu powieszonego", *Polityka* 10 December 1988.

Kursor. "Morderca zamordowany – z prasy polskiej", *Kino* 23: 3 (March 1989): 15-16.

Malatyńska, Maria. "Krótki film o zabijaniu", *Echo krakowa* 16 June 1988.

Pawlicki, Maciej. "List do kata", *Tygodnik powszechny* 8 May 1988.

Peltz, Jerzy. "Wszyscy jesteśmy sędziami", *Kultura* 20 April 1988.

Rymuszko, Marek. "W kręgu zła", *Prawo i życie* 18 June 1988.

Seidler, Barbara. "Nie zabijaj!", *Życie literackie* 8 May 1988.

Sobolewski, Tadeusz. "Wszyscy jesteśmy mordercami", *Kino* 22: 8 (August 1988): 9-11.

—————————. "Kieślowskiego 'dzieje grzechu'", *Przegląd katolicki* 52 (25 December 1988): 8.

—————————. "Blisko Kaina", *Odra* 9 (1988): 82-84.

Szyma, Tadeusz. "Krótki film o zabijaniu", *Tygodnik powszechny* 12 June 1988.

Tronowicz, Henryk. "Krótki film o zabijaniu", *Filmowy serwis prasowy* 34: 6 (640) (6 March 1988): 7-10.

Winiarczyk, Mirosław. "Morderca na szafocie", *Ekran* 21 April 1988: 6-7.

Zawiśliński, Stanisław. "Nie zabijaj!", *Trybuna ludu* 21 March 1988.

Zielińska, Magda. "Krótko o 'krótkich filmach' Kieślowskiego", *Twórczość* 5 (1989): 118-121.

(ii) In French

Bassan, Raphaël. "Tu ne tueras point", *La Revue du Cinéma* 440 (July-August 1988): 32.

—————————. "Tu ne tueras point: 'No future' à l'Est", *La Revue du Cinéma* 443 (November 1988): 20-21.

—————————. "Sexe, mensonges et vidéo: Brève histoire d'amour: Pour une mise en équation des sentiments", *La Revue du Cinéma* 453 (October 1989): 21-22.

Beaulieu, Janick. "Tu ne tueras point", *Séquences* 140 (June 1989): 72-73.

Bradeau, Michel. "Meurtre sans raison", *Le Monde* 18 May 1988: 18.

D.H. "Tu ne tueras point une horreur si ordinaire", *Cinéma 88* 443 (25-31 May 1988): 10.

Estève, Michel. "Autopsie du meurtre", *Esprit* 145 (December 1988): 164-165.

Frois, Emmanuèle. "Kieślowski: la vie au scalpel", *Le Figaro* 16 May 1988.

Magny, Joël. "Rat crevé dans le ruisseau", *Cahiers du Cinéma* 409 (June 1988): 29.

Marsolais, Gilles. "Le cinéma à vif", *24 Images* 39-40 (autumn 1988): 12-13.

Martin, Marcel. "Krzysztof Kieślowski: un cinéma sans anesthésie", *La Revue du Cinéma* 456 (January 1990): 41-45.

M.P. "Meurtres au choix", *Le nouvel observateur* 28 October 1988: 53.

Sineux, Michel. "'Mettre le nez dans son caca'", *Positif* 332 (October 1988): 13-14.

Strauss, Frédéric. "Le nom du crime", *Cahiers du Cinéma* 413 (November 1988): 4-6.

——————. "Le meurtre au travail", *Cahiers du Cinéma* 413 (November 1988): 8-9.

Trémois, Claude-Marie. "Tu ne tueras point", *Télérama* 2024 (19 October 1988): 41.

Valot, J. "Tu ne tueras point", *La Revue du Cinéma*, hors série 35 (1988): 107-108.

(iii) In English

Andrews, Nigel. "Murder turns to overkill", *The Financial Times* 16 November 1989: 29.

Case, Brian. "Rope and Glory", *Time Out* 6 March 1991: 152.

Coates, Paul. "Anatomy of a Murder: A Short Film About Killing", *Sight and Sound* 58: 1 (winter 1988/89): 63-64.

Eidsvik, Charles. "Kieślowski's 'Short Films'", *Film Quarterly* 44: 1 (autumn 1990): 50-55.

Hachem, Samir. "The Unbearable Darkness of Killing", *The Village Voice* 26 September 1989: 64.

Hammond, Wally. "A Short Film About Killing", *Time Out* 1004 (15-22 November 1989): 37.

James, C. "A Polish director's vision of the evil that men do", *The New York Times* 23 September 1989: 9.

Malcolm, Derek. "Mortal sin in close-up", *The Guardian* 19 May 1988: 21.

Pym, John. "Krótki film o zabijaniu (A Short Film About Killing)", *Monthly Film Bulletin* 56: 671 (December 1989): 371-372.

Robinson, David. "Rites and wrongs of killing", *The Times* 16 November 1989: 21.

Yung. "Krótki film o zabijaniu (A Short Film About Killing)", *Variety* 331: 5 (25 May 1988): 18.

(iv) In other languages

Braad Thomsen, Christian. "Klatter fra en hængning", *Kosmorama* 35 (187) (spring 1989): 18-19.

Buchka, Peter. "Weitere Nachricht aus einem kaputten Land: Krzysztof Kieślowski's 'Kurzer Film über die Liebe'", *Süddeutsche Zeitung* 1 June 1989.

Farran-Lee, S. "En liten film om konsten att doda. Diskussion om moral", *Chaplin* 31: 2 (221) (1989): 92-93.

Hamm-Fürhölter, U. "Ein kurzer Film über das Töten", *Filmfaust* 12: 67 (August-September 1988): 48-49.

Karasek, Hellmuth. "Auge um Auge", *Der Spiegel* 23 January 1989.

Meyer, Mark-Paul. "Love and killing", *Skrien* 171 (April-May 1990): 28-31.

Poros, G. "Imperativuszok – halkan, tünödve", *Filmkultúra* 27: 4 (1991): 40-47.

Poussu, Tarmo. "Tappamisen anatomia", *Filmihullu* 4 (1990): 43-44.

Prokopova, A. "Kratky film o zabijeni, Kratky film o lasce", *Film a doba* 36: 6 (June 1990): 341-344.

Stam, H. "Somberheid doeltreffend vergroot", *Skoop* 25 (March 1989): 24-26.

Stempel, Hans. "Ein kurzer Film über das Töten", *Epd Film* 6: 2 (February 1989): 24-25.

Teréus, Roger. "En liten film om konsten att doda", *Filmrutan* 32: 3 (1989): 32-33.

Vandemaele, S. "Gij zult niet doden", *Film en Televisie* 377 (October 1988): 24-25.

Wiegand, Wilfried. "Warschau als Vorhölle", *Frankfurter Allgemeine Zeitung* 25 January 1989.

Zuilhof, G. "Wrede onvermijdelijkheid", *Skrien* 164 (February-March 1989): 22.

No End

(i) In Polish

Dondziłło, Czesław. "W chocholim kręgu", *Film* 40 (1 September 1985): 9-10.

Jackiewicz, Aleksander. "Moje życie w kinie", *Kino* 22: 4 (April 1988): 15-16.

Kałużyński, Zygmunt. "Małpa w kapeluszu", *Polityka* 13 July 1985.

Malatyńska, Maria. "Dylemat", *Życie literackie* 30 June 1985.

Przylipiak, Mirosław. "Nie na temat", *Kino* 20: 2 (February 1986): 8-10.

Sadowski, Marek. "Bez nadziei", *Rzeczpospolita* 11 June 1985.

Sobolewski, Tadeusz. "W samotności", *Kino* 19: 12 (December 1985): 10-13.

──────────────. "Bez końca", *Gazeta wyborcza* 13 December 1989.

Szyma, Tadeusz. "Bez końca", *Tygodnik powszechny* 28 July 1985.

Tatarkiewicz, Anna. "Łabędzi śpiew czy CDN...", *Polityka* 27 July 1985.

Toeplitz, Krzysztof Teodor. "Co dalej", *Miesięcznik literacki* 7 (July) 1989.

Tronowicz, Henryk. "Bez końca", *Filmowy serwis prasowy* 31: 4 (566) (16-28 February 1985): 2-4.

Wiśniewski, Zygmunt. "Bez końca", *Trybuna ludu* 18 July 1985.

(ii) In French

Derobert, Éric. "Le fantôme de Solidarność", *Positif* 334 (December 1988): 44-45.

H.N. "Bez końca", *Positif* 293/294 (July/August 1985): 90-91.

Valot, J. "Sans fin", *La Revue du Cinéma*, hors série 35 (1988): 97.

(iii) In English

Bergan, Ronald. "No End", *Films and Filming* 402 (March 1988): 31.

Canby, Vincent. "Kieślowski's 'No End', from Poland", *The New York Times* 30 September 1986.

Coates, Paul. "Politics of Memory, Ghosts of Defeat: 'No End' by Krzysztof Kieślowski", *The Polish Review* 33: 3 (1988): 343-346.

Genin, Bernard. "No End", *Télérama* 2024 (19 October 1988): 39.

Holl. "Bez Końca (No End)", *Variety* 319: 4 (22 May 1985): 24.

Kaufman, Michael T. "Poland Lets Film Depict Strike Leader's Ordeal", *The New York Times* 29 June 1985: 11.

Malcolm, Derek. "End in view", *The Guardian* 3 July 1986: 13.

Mayne, Richard. "Dissidents' dilemma", *The Sunday Telegraph* 13 March 1988: 21.

Paul, David. "The Esthetics of Courage: The Political Climate for the Cinema in Poland and Hungary", *Cineaste* 14: 4 (1986): 16-22.

Quart, Leonard. "No End", *Cineaste* 16: 1-2 (1987/88): 74.

Robinson, David. "Never mind the plot", *The Times* 10 March 1988.

Sawtell, Jeff. "A denial of hope", *Morning Star* 11 March 1988.

Strick, Philip. "Bez Końca (No End)", *Monthly Film Bulletin* 55: 650 (March 1988): 76-77.

Warchoł, Tomasz. "The End of a Beginning", *Sight and Sound* 55: 3 (summer 1986): 190-194.

(iv) In other languages

Holloway, Dorothea. "Ein Film aus Polen", *Medium* 15: 7 (July 1985): 48.

Kovacs, I. "Az igazsag hasztalan remenye", *Filmvilag* 31: 11 (1988): 24-25.

Norrested, Carl. "Indre emigration", *Kosmorama* 33 (181) (autumn 1987): 16-17.

Widding, A.S. "Att viska i blid", *Chaplin* 29: 1 (208) (1986): 40-41.

Blind Chance

(i) In Polish

Aleksandrowicz, Piotr. "Zgrzyty i szepty", *Sztandar młodych* 13-15 February 1987.

Cegielski, Piotr. "Czy 'Przypadek' to przypadek", *Dziennik wieczorny* 15 February 1987.

Dipont, Małgorzata. "Przypadek", *Życie Warszawy* 24 February 1987.

Dondziłło, Czesław. "Przepowiednia", *Film* 42 (15 March 1987): 6-7.

Jackiewicz, Akeksander. "Moje życie w kinie", *Kino* 22: 4 (April 1988): 15-16.

Malatyńska, Maria. "Przypadek 'Przypadku'", *Życie literackie* 1 March 1987.

Netz, Feliks. "Przypadek", *Tygodnik Tak i Nie* 12 June 1987.

Pawlicki, Maciej. "Wishful thinking", *Kino* 21: 6 (June 1987): 5-7.

Peltz, Jerzy. "Trzy przypadki Witka Długosza", *Kultura* 18 February 1987.

Sadowski, Marek. "Życiorys w trzech odsłonach", *Rzeczpospolita* 7-8 March 1987.

Sobolewski, Tadeusz. "'Przypadek': postscriptum", *Kino* 21: 6 (June 1987): 8-10.

Szyma, Tadeusz. "Przypadek", *Tygodnik powszechny* 22 February 1987.

Zarębski, K J. "Przypadek", *Filmowy serwis prasowy* 33: 5 (1 March 1987): 16-18.

Zawiśliński, Stanisław. "Model – rocznik 56", *Trybuna ludu* 4-5 April 1987.

(ii) In French

H.N. "Przydapek [sic]", *Positif* 317-318 (July-August 1987): 83.

Martin, Marcel. "Le fait du hasard", *La Revue du Cinéma* 429 (July-August 1987): 41.

Masson, Alain. "Nécessité et variations", *Positif* 334 (December 1988): 46-47.

Roth-Bettoni, Didier. "Le hasard", *La Revue du Cinéma,* hors série 35 (1988): 53.

Siclier, Jacques. "Fils espagnol, fils polonais", *Le Monde* 11 May 1987.

Tournès, Andrée. "Le hasard", *Jeune Cinéma* 182 (July-August 1987): 33-34.

T.R. "Le hasard", *Cinéma 87* 400 (May 22-June 2 1987): 11.

Trémois, Claude-Marie. "Le hasard", *Télérama* 2024 (19 October 1988): 40.

(iii) In English

Coates, Paul. "Exile and Identity: Kieślowski and His Contemporaries", in Ruth Dwyer and Graham Petrie (eds), *Before the Wall Came Down: Soviet and East European Filmmakers Working in the West* (Lanham: University Press of America, 1990): 109-114.

Kell. "Przypadek (Blind Chance)", *Variety* 20 May 1987: 30, 34.

(iv) In other languages

Imparato, Emanuela. "Il caso", *Cineforum* 32: 314 (May 1992): 62-65.

Peeters, M. "'Przypadek': een spel met het toeval", *Andere Sinema* 90 (March-April 1989): 25-26.

Persson, A. "Odets nyck. Manniskans standiga tvivel ock kval", *Chaplin* 31: 5 (224) (1989): 262-263.

Putter, J. de. "Verlangen naar licht", *Skrien* 162 (November-December 1988): 22.

Spagnoletti, G. "Przypadek", *Cineforum* 27: 265 (June-July 1987): 23-25.

Camera Buff

(i) In Polish

Horoszczak, Adam. "Amator – czyli optimizm utraconych złudzeń", *Kino* 14: 9 (September 1979): 15-18.

Janicka, Bożena. "Pionek jako figura", *Film* 34: 49 (9 December 1979): 8-9.

Janicka, Bożena. "Amator", *Film* 39: 49 (2 December 1984).

Kałużyński, Zygmunt. "Przebudzenie z apatii", *Polityka* 1 December 1979.

Klaczyński, Zbigniew. "Wejście w świat", *Trybuna ludu* 7 December 1979.

Kłopotowski, Krzysztof. "Amator", *Literatura* 29 November 1979.

Malatyńska, Maria. "Amator", *Echo krakowa* 22 November 1979.

——————————. "Ćwiczenia z perspektywy", *Życie literackie* 11 March 1984.

Płażewski, Jerzy. "'I zstąpmy do głębi'", *Kultura* 2 December 1979.

Raczkowski, Jerzy. "Amator", *Więź* 1 (1980).

Sobolewski, Tadeusz. "Filip i najważniejsza ze sztuk", *Film* 34 (21-28 January 1979).

Szyma, Tadeusz. "Amator", *Tygodnik powszechny* 21 October 1979.

Toeplitz, Krzysztof Teodor. "'Amator' czyli moralność sztuki", *Miesięcznik literacki* 12 (1979): 81-83.

Żaryn, Szczepan. "Przeciw propozycjom współudziału w błędzie", *Ekran* 49 (9 December 1979).

Zatorski, Janusz. "Artysta mimo woli", *Kierunki* 16 December 1979.

(ii) In French

Demeure, Jacques. "Kieślowski, Zanussi et 'le profane'", *Positif* 225 (December 1979): 15.

Douin, Jean-Luc. "L'Amateur", *Télérama* 2024 (19 October 1988): 38.

Gervais, Ginette. "Percée du réalisme dans le cinéma polonais", *Jeune Cinéma* 123 (December 1979/January 1980): 28-30.

Gili, Jean A. "'Un pays si sombre et si triste'", *Positif* 334 (December 1988): 42-43.

J. Ch. "Sur deux films de Krzysztof Kieślowski", *La Revue du Cinéma/Image et Son/Ecran* 361 (May 1981): 117-119.

Piton, J.-P. "L'amateur", *La Revue du Cinéma*, hors série 35 (1988): 13.

Tournès, Andrée. "Vitalité", *Jeune Cinéma* 133 (March 1981): 20-24.

(iii) In English

Andrews, Nigel. "Before the camera froze", *The Financial Times* 2 January 1982.

Brien, Alan. "Poland: the best of all possible worlds?", *The Sunday Times* 3 January 1982.

Canby, Vincent. "Kieślowski's comedy, 'Camera Buff'", *The New York Times* 3 October 1980: C18.

Coleman, John. "In focus", *New Statesman and Society* 1 January 1982: 24.

Elley, Derek. "Camera Buff", *Films and Filming* 329 (February 1982): 26-27.

French, Philip. "Polish metaphors", *The Observer* 3 January 1982.

Gibbs, Patrick. "Another winning view through a Polish lens", *The Daily Telegraph* 31 December 1981.

Holl. "Amator (Camera Buff)", *Variety* 296: 5 (5 September 1979): 22.

Lefanu, Mark. "Amator (Camera Buff)", *Monthly Film Bulletin* 49: 577 (February 1982): 23-24.

Rubenstein, Lenny. "Camera Buff", *Cineaste* 11: 1 (winter 1980/81): 37-39.

(iv) In other languages

Martínez Carril, M. "El cine como ojo", *Cinemateca Revista* 24 (June 1981): 41-42.

Riske, R. "Amator", *Andere Sinema* 17 (March 1980): 34.

Sartor, F. "Amator", *Film en Televisie* 283 (December 1980): 37.

Schepelern, P. "Polsk filmuge", *Kosmorama* 26 (149) (October 1980): 193.

Silber, Rolf. "'Aus anderen Film-Welten': 'Amator' und 'Die Ortliebschen Frauen'", *Filmfaust* 19 (June 1980): 36-38.

Vörös, E. "Hétköznapi kálvaria", *Filmkultúra* 17: 3 (May-June 1981): 39-42.

Wickbom, Kaj. "Ung film i Polen", *Filmrutan* 24: 2 (1981): 18-19.

From the Point of View of the Night Porter

Beaufils, A. "Vu par le portier du nuit", *La Revue du Cinéma*, hors série 24 (1980): 460.

The Calm

(i) In Polish

Krzemiński, Adam. "Pozorny spokój tamtych lat", *Polityka* 27 August 1980.

Kubikowski, Zbigniew. "Sytuacje", *Literatura* 2 October 1980.

Ochalski, Andrzej. "Spokój", *Ekran* 25: 17 (26 April 1981): 12-13.

Raczkowski, Jerzy. "'Spokój' – proszę państwa", *Więź* 10 (1980): 142-143.

Skwara, Janusz. "Niepokój zatrzymanych filmów", *Barwy* 11 (1980).

Sobański, Oskar. "Głos wdeptany w błoto", *Film* 32 (26 October 1980): 9.

Winiarczyk, Mirosław. "Spokój, czyli o solidarności", *Ekran* 25: 31 (5 October 1980): 11.

(ii) In other languages

Holl. "Spokój" ("Calm"), *Variety* 302 (18 March 1981): 154.

J. Ch. "Sur deux films de Krzysztof Kieślowski", *La Revue du Cinéma/Image et Son/Ecran* 361 (May 1981): 117-119.

The Scar

(i) In Polish

Hellen, Tomasz. "Brulion z codzienności", *Fakty* 11 December 1976.

Janicka, Bożena. "Idź sam", *Film* 50 (12 December 1976): 6-7.

Kałużyński, Zygmunt. "Zero do zera", *Polityka* 25 December 1976.

Klaczyński, Zbigniew. "O sprawach pierwszych", *Trybuna ludu* 29 December 1976.

Malatyńska, Maria. "Blizna", *Echo krakowa* 30 December 1976.

Mętrak, Krzysztof. "Chorągiewy na wieży", *Kultura* 2 January 1977.

Płażewski, Jerzy. "W trybie oznajmującym", *Kultura* 23 January 1977.

Robak, Tadeusz. "Śliska droga dyrektorska", *Życie literackie* 9 January 1977.

Skwara, Janusz. "Tropami polskiego kina: *Blizna*", *Barwy* 2 February 1977.

Szczepański, Jan Józef. "Blizna", *Tygodnik powszechny* 2 January 1977.

Wieczorkowski, Aleksander. "Znakomity film trochę niedobry", *Film* 2 January 1977.

(ii) In other languages

Mari. "Blizna", *Variety* 2 February 1977: 24.

Paranagua, Paulo Antonio. "Le technocrate et le cinéaste", *Positif* 227 (February 1980): 21-22.

Plowright, Molly. "Heartbreak in Poland", *Glasgow Herald* 23 August 1978.

Personnel

Eberhardt, Konrad. "Głos niepowołanych", *Kultura* 23 November 1975.

Jazdon, Mikołaj. "*Personel* – credo artystyczne Krzysztofa Kieślowskiego", in Marek Hendrykowski (ed), *Poloniści o filmie* (Poznań: WiS, 1997): 151-161.

Karpiński, Maciej. "O filmie Kieślowskiego", *Literatura* 22 January 1976.

Mari. "Personel", *Variety* 21 April 1976: 23.

Curriculum Vitae

Radgowski, Michał. "Seans", *Polityka* 14 February 1976 [stage version].

Sienkiewicz, Marian. "Sprawa Gralaka, czy zadyszka teatru", *Kultura* 21 January 1978.

Documentaries

Amiel, Vincent. "'Vous ne savez pas, en France, ce qu'il en coûte de vivre dans un monde sans représentation'", *Positif* 409 (March 1995): 58-60.

Biernacki, Jerzy. "Trzeba rąbać nowy chodnik", *Ekran* 37 (1976) (12 September): 18-19.

Janicka, Bożena. "Blisko tego co najważniejsze", *Film* 32 (8 August 1976): 6-7.

Piasecki, Jan. "Taki, jak jego filmy", *Sztandar młodych* 29 November 1977.

Salska-Kaca, Mirosława. "Polski esej dokumentalny", *Film na świecie* 351/352 (1988): 95-112.

First Love

Kałużyński, Zygmunt. "Biurokracja rodzi dziecko", *Polityka* 20 (1974).

Index

Notes on contributors

Paul Coates is Reader in Film Studies in the English Department at the University of Aberdeen. His publications include *The Gorgon's Gaze* (1991) and *Film at the Intersection of High and Mass Culture* (1994), articles in periodicals such as *New Left Review* and *Encounter*, and reviews of Kieślowski's films in *Sight and Sound*, *Film Quarterly* and *The Polish Review*. His links with Poland include a German and Polish BA from Cambridge, a PhD from Warsaw University, and a period as a BBC Monitor of Radio Warsaw in the early 1980s.

Charles Eidsvik is a Professor and independent filmmaker teaching film theory, history and production in the Drama Department at the University of Georgia at Athens. His publications include *Cineliteracy: Film Among the Arts* (1978), and numerous articles on contemporary European cinema in journals such as *Film Quarterly* and *Literature/Film Quarterly*.

Janina Falkowska was born and educated in Poland, teaching in the English Department at the University of Silesia before emigrating to Canada in the 1980s. She is currently an Assistant Professor teaching film in the English Department at the University of Western Ontario, and her publications include *The Political Films of Andrzej Wajda* (1996), and articles on Polish cinema in *Cinema Journal* and *Canadian Women's Studies*.

Alicja Helman, Poland's leading film theorist, is a Professor at the Jagiellonian University in Kraków and at the University of Łódź. Her many books include *Rola muzyki w filmie* [*The Role of Music in Film*, 1964] and *Historia semiotyki filmu* [*The History of Film Semiotics*, 1991-93]. She is the editor of the ten-volume *Słownik pojęć filmowych* [*Dictionary of Film Concepts*], and the author of the majority of its entries. She is also on numerous editorial boards, and reviews regularly for *Kino* and *Tygodnik powszechny*.

Tadeusz Lubelski lectures in the Institute of Film and Television at the Jagiellonian University in Kraków. He is also deputy editor-in-chief of *Kino*, a regular film reviewer for *Tygodnik powszechny* and programme director of the International Short Film Festival in Kraków. He is the author of *Poetyka powieści i filmów Tadeusza Konwickiego* [*The Poetics of Tadeusz Konwicki's Novels and Films*, 1984] and of *Strategie autorskie w polskim filmie fabularnym lat 1945-1961* [*Authorial Strategies in the Polish Feature Film, 1945-1961*, 1992].

Tadeusz Sobolewski worked for Polish Television for many years, during which his articles, interviews and reviews appeared in many Polish periodicals. He is now the regular film reviewer for *Gazeta wyborcza*. The most prolific and influential Polish commentator on Kieślowski's work, he reviewed Kieślowski's films as they emerged, and interviewed him regularly throughout his career.